HOW TO DEFEAT THE SARACENS

DUMBARTON OAKS MEDIEVAL HUMANITIES

Series Editor
Jan M. Ziolkowski

WILLIAM OF ADAM

HOW TO DEFEAT THE SARACENS

Guillelmus Ade, *Tractatus quomodo Sarraceni sunt expugnandi*

Text and Translation with Notes

GILES CONSTABLE

in collaboration with
Ranabir Chakravarti,
Olivia Remie Constable,
Tia Kolbaba,
and Janet M. Martin

Dumbarton Oaks Research Library and Collection
WASHINGTON, D.C.

LIBRARY OF CONGRESS CATALOGING-IN-PUBLICATION DATA

William, of Adam, ca. 1275–ca. 1338.
    [Tractatus quomodo Sarraceni sunt expugnandi. English & Latin]
    How to defeat the Saracens / William of Adam = Tractatus quomodo
Sarraceni sunt expugnandi / Guillelmus Ade ; text and translation with
notes by Giles Constable ; in collaboration with Ranabir Chakravarti . . . [et al.].
      p. cm.
    Includes bibliographical references and index.
    ISBN 978-0-88402-376-0 (hardcover : alk. paper)
1. Crusades--13th-15th centuries--Sources.
I. Constable, Giles. II. Title
III. Title: Tractatus quomodo Sarraceni sunt expugnandi.
      D172.W55 2012
      909.07—dc23
        2011036415

www.doaks.org/publications

Designed and typeset by Barbara Haines

Cover image: MS Paris, Bibl. nat., Lat. 4939 (Paulinus Minorita)

CONTENTS

Preface   vii
Map and Illustrations   viii

Introduction   1
Tractatus quomodo Sarraceni sunt expugnandi   22
How to Defeat the Saracens   23

Abbreviations   119
Bibliography   121
General Index   135

PREFACE

THE TEXT PUBLISHED IN THIS VOLUME was brought to my attention by Professor Ranabir Chakravarti of Jawaharlal Nehru University, New Delhi, who wishes to thank Professor Dietmar Rothermund of the University of Heidelberg for mentioning it to him. The edition and translation were made by myself with the help of Professor Janet M. Martin of Princeton University and Julian Yolles of Harvard University. The notes relating to Mediterranean trade are the work of Olivia Remie Constable of Notre Dame University; those relating to the Greeks and Byzantium, of Tia Kolbaba of Rutgers University; and those relating to India and the Indian ocean, of Ranabir Chakravarti. Marie Favereau-Doumenjou of the Institut français d'archéologie orientale, Peter Golden of Rutgers University, Newark, and Daniel Potts of the University of Sydney, Australia, helped with questions relating to the Mongols. I am indebted for answers to specific questions to Michel Balard, Peter Edbury, Hans Eberhard Mayer, and Jonathan Riley-Smith. Special thanks are also owing to Jan Ziolkowski, the director of Dumbarton Oaks, for accepting the volume into the Dumbarton Oaks Medieval Humanities series and to the anonymous readers, who made many valuable suggestions and corrections.

The two maps reproduced on pages x–xii show the world as it was conceived at the time William of Adam was writing. The modern map on pages viii and ix, which was drawn by Eliza McClennen, includes the places referred to by William.

Attention should be drawn to the notes (apparently the work of Louis de Mas Latrie) to the text of the *Treatise* in the *Recueil*, many of which are still of value but are too long to be fully reproduced here, and also to the introduction by Charles Kohler, which supplements and in some respect corrects the notes to the text, and to his further "Additions et corrections" at the end of the volume.

—*Giles Constable*

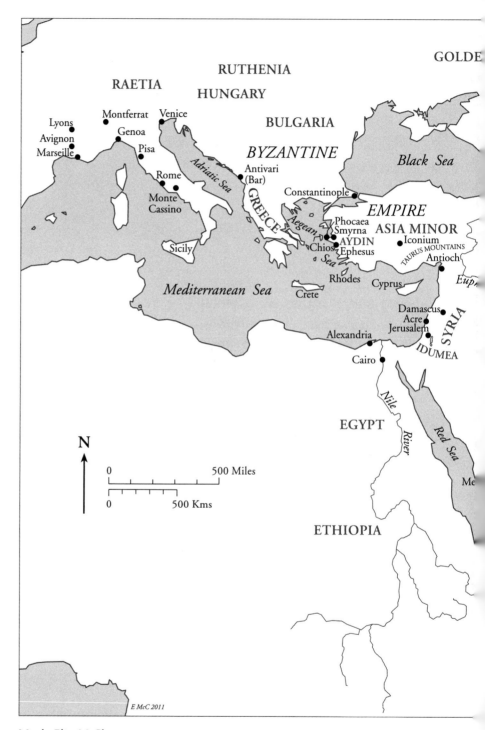

Map by Eliza McClennen.

ORDE

AZARIA

ORGIA

MENIA

Tabriz

Sultanieh

Caspian
Sea

Aral
Sea

TRANSOXIANA

CATHAY
(Great Khans)

Baghdad

PERSIA

Kirman

ALDEA

Persian Gulf

Kish   Hormuz

ARABIA

Gulf of Oman

GUJARAT

Cambay

Diu

Daman   INDIA

Thana

Arabian Sea

KONKAN

GOA

den

Gulf of Aden

Socotra

Laccadive Islands

Calicut

Kulam

MALABAR

Maldive Islands

INDIAN OCEAN

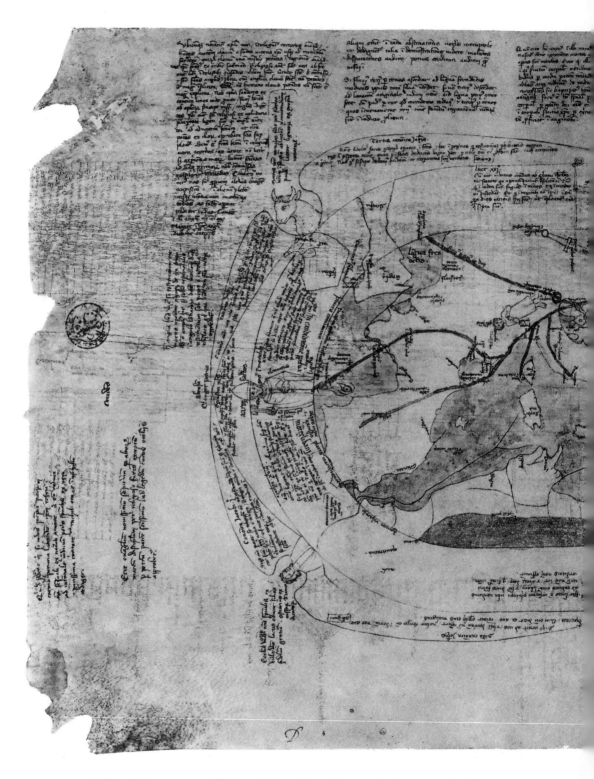

MS Vat. Pal. Lat. 1993, pl. 7 (Opinus de Canistris); see Salomon (1936), 165–68 and pl. V

William of Adam | How to Defeat the Saracens

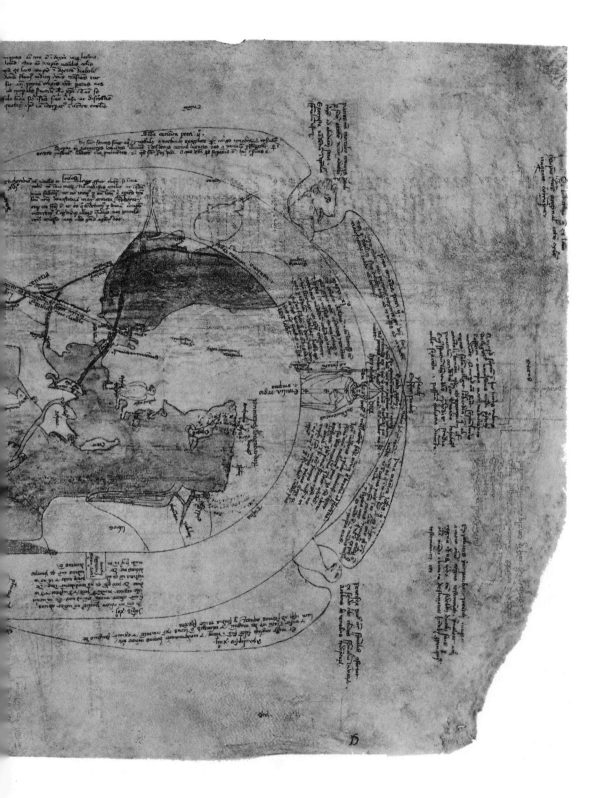

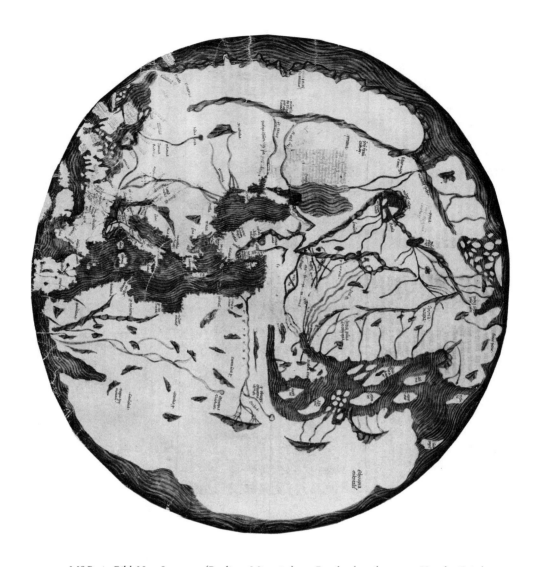

MS Paris, Bibl. Nat., Lat. 4939 (Paulinus Minorita); see Beazley (1906), 521–22; Von den Brinken (2008), 161–65. Another copy is in MS London, BL, Add. 27,376.

INTRODUCTION

❧✦☙

William of Adam

ALMOST NOTHING IS KNOWN about the origin and early life of William of Adam.[1] Even his name is uncertain. He called himself "G. Ade" in the salutation to his *Treatise on How to Defeat the Saracens*, which is edited here, and was addressed as "Guillelmo Ade" in several papal documents in 1318 and 1323.[2] "Ade" may have been a surname (like Adamson), as it was of Salimbene de Adam and other known figures in the thirteenth and fourteenth centuries, or the name of a place, such as Adé in the Hautes-Pyrenées, or his father's name may have been Adam. Scholars, depending on their nationalities, have called him Guillaume, Wilhelm, or William Adam or of Adam or Ada, which preserves the apparent genitive of Ade.[3] Here he will be called William.

He was born in the second half of the thirteenth century, perhaps around 1275, probably in southwest France. A "G. Ade" appears among the students of theology at the Dominican house at Condom in the records of the Dominican general

---

1   The fullest account of William's life and work, with references to previous works, is by Charles Kohler in the introduction to the *Recueil*, clxxvii–cxciv, where the *Treatise* was first published, and idem (1903–4) and (1906), 2:475–515. See also the briefer accounts (some with new information) by Eubel (1897), 183; Hagenmeyer (1908); Dürrholder (1913), 15–16; Golubovich (1919), 173, 180, 404–5; Omont (1921); Abel (1923), 231–32; Altaner (1924), 158; Loenertz (1937), 56, 138, 167–68; Atiya (1938), 64–67; Pall (1942), 546–47, 549–51; Sarton (1947), 414–16; Runciman (1954), 433; Richard (1968), 48–50; Spuler (1968), 234; Kaeppeli (1970–93), 2:81–82; Von den Brinken (1973), 64–66, 118, 275–76, 436–37; Beckingham (1980), 295–99; *Repertorium* 5 (1984), 289; Schmieder (1994), 117–19; Phillips (1998), 85, 98–99, 143; Leopold (2000), passim, esp. 39, 124, 141, 148; Biedermann (2006), 57 and n. 58. In the *DHGE* 1 (1912), 495–96, William was divided into two different men and his *Treatise* was said to be unedited. There is no reference to William in Müller (2002), which is concerned primarily with the thirteenth century.

2   Silvestre de Sacy (1822), 504; Kohler (1903–4), 20, 23, 26.

3   Scholars writing before Kohler's discovery of the papal documents called him Gerard, Georges, and Gaspard: Kohler, in *Recueil*, clxxxi; Omont (1921), 278. On the place Adé see the references in Chevalier (1894–1903), 1:12.

chapter held at Carcassonne in 1302,[4] showing (if this is "our" William) that he was already at that time a member of the Dominican order. A treatise titled *Arbor caritatis* in a fifteenth-century manuscript at Courtrai is attributed to a William Adam who is described in the incipit as "natione Cathalaunum."[5] He seems to have been in Constantinople in 1307, to judge from the *Treatise*, and to have traveled extensively in the east before 1316–17, when he was back in France, probably at Avignon, and wrote the *Treatise*,[6] which was composed after the death of pope Clement V in April 1314 and the election of John XXII in August 1316 and doubtless before William's appointment on 1 May 1318 as one of the six suffragan bishops of the newly created archdiocese of Sultanieh.[7] He may have resigned from the Dominican order at that time owing to the hostility of the Greek emperor and clergy toward the Dominicans.[8] Later that year he left for the east, together with the Dominican Raymond Stephen, the future archbishop of Ephesus,[9] and soon after was appointed bishop of Smyrna. He was back in France in October 1322, when he was named archbishop of Sultanieh, and the following year pope John XXII recommended him to the protection of the king and patriarch of Armenia. In October 1324, when he was again in France, he was appointed archbishop of Antivari (the modern Bar, on the eastern shore of the Adriatic) and lived there until 1329, when he returned to France. A sermon preached at Avignon on 23 October 1334 is attributed to an archbishop of Antivari "of the order of preachers," who was presumably William.[10] He was in Avignon and Narbonne until 1337,

4   Douais (1894), 471.

5   Kaeppeli (1970–93), 2:82. The author is described as a Dominican and archbishop of Antivari, which establishes his identity with "our" William (though not necessarily that he wrote the *Arbor caritatis*).

6   See Kohler, in *Recueil*, clxxxix–cxci, 20 and (1903–4) on the date of the *Treatise*, which was certainly written in the west. William referred twice to "these parts," clearly the west, and also to "the present year" and "this year," without, however, specifying the year. The phrase "alios . . . ordinis mei consocios qui proficiscimur ad infidelium nationes causa fidei predicande," suggests that he was writing shortly before his departure for Sultanieh.

7   On the archdiocese of Sultanieh (Sultania, Sultaniyah, Sultānīye, Sultānīyah), which was established in 1318, see Silvestre de Sacy (1822), 503–5; Eubel (1897), 183, 191–95 (bull of 1318); *Recueil*, 521 n. a and clxxix; Beazley (1906), 206–7, who said that it incorporated "not merely the whole of the Ilkhanate, but also 'Ethiopia,' the Indies, and the North Asian domain of Kaidu"; Golubovich (1919), 198; Cordier (1920), 5; Soranzo (1930), 518 and n. 2; Richard (1977b), 180–95.

8   Delaville Le Roulx (1886), 2, pièces justificatives 11, published a memorandum addressed to Philip VI in 1332/33 in which "the present archbishop of an archdiocese in the empire of Constantinople," who may have been William, was described as "formerly" of the order of preachers. Kohler, in *Recueil*, clxxxiii, knew this document but was apparently unaware of Delaville Le Roulx's edition.

9   On Raymond Stephen (Raimundus Stephani) see Golubovich (1919), 404–5; Abel (1923), 282; Loenertz (1937), 63; Kaeppeli (1970–93), 2:82 and 3:287–88, who said he was archbishop of Corinth.

10   Kaeppeli (1970–93), 2:82: "Dom. XXII p. festum Trin. Sermo archiep. Antibarensis de ordine fratrum predicat," citing two fourteenth-century MSS at Kassel and Vienna.

when he was ordered by the pope to go to Antivari. He died probably in 1338/39 and certainly before the appointment of his successor on 17 December 1341.[11]

William's *Treatise* includes several references to his travels in the east between 1307 and 1316.[12] "I have seen many lands," he wrote at one point, "traveled through many provinces, and experienced the ways of many peoples," and elsewhere he said, "I . . . have traversed the entire empire [of Persia] for as far as it extends. . . ." He gave detailed descriptions of Constantinople, the Bosphorus, the island of Chios, and the islands at the entry to the Red sea. He was familiar with the Balkans, the coast of Asia Minor, and parts of India, and he had, by his own account, visited Ethiopia. He knew a good deal about Egypt, but it is unclear whether he had been there. He was apparently less familiar with Syria and Palestine and says nothing about Greece. Among the most interesting passages in the *Treatise* are William's accounts of his meetings in Persia with a captive Greek woman whose child he baptized and in India with a lapsed Christian who said that God had abandoned him.

In addition to the *Treatise*, and perhaps the other treatise and sermon referred to above, William may also have written several liturgical works which have been traditionally attributed to him but of which the authorship is uncertain.[13] His name has also been associated with the *Directorium ad passagium faciendum*, which will be discussed below, and with a work entitled *Livre de l'Estat du grand caan*, which was written at the order of pope John XXII in 1330/34 and survives only in a French translation.[14]

Opinions differ with regard to William's literary abilities. Whereas Omont considered it difficult to call the *Treatise* "a literary work," Leopold said that William "had more literary style" than the authors of more concise and practical treatises on the crusades.[15] He was without question, however, a trained writer, as some of his rhetorical protestations to the contrary (such as the reference to his *incomposita et incompacta uerba*) show. He used a highly articulated structure for his presentation, which is broken down into numbered sections and, sometimes, subsections. He called the treatise a *libellus* and *opusculus* and referred to

---

11   On the date of William's death, see *Recueil*, cxciii n. 3; Omont (1921), 280, who dated it "sans doute en 1341."

12   On the references to William's travels in the *Treatise* see, in addition to other works cited in n. 1, Soranzo (1930), 558; Biedermann (2006), 57 and n. 58, on his time on the island of Socotra. Omont (1921), 282, said that "On chercherait vainement dans le *De modo Sarracenos extirpandi* ces observations personelles, ces descriptions des contrées et des choses merveilleuses de l'Orient qui ont assuré à d'autres relations des missionaires ou projets de croisade contemporains un intérêt et un succès plus durables." This is a question for readers of the *Treatise* to decide, though it is true that it includes no descriptions of the "marvels" of the east.

13   *Recueil*, cciii; Omont (1921), 283–84; Sarton (1947), 416; Kaeppeli (1970–93), 2:82.

14   Moule (1930), 249 n. 8 (attributing it "probably" to John of Cora, archbishop of Sultanieh); Richard (1977b), 180 n. 40.

15   Omont (1921), 281; Leopold (2000), 39.

the *libelli modum*, which implied a short work. In spite of his stated desire for *brevitas,* which was a well-established stylistic ideal in the middle ages,[16] he frequently repeated himself and used the terms *dictus, predictus,* and *supradictus,* in various forms, almost fifty times; *nominatus* five times; and *premissus* three times, not all of which are translated here. He often linked synonyms, known technically as hendiadys (*uolo et cupio, reiciant et repelant, dico et assero, promoueri et extolli, debiles et infirma*), even when the second element adds little in meaning to the first;[17] and he used the construction *non dico . . . sed* to emphasize a point, as when he wrote of the Greeks, "I do not say their strength but their cowardliness of spirit," and of the famine in Egypt, when grain could not be found, "I do not say for food but not even for seed." He made considerable use of direct speech and was fond of figures of speech and metaphors, including images of the mover and the moved, the glutton eating his food, the digestive tract, the organic structure of society, and a father chastising his son. He particularly liked medical terminology and referred to diseases (*morbus*) and to the remedies and medicines for various maladies. He occasionally made use of irony, saying that the emperor of Persia would receive his enemies *curialiter,* and of word-play, as when he said *inpudenter et imprudenter.* He cited the Bible sparingly and made use of relatively few other works, aside from some references to the history of the first crusade. He liked to cite his own experience in contrast to the hear-say reports of others and clearly felt that his arguments could stand on their own without other evidence.

The *Treatise on How to Defeat the Saracens*

William gave no title to his work. He wrote at the beginning that he intended it to serve as "a guide for a general crusade," which, here and elsewhere, he called a *passagium.* In other places he said that its purpose was that the strength of the Saracens "may be reduced or even annihilated," "that the Saracens may be more quickly and effectively destroyed," and that "our men" may "extirpate all the Saracens from the Indian sea and its coastal cities."[18] In the printed edition in the *Recueil* it is entitled "Tractatus quomodo Sarraceni sunt expugnandi" and "De modo Sarracenos extirpandi," which the editor called "titre moderne," without saying whether it was his own or another's.[19] In MS B it is entitled in a later (but still fifteenth-century) hand "Tractatus quomodo Sarraceni sunt expugnandi,"

---

16 Curtius (1990), 487–94.

17 Pp. 24, 46, 82, 104. See also *obruere, conterere, et calcare, exilis et paruus, tantus et talis,* etc. On this practice see Schon (1960), 180–81 (citing Latin examples), 205–38.

18 *Recueil,* 522, 534, 555. William, like other contemporaries, seems to have felt no incompatibility between mission and crusade: see Siberry (1983).

19 This has been translated in several ways. Housley (1992), 28, 381 called it "How to destroy the Saracens."

which can be translated "On How to Defeat the Saracens." Here it is called the *Treatise*. It occupies a special place in the crusading literature of the late thirteenth and early fourteenth centuries owing to the extent to which William drew on his own experience and expressed his personal feelings. Time and again he used the first person and stressed that he was writing on the basis of what he had himself seen, not what he had heard or read.[20]

The fall of Acre in 1291 promoted, as Joshua Prawer put it, "a flood of projects on the *Recuperation of the Holy Land*."[21] Among the most important of these were the works of Fidenzio (Fidentius) of Padua, Ramón Lull, Pierre Dubois, William of Nogaret, the Armenian Haython (Hethoun, Hayton, Het'um), the *Directorium ad passagium faciendum*, and the *Liber secretorum fidelium Crucis* by Marino Sanudo. William shared many ideas with the authors of these works, and with later writers like Philip of Commines and Philip of Mézières, who, like William, tended to attribute the failure to launch a crusade to the reluctance of the western rulers to take the initiative. The contents of these works have been analyzed by several scholars and do not need, with one exception, to be studied here.[22]

The exception is the *Directorium*,[23] or *Directory*, as it will be called here, which was written probably in 1332 and which has been attributed to William by several scholars. Charles Kohler in particular compiled a list of factual parallels between the *Directory* and the *Treatise*, of which the authorship is undoubted. To these can

---

20 See Schmieder (1994), 314 n. 607. On the importance of eyewitness evidence in medieval historiography, see Hartog (2005), 199–207; Lapina (2007), esp. 118–20; Carozzi and Taviani-Carozzi (2007); and esp. Dagron (2007). On the use of the first person by late medieval French historians, see Guenée (2005).

21 Sanudo (1972), vii. On Sanudo see Magnocavallo (1901) and Tyerman (1982).

22 See Delaville Le Roulx (1886); Röhricht (1890), 75; Norden (1903), 676–93; Bréhier (1928), 248; Setton (1976), 166, 174; Tyerman (1985); Housley (1992), 383–84; Schmieder (1994), 110 n. 176; Housley (1996); Leopold (2000), ix–x (list of publicists) and *passim*. On William of Mende, see Dürrholder (1913), 109–10; Viollet (1921), 129–34; Fasolt (1991), 80–81, 305–6, 312–14; on Lull, see Gottron (1912); on Pierre Dubois, see Dubois (1956); on Hayto, Giese (1978); on Sanudo n. 21 above; on Philip de Mézières, Williamson (1994). To these should be added the treatise by bishop Garcias de Ayerbe of León, published in Dürrholder (1913), 110–17, cf. Schmieder (1994), 113, and the collection of crusading texts made for Charles IV probably in 1311/13 and preserved in MS Paris, Bibl. nat., Lat. 7470, on which see Rouse (2006) (I owe this reference and further information on this manuscript to Elizabeth A. R. Brown).

23 There are two more or less contemporaneous editions of the *Directory*: (1) in 1906, which is based on three manuscripts in Vienna, Basel, and Brussels and (2) with some omissions in 1906–8, which is based on two manuscripts in Oxford and Paris. Beazley (1906), 548, listed fourteen manuscripts of the *Directory*, of which he had inspected six. See also *Recueil*, clxiii–clxviii; *Repertorium* 4 (1976), 207–8, with further references to manuscripts of the *Directory*. It is dated 1330 in two manuscripts (Paris, Bibl. nat., Lat. 5138 and Brussels, Bibl. royale, 5900) and 1332 in others: see *Recueil*, clxvii, who considered 1330 "une erreur du scribe," and Beazley in *Directorium* (1906–8), 66 n. 2.

be added some textual similarities, to which Kohler did not draw attention. The most striking of these are the passages describing the promises made by the Byzantine emperor Andronicus Paleologus at his accession.

Treatise	Directory
	(1906), 434; (1906–8), 850–51

Prima conditio *fuit quod fidem* et obedientiam *romane ecclesie* abnegaret et insuper anathematizaret et *malediceret* omnes communionem et obedientiam et fidem romane ecclesie profitentes. *Secunda quod numquam uerbo uel* opere *Grecorum fidei* immo perfidie *in aliquo contrairet. Tertio quod, quia pater eius fidem* catholicam susceperat *et mortuus fuerat in eodem, ipsum malediceret et excommunicaret* et anathematizaret aut *anathemati perpetuo obligaret. Quarta quod* quia idem pater suus multos monachos piscibus maris et uolucribus celi et terre bestiis tradiderat deuorandos, *numquam* in perpetuum eundem *permitteret sepeliri. Quinta quia* monachi illi timebant ut cum iste esset in imperio confirmatus contra eos, sicut pater eius fecerat, dampnis et iniuriis anhelaret, quod *numquam mortis uel sanguinis,* nec *per se* nec *per alium in* toto suo imperio *iudicium promulgaret. . . . Has autem* conditiones iniquas *ita stricte et cum tanta* diligentia *obseruauit usque ad hanc diem* ut in hiis *dispensatio nulla* cadat.	*Primum* iuramentum *fuit quod Romane ecclesie [fidem]* nunquam reciperet, sed ipsam excommunicaret cum omnibus sibi adherentibus et *malediceret* in eternum. *Secundum* [fuit] *quod Grecorum fidem nunquam* desereret nec ei *verbo uel* facto *in aliquo contrairet. Tertium* [fuit] *quod quia pater eius fidei* Romane adheserat *et mortuus fuerat in eadem ipsum malediceret et excommunicando* [eum] *perpetuo anathemati obligaret. Quartum* [fuit] *quod* in detestationem Romane fidei et ecclesie eundem patrem suum *nunquam permitteret sepeliri. Quintum* [fuit] quod *quia* pater suus multum effuderat sanguinem monachorum, quia nitebantur predictam unionem cum Romana ecclesia impedire, *nunquam per se* uel *per alium iudicium mortis uel sanguinis promulgaret.*
	Hec *autem* iuramenta *ita stricte et cum tanta* perseuerancia *obseruauit* quod per ipsum *usque ad hanc diem dispensacio nulla* fuit.

Other examples of textual resemblances are found in the descriptions of the Byzantine plots against the crusaders, where both texts read "Quod et factum fuisset nisi Deus [Dominus] consilium malignantium detexisset" and of the German wife of Andronicus III, who "Greca perfida est effecta."[24]

Since the *Directory* was written twelve to fifteen years after the *Treatise*, there seem to be only three possible explanations for these resemblances: (1) the two works were written by the same author, (2) they were based on the same or similar sources, or (3) the author of the *Directory* made use of the *Treatise*. Scholarly opinion has differed sharply over this question. Delaville Le Roulx, writing in 1886, before the publication of the two works in the *Recueil des historiens des croisades*, stressed the distinctiveness of William's views, especially on the need to conquer Constantinople, which differed "sensiblement," he said, from the view of Brocardus, to whom the *Directory* was attributed at that time and in the *Recueil*.[25] Kohler, on the other hand, argued vigorously, on the basis of the evidence cited above, that William wrote both works,[26] and he has been followed (with occasional expressions of doubt) by most scholars.[27] Others have adhered to the traditional attribution to Brocardus (Brochard, Burchard), sometimes calling him Brocardus the German or pseudo-Brocardus in order to distinguish him from the well-known Carmelite Brocardus of Mount Sion.[28] Beazley, who was writing

24 Charles Kohler in *Recueil*, clv, and idem (1909–11), 104–11. See also the passages relating to travels in Persia (*Recueil*, 514), the hardships of travel by sea (*Recueil*, 412), and the lack of Christian ports between Constantinople and Alexandria (*Recueil*, 510), though elsewhere William stressed the advantages of Chios as a base for the crusade. See Leopold (2000), 89–90, 94–95, 100, 113, 151 on these and other parallels between the two works.

25 Delaville Le Roulx (1886), 1:70, 75, 94 n. 2. He may, however, have had access to the proofs of the *Recueil*: see n. 53 below.

26 See n. 24 above. This view is supported by the fact that copies (one incomplete) of the *Directory* are found in all known manuscripts of the *Treatise*.

27 See among others the reviews of *Recueil* by Chabot (1905–8), 492 and by Hagenmeyer (1908), 521–24; Altaner (1924), 158; Bréhier (1928), 249; idem, in *DHGE* 10 (1938), 793; Ferrand (1922), 307; Soranzo (1930), 375 n. 5, 380, 395, 518 n. 2; Pelzer (1947), 151; Kammerer (1950), 47, 51 (William or Pseudo-Brocardus); Pelliot (1951), 125 n. 1 (probably by William); Hennig (1953), 180–84; Alphandéry (1954–59), 2:241 n. 2 (saying that he followed Kohler fully and that a comparison of the two texts left no doubt that they were by the same author); Von den Brinken (1973), 6, 64–66, 96 (dated 1332), 145, 148, 152 (dated 1332); Geanakoplos (1975), 51 n. 77, 52 n. 84 (citing some contrary views); see also Geanakoplos (1966), 2 n. 3, accepting the attribution of the *Directory* to "the Dominican Brocardus," cf. 103 n. 74: "Brocardus or possibly by the Dominican Guillaume d'Adam"; and idem (1976), 16, 18, where the *Directory* is attributed to William; Dalché (2008), 78 (calling William a Franciscan).

28 These include not only older authors, such as Röhricht (1890), 74–76; Mas Latrie (1891); Magnocavallo (1901), 128; and Molinier (1903), 109–10, no. 3549, who all were writing before the publication of Kohler's work, but also Atiya (1938), 96–98, supporting the authorship of Burchard and denying that of William; Pall (1942), 549–50 (with further references); Sarton (1947), 391, who attributed the *Directory* to pseudo-Brocardus but said that in spite of the "striking resemblances"

before Kohler's works were published, suggested either Burchard or John of Cora, William's successor as archbishop of Sultanieh, as possible authors of the *Directory*.[29] Some scholars proposed Raymond Stephen, who accompanied William to the east in 1318,[30] and yet others, finally, gave up the search and left the question of the authorship of the *Directory* open.[31] This uncertainty has led to the conflation in some works of the views of William and the author of the *Directory*.[32]

Personally I lean toward the view (no. 3 above) that the author of the *Directory*, whoever he was, knew and made use of the *Treatise*. In spite of their similarities, there are too many differences to attribute them to the same writer, even writing many years later.[33] In the passages cited above the different reasons given for the conditions imposed on the emperor, especially the prohibition to bury his father, suggest different authors, since it is unlikely that a writer would change his mind on such a subject. More fundamental, even taking into account the differences in date and circumstances, is the contrast in point of view between the two authors. William took an economic approach and was particularly concerned to cut off material and military support to Egypt, whereas the writer of the *Directory* had a more political approach and seems to have traveled further than William down the eastern coast of Africa.[34] The most likely candidate among those who have been proposed as author of the *Directory* seems to be Raymond Stephen, who may have been with William on some of his travels and had access to the *Treatise*, but unless further evidence comes to light (as in one of the unpublished manuscripts of the *Directory*), the matter must remain uncertain.

---

between the two works the divergencies "leave some doubt on the question of authorship"; and, with reservations, Geanakoplos (1966), 2 n. 3.

29   *Directorium* (1906–8), 811–12. On John of Cora, see Soranzo (1930), 518 n. 2.

30   In addition to the references on Raymond in n. 9, see Abel (1923), 232 (saying that Kohler's arguments were not so convincing as to eliminate Raymond); Pall (1942); Richard (1960), 328 n. 25, (1968), 48, and (1977b), 170 (Raymond Stephen or William); Sinor (1975), 543 ("William Adam or (more probably) Raymond Etienne"); Richard (1984), 122 n. 11.

31   Omont (1921), 283; *Repertorium* 4 (1976), 207; Schein (1991), 206 n. 47 ("anonymous"); Schmieder (1994), 117, who distinguished William from the author of the *Directory*. Leopold (2000) did not discuss the question of authorship but by treating the *Directory* and *Treatise* separately implicitly distinguished their authors.

32   Hennig (1953), 3:180–84, confused the two works, saying that William traveled into southern east Africa, as did Richard (1977a), 15.

33   The writers mentioned in nn. 28–31 above, most of whom questioned the attribution of the *Directory* to William, pointed out specific differences between the two works. Atiya (1938), 97–98, cited the participation of the author of the *Directory* in the conversion of the Armenians as "a direct proof" that he was not William. The author of the *Directory* appears to have traveled further than William and to have had a knowledge of astronomy and navigation of which there is no evidence in the *Treatise*: see Mas Latrie (1891), 22 and Kammerer (1950), 51–53, who attributed it to travelers' tales.

34   See Ferrand (1922), 307–8.

William gave a brief summary of the *Treatise* toward the beginning, where he outlined the five ways to cut off the support given to the sultan of Egypt: "first, by the merchants subject to the Roman church; second, by the pilgrims of our church; third, by the emperor of Constantinople; fourth, by the emperor of the northern Tartars; and fifth, by the merchants of the Indian ocean"; and he devoted a section of the work to each of these objectives.[35] The first was the need to enforce the established prohibitions against trading with Egypt, especially by the Genoese merchants whom William called *Alexandrini* because they sailed to and from Alexandria and who provided the Egyptians with wood, arms, and other supplies, including children, whom they used for immoral purposes and for service in the army.[36] The second objective was to stop the flow of pilgrims to the Holy Land who paid fees to the sultan. The third was to prevent the Byzantine emperor from helping the sultan and to capture Constantinople, without which no crusade could succeed, in William's view, because of the hostility to the crusaders of the emperor and the Greeks. The fourth objective was to exploit the divisions between the four rulers of the Tartars and in particular to prevent the khan of the Tartars of the north from helping the sultan of Egypt. The fifth and final objective was to blockade trade on the Indian ocean, especially at the entrance to the Red sea, in order to prevent merchants from India coming to Egypt with the goods which the *Alexandrini* then carried to Europe. William described this trade by the metaphor of food going from the mouth (India) down the throat (the Red sea) into the stomach (Egypt) and from there to other parts of the body.

These objectives were not new. The popes had long prohibited Christians from trading with the Muslims and tried to restrict pilgrimage to the Holy Land, which was a source of profit to the Muslims. Hostility to the Byzantine emperor and the idea of taking Constantinople as preliminary to the recovery of Jerusalem went back to the beginning of the crusades. The west had also long looked to the Mongols as possible allies against the Muslims. Several contemporary crusading theorists, including Marino Sanudo the Elder and Fidentius of Padua, advocated an economic blockade of Egypt. Fidentius went further in saying that the commerce from India to Egypt should cease.[37] None of these writers went into the same detail as William, however. He seems, indeed, to have been the first to bring

---

35 There are brief summaries of the *Treatise* in *Recueil*, cxliv ff., and Omont (1921), 281–82. On regarding Egypt as the object of a crusade and the need to conquer Constantinople, see Lloyd (1995), 39; G. Constable (2008), 329 (and n. 35) and 342–43, with further references.

36 These passages in the *Treatise* have attracted the attention of many scholars, including Golubovich (1919), 180; Brătianu (1929), 229–30; Daniel (1975), 221–22; Boswell (1980), 282–83; Trexler (1995), 40; Leopold (2000), 89–90

37 Fidentius of Padua, *Liber*, 68, in Paviot (2008), 141: "Et ideo oportet quod illa via de India in Egiptum cessare debeat, sicut cessare debet via Christianorum ad terram Egypti." To these should be added, on the practical side, the failed undertaking of the Genoese, to which William refers, to put a Christian fleet in the Indian ocean.

together these ideas into a comprehensive plan, which has a special interest owing to his personal knowledge of the regions and circumstances of the undertakings he advocated. He was certainly well informed, though not necessarily always correct, and on several matters he is the only known historical source. He was one of the first writers on the crusades to put the new geographical knowledge to a military end.

His attitude toward Byzantium was based, from William's point of view, on facts, but his tone of disapproval reflected the western failure to understand the empire's situation.[38] From the seventh century on, Byzantines often treated with Islamic powers to the east; treaties, as well as exchanges of prisoners from the intermittent wars, required regular embassies; embassies carried gifts, including human beings; trade between Byzantines and Muslims included food and arms. In the middle Byzantine period, from about 843 to about 1050, Byzantine protocol books and other sources show a clear sense that the caliphate in the east was the only other civilized power in the world. Although some crusaders were appalled by Byzantine relations with the Muslim world, from a Byzantine perspective these interactions were simply acceptance of the new world order that followed the Islamic conquests. Embassies to and treaties with Islamic powers had a long history before the crusades began, and their continuation during the period of the crusades was seldom aimed at forming an alliance against the crusaders.[39] Treaties with Islamic powers, however, could be interpreted by crusaders as directed against them, as in the case of the Byzantine treaty with the Seljuks of Iconium before the second crusade.[40]

By William's time, Byzantine emperors had confirmed crusader suspicions when both Andronicus I Comnenus and Isaac II Angelos sought alliances with Saladin. Emperors and sultans had common interests in fighting the Turks who ruled Asia Minor, the crusader kingdoms, and the third crusade (itself allied with the Seljuk Turks who ruled Asia Minor). Latin propaganda magnified this evidence of collusion between Constantinople and the infidel even to the point of blaming Isaac for the fall of Jerusalem to Saladin in 1189.[41] Together, truth and elaboration on the truth led to William's bitter conclusion that only by defeating the Greeks could a crusade hope to succeed.

38 This and the following paragraph are largely the work of Tia Kolbaba.
39 Honigmann (1935); Vasiliev (1935–68); Shahîd, Kazhdan, Cutler (1991); Laiou (2002b), esp. 692–93; Oikonomides (1991a) and (1991b); al-Qaddumi (1996); Cutler (1996); Grabar (1997).
40 Odo of Deuil (1948), 54–55; Lilie (1993), 146–47. On diplomatic relations between Christians and Muslims in the western Mediterranean in the thirteenth and fourteenth centuries, see Jaspert (2008).
41 The account of this treaty in Brand (1962) must be read in the light of the more skeptical observations of Lilie (1993), 42 and Harris (2003), 127–36.

The most original feature of William's treatise was the link he saw between the crusade and Indian ocean commerce.[42] During William's own lifetime, however, his plans seem to have fallen on deaf ears. There was a flurry of interest in crusading in the early fourteenth century, as shown not only by the treatises cited above but also by the collection of crusading texts compiled for Charles IV probably in 1311/13,[43] but no one seems to have paid any attention to William's work. Aside from the author of the *Directory*, who must have known the *Treatise* (if he did not write it), the only possible contemporary mention of William's work is in a memorandum addressed to king Philip VI in about 1332 concerning the route of his proposed crusade. It includes a reference to a book "which a wise prelate, who was formerly [a member] of the order of preachers and is presently an archbishop of the empire of Constantinople and who walked beyond there, composed and sent to him [the king]."[44] This could refer to either the *Treatise* or the *Directory*, but it had no known influence on royal policy. The *Treatise* was not entirely forgotten, however. The surviving manuscripts were all associated with the council of Basel, which met from 1431 to 1449, and one of them belonged to the president of the council and includes notes in his hand, but so far as is known it had no practical effect.

Manuscripts

The three known manuscripts of the *Treatise* are referred to here as A, B, and C, following the *Recueil*, where they are described in detail.[45]

A: Basel A.I.28, ff. 232^v–54^v.[46]
A collection of texts written on paper (30 × 20 cm) in a single cursive gothic hand of the early fifteenth century, probably from north of the Alps. The contents include the acts and decrees of the general councils from 869 to 1415 (3^r–172^v),

---

42 In addition to the notes to the text, see the forthcoming article by Ranabir Chakravarti on William's account of the Indian ocean and Indian trade.

43 See n. 22 above and Kedar and Schein (1979).

44 See n. 8. Delaville Le Roulx identified this archbishop with William, perhaps because the memorandum may have been written before the *Directory*.

45 I am indebted to Laura Light and Peter Godman for advice on the date of the manuscripts and to Steven Rowan for obtaining a copy of the Rome manuscript (C).

46 Haenel (1830), 553; *Recueil*, clxiv–clxv; and the typewritten *Beschreibungen* in the Handschriftenabteilung of the Öffentliche Bibliothek of the University of Basel. An early list of contents on f. 1^r calls the *Treatise* "opus cuiusdam fratris ordinis predicatorum de infidelitate sarracenorum de modo eosdem extirpandi." A later table of contents (made by Paul Riant, dated 28 September 1877, and pasted on the inside of the binding) listed William as dead in 1327. There is a nineteenth-century copy of this manuscript, made for Paul Riant, in Paris, Bibl. nat., N.a.l. 1775: see Omont (1898), 19; and idem (1921), 280 n. 3. This may be the copy consulted by Delaville Le Roulx (1886), 70 n. 2 (cf. *Recueil*, clxxviii n. 1). There is no reference to it in de Germon and Polain (1899).

Burchard of Mount Sion, *Descriptio terrae sanctae* (195^r–232^r), and the *Directory* (254^v–91^v). Provenance: "Iste liber est fratrum Predicatorum domus Bas[iliensis]."

B: Basel A.I.32, ff. 139^r–63^r.[47]

A collection of texts written on paper (29.5/30 × 21 cm) in the second quarter of the fifteenth century in several hands, all gothic minuscule except for the *Treatise*, which is in a semi-humanist (Italian?) cursive script. It includes several treatises written against the Greeks, Armenians, and Jacobites and a fragment of the *Directory*. Provenance: "Iste liber est fratrum Predicatorum Bas[iliensis]."

C: Rome, Bibl. Vat., Cod. Palat. 603, ff. 111^v–33^v.[48]

A collection of texts written in several hands in the first half of the fifteenth century. They include the *Directory* (73^r–111^v) and various works concerning the council of Basel (199^r–261^r). There is no mark of provenance aside from a note in an early humanistic hand on the inside of the binding: "Lectura in ius canonicum S. de Monte Landino et alia," which refers to the first text. The text of the *Directory* may derive from a manuscript described in the catalogue of the papal library at Avignon in 1375.[49]

Two general points about these manuscripts are that they all date from about a century after the *Treatise* was written, showing the continued interest in the crusades in the fifteenth century, and, more particularly, that they all have a connection with the council of Basel. It should also be noted, as mentioned above, that each of them includes a copy (in one case incomplete) of the *Directory* as well as the *Treatise*, showing the close connection between the two works.

No one of the three manuscripts is a direct copy of another, and it is hard to establish the relationship between them, except that there are more agreements between A and C than between A and B or between B and C. When B and C agree A agrees with them in all except two cases (plus three uncertain readings), of which neither is significant (an added *ad* and *uel* for *nec*). An agreement between all three manuscripts is therefore as a rule sufficient to establish the text, though

---

47 Haenel (1830), 553; *Recueil*, cciv–ccvii; *Beschreibungen* (cited n. 46 above), where the *Treatise* is described in a fifteenth-century list of contents on f. a and again on f. 139^r as "Tractatus quomodo Sarraceni sunt expugnandi." See *Monumenta* (1857), xvii–xviii, on this manuscript, which belonged to John of Ragusa, the president of the council of Basel (and includes his notes), before it came into the possession of the Dominicans of Basel: Leopold (2000), 195. The fact that the first six and last three folios of the *Treatise* are separately paginated in the extreme right-hand corner suggests, as does the distinctive script, that it was copied separately.

48 Stevenson and de Rossi (1886), 209–10; *Recueil*, clxvii–clxviii. I was unable to inspect this manuscript personally owing to the closing of the Vatican Library in 2007.

49 Ehrle (1890), 503, no. 724, cf. 505, no. 766. See Pelzer (1947), 151, who drew attention to the "paruus liber dictus decretorum ad passagium" (no. 2001 in the catalogue of 1369: Ehrle, 429), where "decretorum" may be an error for "directorium."

not necessarily what William wrote. The readings *flamis* (*flammis*) for *famis*, for instance, *in te* (*inte*) for *inde*, and *exempto* for *exemplo* are certainly incorrect. *Intendere* for *incendere* and *ciuium* for *ouium* (which is found in all three manuscripts) are explained by the similarity of *c* and *t* and of *ci* and *o*, but the context shows the manuscripts are wrong. C in particular has many distinctive readings, some of them clearly errors, and one important omission: the long passage describing the *Officium Robariae* at Genoa. If this is a later addition, C may be a poor copy of an earlier (and perhaps inaccurate) version of the text, in which case its readings must be treated with respect, especially since it has a number of readings superior to AB.[50] A and B each also have errors and distinctive readings, fewer than C but enough to suggest that they are independent, though possibly deriving from a common ancestor.

A and C, though (perhaps because) both were written by professional scribes, are hard to read owing both to the similarity in form of some letters, which will be discussed below, and their use of the same abbreviation mark for different words or letters, which the reader was presumably expected to know. A, for instance, uses an umlaut for *ma* (röne = romane), *or(i)ta* (aüctis = auctoritas), *tra* (ëx = extra), and *uas* (qï = quasi). B is much easier to read but also less accurate. It occasionally misled the editor of the printed text in the *Recueil*, who for instance put *Deinde* (with no variant), which is spelled out in B, when A and C have *dni*, standing for *Domini*,[51] which is the correct reading. The scribe of B was presumably presented with a difficult abbreviation for *domini* and read it as *deinde*.

All three scribes made errors of homoeoteleuton, which are noted in the apparatus, and each of them apparently found the text hard to read and left gaps when they could not decipher a word: six in B, two in C, and one in A.[52] They had special difficulty with the word *Mediterraneum*: the scribe of A wrote *m* (or *in*) at the end of one line, left a space at the beginning of the next line, and then wrote what appears to be *francum*; the scribes of B and C both wrote *m* followed by a space and then *terraneum*. *Internuncios* also gave trouble: it is correct in A; B has a space; C has five minims (with no abbreviation mark, which cannot read *nunci*) between *inter* and *os*. A more complicated case is presented by the passage

50 For example: *celatur* for *colatur* (38[a]), *terras* add. (70[g]), *destruxit* for *destruxisset* (82[w]), *nomen Domini* for *non Dominum* (84[f]), etc. In eight cases the scribe of C (owing either to inadvertence or to differences in his model) added or omitted the prefix *im-*, *in-*, and *ir-*, which reversed the meaning of the word, as in putting *reuerantiam* for *irreuerentiam*, *pietate* for *impietate*, and *iustum* for *iniustum*. C has a number of idiosyncratic spellings, such as Iorzuntz (Hormuz) and Gelphos (Guelfos), not all of which are noted in the apparatus. It also has over forty differences in word order, including two which have been changed (or corrected) to the order in A and B.

51 It is hard to read in A. The editor doubtless thought it stood for *Deinde* and gave no variant.

52 A 250[v]; C 123[r], 129[v]; B 139[r], 142[v], 144[r], 157[r], 158[r], 159[v].

which reads "quantum dedecus Christi nominis, quantum fidei detrimentum" in B; A has "quantum dedecus Christi nominis, quantum dedecus Christi nominis, quantum fidei detrimentum," which (coming at a break of a page) looks like a simple repetition, except that C has "quantum dedecus Christi nos, quantum dedecus Christi nominis, quantum fidei detrimentis," where *nos* is clear (and different from the abbreviated *noīs* a few words later) and *Christi* has an *s* crossed out at the end. The *nos* here may be an error for *nominis* and *detrimentis* for *detrimentum*, and the first phrase, as in A, a repeat, suggesting that C was related to A, but it may be the other way around and that C represents a garbled form of a different version of the text.

Although B has more incorrect readings than A and C, it occasionally has preferable readings, such as *improhibitus* where A and C have *prohibitus* and the inclusion of *et uino*. It is not always easy to distinguish the preferable readings, as between *celatur* in C and *colatur* in AB, both of which make sense, as do *auro* in B and *caro* in AC, and the inclusion or omission of *et* in "hostes illi crucis et Christi." Some not very clear guidance is given by errors, changes, and "corrections" in the text. At the beginning of part III, for example, C has *autem* after the word *imperator*, A has *autem* crossed out, and B has nothing, which suggests that A was related to a manuscript of the C family and that B was independent. In part IV, where A has *iniantes*, B a space, and C *iuuantes* (the preferable reading), it looks as if the archetype was hard to read, the scribe of A made a mistake, and the scribe of B gave up. A few lines later A has *villa* changed to *via* (the correct reading), B has *via*, and C has *villa*. This again suggests the priority of version C to version A, though the omissions in C show that A did not derive from C and that the two versions are independent.

The *Recueil* Edition

The only printed edition of the *Treatise* is in the second volume of the *Recueil des historiens des croisades. Documents arméniens*, which was published in its entirety in 1906, but of which parts were printed previously and may have circulated as early as the 1880s.[53] The long and drawn-out publication of the volume was plagued by the deaths and withdrawals of successive editors and collaborators,[54] as explained

53 According to *Recueil*, ii, the texts of Dardel (1–109) and Haython (111–363) were in "bonnes feuilles" (that is, printed and ready to bind) in 1888. Mas Latrie (1892), 266 n. 1, referred to the passage on the *Officium* in the *Treatise* with the correct volume and page number in the *Recueil*. Omont (1921), 280–81 said that the text of the *Treatise* was printed but not published before the appearance of the volume. There is no substantive information on the publication history of this volume in Faral (1947) or Cahen (1970). The article of Dehérain (1919) is concerned with the origins of the *Recueil*.

54 Faral (1947), 87 said that "les difficultés se soient produites de plus en plus nombreuses et

in the anonymous preface. It was begun in 1879 by E. Dulaurier, who died in 1881. It was then taken up by Paul Riant, who withdrew in 1882, and by Charles Schefer, and after 1885 by Louis de Mas Latrie, in collaboration (for the French texts) with Gaston Paris and with the assistance, until 1896, of Ulysse Robert, who worked on several of the texts, including the *Treatise*, and whose contribution was described as "certainement considérable." In principle Schefer was responsible for the notes and Mas Latrie for the texts, but "on constatera sans peine que la presque totalité des notes est de lui," that is, Mas Latrie. Mas Latrie died in 1897, however; Schefer in 1898; and Paris in 1903, leaving the volume something of an orphan and without notes and instructions (except for the *Gestes des Chiprois*) for the preface, which was written and the volume completed by Charles Kohler. At several points in the introduction Kohler specifically disassociated himself from "the editors of the present volume," presumably referring to Schefer, Mas Latrie, and Robert, and corrected and supplemented their work.[55] At this distance of time (and perhaps even at that time) it is impossible to distinguish the contributions of the various collaborators, but it seems that the text of the *Treatise* was the work of Mas Latrie and Robert, the notes of Mas Latrie, and the introduction (and "additions and corrections") of Kohler, who completed his work in 1902.

The author of the preface acknowledged that the *Treatise* and *Directory* had nothing to do with Armenia, with which the texts in this volume were ostensibly concerned, and that they might have been better published in a volume devoted to the expeditions of western crusaders against the Byzantine empire. The Académie des Inscriptions et Belles-Lettres, however, having had the volume on its hands, and much of it in print, for many years, decided to publish these texts in what proved to be the last volume of the folio series of the *Recueil*.[56] As a result the *Treatise* and its learned notes and introduction are less well known than they deserve.

The edition of the *Treatise* in the *Recueil* was based on two of the three manuscripts described above, A and B, and for A perhaps on the copy made for Riant and now in the Bibliothèque nationale.[57] It is a competent piece of work, which has served scholars well for over a century, but it suffers both from the reliance of the editors on B, which is easier to read but less accurate than A, and from their

---

gênantes" (which he did not specify) and delayed the publication, cf. 88. See also the review by Chabot (1905–8), 190.

55 *Recueil*, cxc n. 6, cxci n. 9, cxcii nn. 3, 11, etc. See also the "Additions et Corrections" (1036). As a result the notes and the introduction do not always agree.

56 Faral (1947), 87; Kammerer (1950), 47, who suggested that the editors did not have enough material to fill the volume.

57 The editor (Mas Latrie or Robert) may have transcribed manuscript B in Basel and compared it with Riant's copy of A in Paris. This is a conjecture, but it conforms to some of the evidence presented above, such as the inclusion of an obvious error like *Deinde* from B.

failure to make use of C, which in spite of its peculiarities is a useful check on A and B, especially when A is hard to read.

The Present Edition

The present edition is based upon a comparison of the three manuscripts described above, no one of which can be relied upon for an authoritative text. All significant differences among them are listed in the apparatus, including differences in word order. Obvious errors, especially in C, are not included unless they might be of use in establishing the relationship of the text to the existing manuscripts if another manuscript is found. Very occasionally, when all three manuscripts agree on an error (like *ciuium* for *ouium*, where both the context and sense of the passage require "of sheep" rather than "of citizens") the correct reading has been inserted into the text, with a variant marked ABC,[58] or the reading required by sense or grammar is in the apparatus marked *recte*. In a very few cases a grammatically incorrect reading has been preserved in the text, when the meaning is clear and there is no obvious emendation, as in the phrase beginning "Illi vero" (p. 56), where the verb (*est*) does not agree with the subject (*Illi*) and may refer to the following singular *imperator*.

The manuscripts give no satisfactory guide to spelling, punctuation, or text division. Each has its own idiosyncrasies and inconsistencies. They all lack some or (in the case of C) all the rubications, and the missing initial has to be supplied (usually without difficulty) from the subsequent letters.[59] B at one point has *[T]ertia* for *Sexta*.

The spelling is inconsistent both in the individual manuscripts and between them, and in the printed edition some hard choices have to be made in the interest of consistency. The division of words varies. In this edition, for instance, *plus quam* and *procul dubio* are used in place of the *plusquam* and *proculdubio*, which are also found in the manuscripts. Many letters are doubled,[60] added, or omitted,[61] and used in alternative forms,[62] so that it is impossible to establish which spelling, if any, is "correct." *Galilee* is used alternatively with *galie*, and *Chaym* with *Cain*. In manuscript A *c* is often indistinguishable from *t* and *e* from *i*; in B, which is on the whole very clearly written, it is hard to tell *b* from *h* and to separate multiple minims (as in successions of *i, m, n,* and *u*); and in C the vowels are easily confused, as are *c/t, r/n,* and *i/m/n/u*, and the prefex *in-* is often separated from the word with which it belongs, as *in composita* and *in nitu*. In all the manuscripts *t* and *d* are

58 Such as *flam[m]is* and *ouium* mentioned above.
59 These missing initial letters are not indicated in the apparatus.
60 Especially *c, d, l, m, n* (as in *innimicus*), *r* (regularly in *Sarraceni*), and *u*.
61 Such as *a* (*Alamani*), *b* (*obmitto*), *c* (*aquilonis*), *e* (*uiperarum*), *h* (*anhelare, hyeme, Turchi*), *p* (*sollempnis*).
62 *b/p, c/sc, c/ss* (as in *Rassia*), *c/t, d/t, f/ph, f/v, i/y, m/n, ss/x* (as in *lassati*).

used interchangeably, as in *apud/aput*. The similarity of *c* and *t* is particularly confusing, as in the distinction, mentioned above, of *intendere* from *incendere*. The spelling *encenia* for *exenia* presumably arose from the confusion of *nc* and *x*. The similarity of *n* and *u* is occasionally puzzling: *nolente* and *uolente*, for example, have diametrically opposite meanings.

The abbreviations are often confusing, and the same mark can be expanded in several ways. A line over a word can indicate almost any letter, and a *p* with a line through the leg can stand for *par-, per-, pir-,* or *por-*.[63] In all three manuscripts the abbreviations for *causa* (*cā*) and *tam* (*tā*) are similar, and in C a lying-down hook (⌒) covers a variety of missing letters. In the present edition abbreviations have been expanded *ad sensum*, with a few cases of doubt indicated in the apparatus.

The spelling has been revised to conform with commonly accepted standards, including the use of capital V and lower-case u and of i in place of j and y, which are used in the manuscripts. There is a wide variety of spellings even in the same manuscript, and attention should be drawn to a few cases where compromises have been made: (1) *ch* is used in *Antiocha, brachium, christianitas, machinatur, mechanicus, monachus,* and *nichil,* but not in *mihi, pulcra, serica,* or *Turci,* which is often spelled *Turchi* and *Turki* in the manuscripts; (2) *h* is used in *adhibere, anhelare, exhibere, habeo, habundantia, heremus, hiems, historia, honestus,* and *hostis*; (3) *m* is usually preferred to *n* in words like *numquam* and *umquam,* but some variation may persist; (4) *ph* is used rather than *f* in *Ephesus* and *guelphus* but not in *gulfus* or *nefandus*; (5) *t* is used rather than *c* in all except a few words, like *audacia, contumacia, iusticia, officium, prouincia, sancio,* and *suspicio*; (6) *th* is used in *catholica, Sathanas,* and *thronus*; (7) *d* is used in *apud,* and *t* in *caput*. Some letters are regularly doubled, including *l* in *sollemnis* (*sollempnis*), *m* in *communis* and *immo* (*imo, ymo*), *r* in *Sarracenus,* and *t* in *lettera, littera,* and *quattuor,* but not in *comodus* (*commodus*), *necessarius* (*neccessarius*), *oceanus* (*occeanus*), or *oculus* (*occulus*). Dipthongs such as *ae* for *e* and diagraphs such as *ph* for *f* (mentioned above) appear occasionally. Some unassimilated spellings have been retained, especially in words beginning with *ob* (*obmitto, obprobrium, obpugnare*) and *sub* (*substineo*), and the additional *p* in *contempno, dampno, sollempnis,* and *sumptus,* but it is hard to impose complete consistency, and some flavor of the variation in the manuscripts persists.

Capital letters also pose a problem, since usage varies not only in the manuscripts but also in the printed text. Proper nouns used as names are capitalized here, but not (following the usage of the manuscripts and as a rule the *Recueil*) the

---

63   A mark that looks like a cursive *z* (ʒ) stands for *ad, atet* (as in *pz*), *ed, et, ibet, m, ue,* or for longer abbreviations, as in B, where *pz* stands for *patebit*. It is also used for *z,* as in Hormutz. In B and occasionally in C a mark resembling the numeral 2 or a capital Z is placed before a capital B (but not a lower case *b*) as in *Babilon, Baldacum, Barones, Bartholemeus, Benedictus,* and *Bulgari*. Its meaning is uncertain, and it is omitted here.

adjectives derived from them, such as *christianus*, *romanus*, and *sarracenus* when used as adjectives, though the distinction is not always easy to determine. *Turci sarraceni* may thus mean either "Turks [who are] Saracens" or "Saracens [who are] Turks," and *christianos Grecos* either "Greeks [who are] Christian" or "Christian Greeks." The common phrase *nostri Romani*, likewise, may mean "our men [who are] Romans" or "our Romans." The difference is not great but occasionally significant. William as a rule uses *sarraceni* alone for the Egyptians and as a modifier for the Turks and Tartars, who were often enemies of the (Egyptian) Saracens. At one point at least he contrasts the *Sarraceni* of Egypt with the *Turci* of Asia Minor, though they were both Muslims. He regularly calls the Mongols "Tartars."

The form of the numerals found in the manuscripts varies. The dots between the figures are sometimes medial, sometimes on the line, and sometimes omitted (especially before the initial figure), and the figures, especially in B, are occasionally spelled out (*milia, uiginti*). The system of medial stops used here corresponds to that found most frequently in the manuscripts.

The most useful indications of divisions in the text, besides William's own system, are the capital letters, though each manuscript has its own peculiarities. The divisions in the printed edition in the *Recueil* probably derive from B, which has a number of very short paragraphs (as on f. 159^r). Manuscript A has fewer divisions than either B or the *Recueil*, but the major divisions into parts I–V are clearly indicated and some of the shorter ones (as on ff. 230^v, 238^v, and 251^v) are set off. There are some very long paragraphs in A, as from the bottom of 246^r to 248^r and from 248^r to 250^v, which has four divisions in B and eight in the *Recueil*. The divisions in C correspond closely to those in A—thus incidentally confirming the relationship between the two manuscripts—except in three cases, where a division is added and two are omitted. The *Treatise* is on the whole a clearly articulated text, established by the author, and the divisions in the present edition follow those in A and C, though it involves a few very long and short paragraphs.

The punctuation here is based on the author's divisions and the manuscripts, with some supplements *ad sensum*. The scribe of A made use of a short vertical line between words as a punctuation mark. Scribe B used the conventional medial stop and slash. There is almost no punctuation in C, but the sentences are reasonably clearly divided by initial capital letters.

Translation

An effort has been made in the translation to stay as close as possible to the original in order to preserve some of the character of William's text. Some long sentences have been divided, and the passive tense has occasionally been changed to the active in order to make the meaning clear. For the same reason a specific subject, such as "the emperor" or "the patriarch," has in places been substituted for an

indefinite "he." Some of the uses of "aforesaid," "as I said before," and the like have been omitted, as have uses of *enim*, *ergo*, and *igitur*.

As a rule the same English word is used for the same Latin word, but this is not always possible, because William sometimes used the same word in several senses and different words for the same thing. *Christianitas* and *Christianorum nomen* mean both Christianity and Christendom; *Grecia*, *Romania*, *Romanitas*, and (once) *imperium romanum* all refer to what is now called Byzantium (a term he did not use) and are translated here as Greece in order to avoid confusion with the western Roman empire. The crusaders are called *nostri Christiani* and *nostri Romani*, and once *sancti*, to distinguish them from the Muslims. The army of the crusaders was the *exercitus Domini* and *castra Dei*. William's usual word for a crusade is *passagium* (or *generale passagium* for a general crusade),[64] but he also used *transitus* and *transire* and more general terms for traveling, way, voyage, or journey, such as *uia* (which also means "road" or "route"), especially across the sea. The more general term *negotium*, meaning an "enterprise," "business," or "undertaking," may also refer to a crusade. *Serui*, *emptitii*, and *uenditi* are hard to distinguish and may be interchangeable. They all indicate servitude (perhaps in different degrees) and can be translated as "slave," since they were all bought and sold, though this term may be too strong (as "unfree" or "serf" are too weak), since some of them, especially in Egypt, occupied positions of wealth and power, like *ministeriales* in the west, and enjoyed a degree of freedom.[65] *Habere* with an infinitive covers a range of meanings, like the modern "have to," ranging from "should" to "ought" and "must," and is translated accordingly. *Villa* and *castrum* are both problematic: *uilla* covers a variety of meanings from "land" and "estate" to "farm" or "manor" or even "surroundings," and *castrum* means "forces" and "army" as well as "fort" or "camp." *Dominium* likewise seems to cover "rule," "power," "control," and "domain" in addition to "dominium" or "rule" in the modern sense. *Modus* means "way," "method," "manner," and, as in the title to the *Treatise*, "how to"; *fauor* covers "support" as well as "favor"; *uirtus* usually means "strength," "courage," and "manliness" (rather than "virtue" or the Italian *virtù*) and *uiriliter*, "strongly."

---

64 On the use of *passagium* for crusade and the distinction between a *passagium generale* and *passagium particulare*, see Hölzle (1980), 34, and Jaspert (2003), 49. It is sometimes hard to tell whether *passagium* should be translated as "a" crusade or "the" crusade that William was planning.

65 *Serui* here, unlike western Europe, carries no implication of attachment to the land.

HOW TO DEFEAT THE SARACENS

GUILLELMUS ADE

TRACTATUS QUOMODO SARRACENI SUNT EXPUGNANDI

Venerabili in Christo patri ac reuerendissimo domino, domino[a] R.[b] de Fargis, tituli Sancte Marie Noue diacono cardinali, frater[c] G. Ade ordinis fratrum Predicatorum, eius seruus humilis et indignus, Ihesum Christum et dignis actibus et prudentia eius fidem extollere, qui solus debet extolli laude digna, honore summo, uirtute perpetua, grandi potentia et fortitudine inconcussa.

Vox flentis ecclesie cum Rachele, uox oppressi populi christiani, uox deceptorum sarracenica seruitute, uox terre Christi sanguine consecrate mundum replent crebris, amaris altisque gemitibus intonantes. Clamat ecclesia in excelsis nec est qui audiat quod filii eius magnifici de medio sunt[d] sublati. *Paruuli eius ducti sunt in captiuitatem ante faciem tribulantis*, nec est eis requies propter afflictionem et multitudinem seruitutis. Clamat oppressus populus christianus, nec est qui liberet, quod inimici eius locupletati sunt, factique sunt[e] ei in capite; ceditur, illuditur, affligitur atque ad amaritudinem ducitur uita eius dure operibus seruitutis, nec est qui eum inter tantas angustias consoletur. Clamat denique Terra Sancta, quod eam, *coram nobis, alieni deuorant, desolatur in uastitate hostili* et *absque habitatore* debito *sabbatizat*. Transit per eam et inhabitat incircumcisus populus et immundus qui polluit templum et conculcat sancta. Habitant in ea qui suorum filiorum christianorum in circuitu Iherusalem tamquam aqua[f] sanguinem effuderunt. Clamant[g] insuper omnes simul, aures uestras rugitu inconsolabili propulsantes, celum internis et frequentibus suspiriis penetrantes, quod non solum patiuntur hoc corporis durum iugum, sed anime penis, dum coguntur alienam legem suscipere quam non coluerunt patres eorum, colere et obliuisci Domini creatoris, quem cum amara necessitudine coartantur

SIGLA: A   MS Basel A.I.28   B   MS Basel A.I.32
         C   MS Rome, Bibl. Vat. Cod. Palat. 603   R   *Recueil*

---

a domino *om.* C   b .N. B   c frater *om.* C   d sunt *om.* C   e sunt *om.* C
f *recte* aquam   g Clamat B

HOW TO DEFEAT
THE SARACENS

To his venerable father in Christ and most revered lord, lord R. of Farges cardinal deacon of the church of Sta Maria Nova,[1] brother G. of Adam of the order of preachers, his humble and unworthy servant, to exalt by worthy deeds and prudence Jesus Christ and His faith, Who should alone be extolled by worthy praise, highest honor, perpetual virtue, great power, and unshaken fortitude.

The voice of the church weeping with Rachel, the voice of the oppressed Christian people, the voice of those trapped in servitude to the Saracens, the voice of the land consecrated by the blood of Christ fill the world and resound with frequent, bitter, and loud laments. The church cries to the heavens, and there is no one to hear that her splendid sons have been taken. *Her children are led into captivity before the face of the oppressor,*[2] and there is no peace for them on account of the affliction and extent of servitude. The oppressed Christian people cry, and there is no one to free them, because their enemies are rich and govern them; their life is shattered, mocked, afflicted, and embittered by their harsh servitude, and there is no one to comfort them amid such great troubles. Lastly the Holy Land cries that *strangers devour it before our face;*[3] it *keeps a Sabbath in the enemy's* land[4] and *remains without its due inhabitant.*[5] It is crossed and occupied by uncircumcised and impure people, who pollute the temple and trample on holy things. It is inhabited by men who have shed like water the blood of their own Christian sons in the surroundings of Jerusalem. Furthermore, everyone cries together, beats your ears with inconsolable weeping, and penetrates the heavens with many inner sighs that they suffer not only this harsh yoke on their bodies but also punishment of their spirits, since they are forced to accept and practice an alien law which their fathers did not observe and to forget the Lord their creator, Whom they are forced

---

1   On Raymond of Farges, the nephew of pope Clement V, see *Recueil*, clxxviii n. 1, and 521 n. a; Hagenmeyer (1908), 524; Omont (1921), 281.

2   Lam. 1.5.   3   Is. 1.7.   4   Lev. 26.35.   5   Jer. 4.7.

blasphemare pariter et negare. Clamant[h] et querelas ingeminant et dolor intolle-
rabilis mestos reddit, quod, per gentem peccatricem, inimicum populum, filios
sceleratos, falsos uidelicet christianos, uerbo fidem romane ecclesie profitentes,
sed eam operibus abnegantes, inimicis eorum oppressoribus qui hereditatem
Domini deleuerunt, stimuli, iaculi et gladii ministrantur, quibus inimici Domini
eos cedunt usque ad internectionem[i] anime et spiritus penetrantes. Igitur, benigne
pater et domine reuerende, si tacuero sceleris reus ero.

Inter alios enim ordinis mei consocios qui proficiscimur ad infidelium nationes, causa fidei predicande, plures uidi terras, lustraui prouincias, moresque mul-
tarum gentium sum expertus, et frequentius aures meas tales gemitus repleuerunt,
quibus fui sepius ad interiores cordis amaras lacrimas prouocatus, plus eorum
anime quam corporis seruitutem, oppressiones et miserias miseratus. Et tanto
coram Deo dampnabilior apparebo, quanto de talibus plura uidi, si non annun-
tiauero illis qui mundum regunt et ecclesiam ordinant et gubernant. Vobis ergo
quem non ambigo[k] fidei honor, ueritatis cultus, miserorum compassio, confessio
unitatis et zelus parentum comedit animarum, denuntio, et per uos ecclesie capiti,
rectori mundi et domino, uicario Ihesu Christi et preposito domus sue; denuntio inquam de dampnis ecclesie reparandis, de gemitu pauperum consolando, de
membris dolentibus, de inordinata familia, de seruis inobedientibus qui gremium
matris ecclesie fugiunt et obedientiam derelinquunt; ut hii dolores pietatis et ope-
ris medicamine limantur et cornua delinquentium correctionis baculo depriman-
tur, et per inobedientiam oberrantes, uirga directionis reducantur ad equitatem
iustitie, uel[l] inuiti.

Intentionis autem mee est que inferius ponuntur ad generalis passagii
quoddam preambulum texere, que oro ueritate fulciri et uolo et cupio breui-
tate succindere, ut ueritas attrahat ad legendum et breuitas[m] condelectet. Et ne
oporteat eadem multotiens replicari hunc modum apposui, ut primo dicam
quantum ad presens spectat unde pestis sarracenica roboratur uel etiam enu-
tritur; secundo quomodo eorum fortitudo quam per quorumdam fauorem acquirunt, ualeat minorari, uel etiam annullari, ut agnito morbo uideatur

h   Clamat C   i   intenectionem A, *om.* (*cum spatio*) B, insenectionem C, inte[r]nectionem R
k   ambigu[u]s R   l   uel *om.* C   m   ut breuiter C

out of bitter necessity to blaspheme and deny. They weep, complain, and are saddened by unbearable grief that a sinful race, a hostile people, accursed sons, that is, false Christians who profess fidelity to the Roman church by word but deny it by deed, supply their oppressors, who have destroyed the inheritance of the Lord, with the darts, spears, and swords with which the enemies of the Lord kill them and exterminate their souls and spirits. If I am silent, therefore, benign father and revered lord, I shall be guilty of a sin.

Among other members of my order who go to the nations of the infidels to preach the faith, I have seen many lands, traveled through many provinces, and experienced the ways of many peoples, and often such laments have filled my ears, often they have moved me to bitter inner heartfelt tears, and I have pitied their spiritual more than their physical servitude, oppressions, and sufferings. And the more I have seen of such things the more damnable I shall appear in the eyes of God if I do not make them known to those who rule the world and who order and govern the church. I therefore declare to you, whom I know to be consumed by unwavering honor of the faith, cultivation of truth, compassion for the suffering, confession of unity, and zeal for the souls of our ancestors, and through you to the head of the church, the rector and lord of the world, the vicar of Jesus Christ, and provost of His house; I denounce, I say, the damages to the church that need to be repaired, the laments of the poor to be consoled, the suffering members, the disordered family, and the disobedient servants, who flee from the bosom of their mother church and desert their obedience, in order that the medicine of piety and good deeds may relieve these griefs, the staff of correction may bring down the horns of the offenders,[6] and the rod of righteousness may lead back to the equity of justice even against their will those who are erring through disobedience.

I intend that what is written here should serve as a guide for a general crusade, and I pray to support it with truth, and I wish and desire to bind it with brevity so that the truth may attract the reader and the brevity may give pleasure. In order not to have to repeat the same things many times my procedure will be to say, first, what applies to the present, how the pest of the Saracens is strong and even growing,[7] and, second, how their strength, which they are acquiring with the support of certain people, may be reduced and even annihilated, so that when the

---

6   Cf. Zach. 1.21.

7   At the time William was writing, new powers had recently appeared in the Muslim world. The Mongols had taken control in many regions, and one Mongol group, the Ilkhānids, was ruling in former Abbasid domains and in eastern Anatolia, forcing the local Seljuk rulers to pay them tribute and creating anxiety among western Christian observers. William provides more data on the Mongols (whom he calls Tartars) later in his text. By the early fourteenth century, the early Ottomans also began to gain power in central and western Anatolia in the wake of Seljuk decline. Meanwhile, Egypt and Syria had been ruled by the Mamluks since 1250. In 1317, the Mamluk sultan Muhammad I b. Qalāwūn held the throne.

quomodo apponi debeat medicina, et rami deficiant et arescant sublato a radicibus nutrimento.

Nouerit ergo uestra sanctitas quod per multas uias et per[n] multos modos et per multas gentes, Sarracenis Babilonis fauor acquiritur in magnum dispendium Terre Sancte. Primo per mercatores subditos romane ecclesie, secundo per peregrinos nostre ecclesie, tertio per imperatorem Constantinopolitanum, quarto per imperatorem Tartarorum aquilonis, quinto per mercatores[o] maris Indie.

I

Primo igitur ministrantur necessaria Sarracenis per mercatores Catalanos, Pisanos,[p] Venetos et aliorum maritimos mercatores et maxime Ianuenses. Ad quod sciendum quod Sarraceni Egipti non habent ex se ferrum, nec ligna, nec picem naualem, nec pannos laneos ad induendum, nec oleum, uinum, nec bladum interdum ad comedendum, nec sufficienter homines ad eam inhabitandum; sed per predictos mercatores, ministros inferni, falsos Christianos, hec omnia ministrantur, et tam habunde ut aliquando de hiis in Alexandria Egipti, que ad hoc portus et

n multas uias et per *om.* B   o imperatores magis *pro* mercatores C   p Pisanos *om.* B

disease is recognized the remedy to be applied may be clear, and the branches may weaken and dry up when nourishment is taken from the roots.

Your Sanctity should therefore know that, to the great detriment of the Holy Land, support is being given to the Saracens of Babylon in many ways,[8] by many methods, and by many peoples: first, by the merchants subject to the Roman church;[9] second, by the pilgrims of our church; third, by the emperor of Constantinople; fourth, by the emperor of the northern Tartars; and fifth, by the merchants of the Indian ocean.

I

First, therefore, the Catalan, Pisan, Venetian, and other maritime merchants, and above all the Genoese, supply the Saracens with necessary goods. For it should be known that the Saracens of Egypt do not have iron, wood, or naval pitch of their own, nor woolen materials to wear, nor oil, nor wine, nor at times grain to eat, nor enough men to populate the land.[10] All of these are supplied by the aforesaid merchants, ministers of hell, false Christians, and in such abundance that they are sometimes available in Alexandria in Egypt,[11] which is the port for this and

8   William is referring to the Mamluks, whose capital city, Cairo, was often called Babylon in western sources.

9   By the later middle ages, most of Mediterranean maritime trade was controlled by western Christian merchants and ships from Genoa, Pisa, Venice, Barcelona, Marseille, and other cities. In spite of papal disapproval, these merchants maintained close commercial ties with Islamic markets in the eastern Mediterranean. On western trade with Egypt and Syria in this period, see Kedar (1976) and Ashtor (1983), 3–63.

10   William cites a common list of prohibited trade items. Since the later twelfth century, the papacy had sought to prevent European merchants from supplying Muslim states with war materials, naval supplies, staple food stuffs, slaves, and other goods. Alexander III had imposed a ban on trade in arms, iron, and timber both at a synod in Montpellier in 1162 and at the Third Lateran Council in 1179: Mansi (1901–27), 21:1159 and 22:230, canon 24. In 1215, at the Fourth Lateran Council, Innocent III had likewise excommunicated and anathematized "those false and impious Christians who against Christ Himself and the Christian people carry arms, iron, and timber for galleys to the Saracens; those too who sell them galleys or ships . . . or give them any advice or help with [war] machines or anything else" (ibid., 22:1066). Similar strictures were repeated throughout the thirteenth and fourteenth centuries. Shortly before William was writing, a memorandum sent in 1311 by Henry II of Cyprus to the council of Vienne condemned the "evil and false Christians" who carried slaves, wood, iron, pitch, food, and other necessities to Muslim markets: Heyd (1885–86), 2:24–27; Purcell (1975), 171–81; Richard (1984), 124–25; Edbury (1991), 133–34; Salonen and Schmugge (2009), 42–43.

11   Alexandria was the main Muslim port visited by European traders in the eastern Mediterranean, and the Mamluk government encouraged western commerce with this city. Several European states, including Genoa, Barcelona, Venice, and Marseille, were granted trading houses (*funduqs*) in Alexandria, where they maintained their own consuls and small resident merchant communities with western support staff. Customs facilities, warehouses, translators, and various types of commercial agents were also all available in Alexandria to facilitate, regulate, and oversee western trade. A contemporary of William, the Irish pilgrim Symon Semeonis, visited Alexandria in 1321

porta dampnationis est, tanta habundantia habeatur, ut pro paruo pretio et^q quasi pro nichilo habeantur. Portatur ergo eis ferrum et omnia que de ferro fiunt, ut sunt gladii, lancee, ferra iaculorum et telorum, lorice, galee et alia que necessaria esse possunt ad inuadendum Christianos uel eisdem^r resistendum si passagium esset, uel ad defensionem propriam et munimen, ita quod si hec per illos, ut premittitur, non portarentur in Egiptum, non inuenirentur in ea lancee nec ligones. Portantur etiam ligna ad domificandum, aste pro lanceis, pro sagittis, pro iaculis, buxum et alia ligna^s apta pro arcubus et balistis, tabule pro galeis, nauibus et lignis piraticis, et etiam ipsimet Christiani nequam talia uasa eisdem Sarracenis comperiunt et fabricant, et fabricare insuper eos^t docent, uel huiusmodi uasa iam facta in hiis partibus eis uendunt, que Sarraceni a seipsis haberi nequeunt^u nec fabricare sciunt. Et, quod horrendum est, se eis iungunt ad exequendum nauale officium et piraticum, ad expoliandum Christianos uel etiam captiuandum. In Egipto iterum non pluit quod sufficiat, nisi quando fluuius qui Nilus dicitur perinde transiens super excrescit et Egipti prouinciam irrigaret, et ideo fame tabescerent et deficerent in seipsis nisi predicti falsi Christiani in Egiptum uictui necessaria apportarent.

Sed adhuc predicta peccata sequentis superat sceleris magnitudo, quod quidem predicti falsi Christiani in irreuerenciam Dei et offensam ecclesie et dedecus humane nature perpetrant, dum Sarracenis uendendo homines Christi redemptos sanguine uel regeneratos baptismate et babilonicum imperium forte^v reddunt et exhibent multis et inauditis criminibus detrimentum. Circueunt^w enim mare, lustrant prouincias et de diuersis mundi partibus emunt pueros et puellas, Grecos uidelicet, Bulgaros, Rutenos, Alanos, Vngaros Minoris Vngarie, qui omnes gaudent sub nomine christiano, uel Tartaros et Cumanos uel quoscumque alios paganos quos uenales exposuit paterna impietas, ut predictorum paganorum moris est, uel quos clades tartarica uel turcica uel aliqua alia hostilis impietas subiugauit.

q   et *om.* C   r   eis C   s   aptum *add.* AC   t   eos insuper C   u   nequiunt AC
v   fortem AB, fortem *corr.* forte C   w   circumeunt C

the port of damnation, for a small price or almost nothing. Iron is brought to them, therefore, and all things that are made of iron, such as swords, lances, spear-heads, arrows, corselets, helmets, and other things that they need to attack the Christians, to resist them if there is a crusade, and to defend and protect them-selves. There would be no lances or spades in Egypt if they were not brought there by those men.[12] They also bring wood for building; shafts for spears, arrows, and darts; box and other woods suitable for bows and military machines; planks for galleys, vessels, and pirate ships; and the same evil Christians also obtain and make such vessels for the Saracens, teach them how to make them themselves, and sell them vessels of this sort already made in these parts, which the Saracens cannot have for themselves and do not know how to make.[13] And, which is horrible, they join them in naval and piratical expeditions to rob and even capture Christians. Moreover, since there is insufficient rain in Egypt except when the river which is called the Nile, flowing through, floods and irrigates the province of Egypt, the Saracens would waste away from hunger and be in need for themselves if the afore-said false Christians did not bring the necessities of life to Egypt.

Even greater than these sins is that the false Christians, to the irreverence of God, offense of the church, and disgrace of human nature, both strengthen the Babylonian empire and do harm by many and unheard-of crimes by selling to the Saracens men redeemed by the blood of Christ and regenerated by baptism. For they traverse the seas and travel through provinces, and from diverse parts of the world they buy boys and girls, that is, Greeks, Bulgars, Ruthenians, Alans, and Hungarians from lesser Hungary, who all rejoice in the Christian name, or Tar-tars, Cumans, and any other pagans whom their impious parents have offered for sale, as is the custom of these pagans, or who have been defeated or subjugated by the Tartars, Turks, or other impious foes.[14]

---

and described the western colonies in the city and their commercial activities, including traffic in timber and slaves: Symon Semeonis (1960), 45–65.

12 On war materials, see Jacoby (2001).

13 According to Fidentius of Padua, *Liber*, 9, in Paviot (2008), 63, "There are . . . some Latins, cursed by God and by the church, who carry iron, arms, wood, and other prohibited goods to the Saracens and give to the Saracens the means with which to murder and kill the Christians." Wood was rare in Egypt, and much of the timber suitable for shipping and building had to be imported from elsewhere: Lombard (1958) and Jacoby (2001).

14 Because the Mamluk political system was not dynastic but based on training and promot-ing military slaves to enter the elite levels of government, the Mamluk state was dependent on the continuous importation of young male slaves from non-Muslim lands. Many of these young men came from regions north, east, and west of the Black sea, and some may have been Christian. Geno-ese traders were heavily involved in transporting these slaves to Egypt, and although they claimed that they were careful to remove any Christians from their cargoes, there were ongoing accusations in line with those made here by William. On the Mamluk slave system, see Ayalon (1994). On the slave trade, see Heyd (1885–86), 2:555–63; Brătianu (1929), 229; Ayalon (1951); Richard (1974), 13, 20; Balard (1978), 1:289–310; Schmieder (1994), 161; Epstein (1996), 179; O. Constable (2003), 273–74.

Isti igitur pueri sic uenditioni expositi per hostes ut[x] Christiani uel per patres
ut pagani per nostros mercatores emuntur, qui sibi de talibus mercimoniis lucrum
statuunt et meritum dampnationis acquirunt cum predictos pueros *ori draconis*
denuo offerunt deuorandos, et Sarraceni emunt a predictis mercatoribus mini-
stris Sathane atque eos deputant non cuique usui, sed sceleroso, nefario, immundo
pariter et dampnoso. Quod certe cum rubore et horrore nimio profero, cum
uestris sanctis auribus proponere habeo turpia uerba, turpiora facta, nisi quia
uestram preeminentiam scire conuenit, ut hiis tantis malis remedium apponatur,
et me dicere expedit, ut conscientie mee stimulus quietetur. Dampnosa est Christianitati hec negotiatio, quia Egiptus terra est que suos habitatores deuorat et con-
sumit, quia *non dabunt radices altas uiperarum genimina abortiu*a, et ideo Egiptus
paulatim sine cultore et habitatore tabesceret, nisi per istos[y] emptitios habitantium in ea numerus augeretur. Gens etiam egiptiaca utpote carnali luxui dedita
minus est apta ad actus militie exercendos. Et idcirco pueros predictos emunt
libenter[z] ut in armis et rebus bellicis, secundum morem eorum plenius eruditi,
ubicumque oporteat contra Christianos uel quoscumque alios babilonicum exercitum antecedant. Et hii postmodum efficiuntur domini Egipti, admirati et principes et rectores, sicut in presenti ille qui modo est soldanus fuit de illis emptitiis
procreatus. Igitur quilibet potest attendere quantum sit dispendium Terre Sancte,
quanta Christianitatis minoratio, quantum fidei et ecclesie detrimentum, quod sic
per istorum maledictorum studium et iuuamen secta sarracenica augeatur. Nullus
istorum uenditorum numerus[a] scire potest, quia per diuersos et diuersis temporibus multa milia sunt sic transducta et uendita in Egiptum, ita ut illorum solummodo qui de predictis emptitiis apti nunc ad arma dicuntur quadraginta milium
excedant numerum.

Sed et adhuc maior macula in gloria Christianitatis ponitur, dum per huiusmodi negotiationes illicitas christianum nomen exponitur obscenis ludibriis
peccatorum.

Apud sectam Sarracenorum actus quicumque uenereus non solum est in-
prohibitus,[b] sed licitus et laudatus. Vnde preter meretrices innumerabiles que apud
eos sunt homines effeminati sunt plurimi qui barbam radunt, faciem propriam
pingunt, habitum muliebrem assumunt, armillas portant ad brachia et ad pedes,
et ad collum torques aureos ut mulieres, et ad pectus monilia circumponunt, et sic
sub[c] peccato uenumdati contumeliis afficiunt sua corpora et exponunt, et *masculi
in mascul*um *turpitudinem operantes, mercedem* iniquitatis et *erroris recipi*unt

---

x   uti BR   y   ipsos CR   z   libenter emunt C   a   *recte* numerum
b   prohibitus AC   c   cum *pro* sub C

These boys are offered for sale by enemies, when they are Christians, or by their fathers, when they are pagans, and are bought by our merchants, who by such transactions make money and acquire a deserved damnation, since they offer the boys to be devoured in the mouth of the dragon,[15] and the Saracens buy them from the merchants, the ministers of Satan, and devote them not to some general use but to evil, nefarious, unclean, and damnable use. I say this with great shame and horror, since I have to report to your holy ears shameful words and yet more shameful deeds only because Your Preeminence should know that a remedy can be found for such great evils as these, and I must speak in order to quiet the voice of my conscience. This business is damnable to Christianity, since Egypt is a land that devours and consumes its inhabitants, because *an untimely generation of vipers*[16] *shall not take deep root*,[17] and it would therefore slowly decay without cultivation or inhabitants if the population were not increased by these purchased children. The Egyptian people are devoted to carnal pleasure and are not suited for military activity. They therefore eagerly buy the aforesaid boys so that after they have been fully trained in arms and military matters according to their custom they may go before the Babylonian army wherever it is needed against the Christians or any others. And these men later become the lords of Egypt, admirals, princes, and rectors, just as the present sultan was born from among these boys who had been bought.[18] Anyone can observe therefore the loss of the Holy Land, the diminution of Christianity, and the damage to the faith and to the church because the Saracen sect is thus augmented by the effort and aid of these accursed men. No one can know the number of these slaves, since by different men and at different times many thousands have been transported and sold in Egypt, but the number just of those slaves who are said to be now fit to bear arms exceeds forty thousand.

But a still greater stain is placed on the glory of Christianity when illicit business of this sort exposes the Christian name to the obscene insults of sinners.

In the sect of the Saracens any sexual act is not only not prohibited but is permitted and praised. Consequently in addition to the innumerable female prostitutes among them, there are many effeminate men who shave their beards, paint their faces, assume female costume, and wear bracelets on their arms and feet and golden necklaces on their necks, like women, and they place jewels on their chests. They afflict and expose their bodies to contumelies by the sin of offering them for sale, and *men with men, working that which is filthy,* they *receive in themselves the*

---

15 Cf. Dan. 14.26.   16 Matt. 23.33; cf. Job 3:16.   17 Wis. 4.3.
18 William provides a reasonably accurate description of the Mamluk system, although he is in error about the current sultan, Muhammad I b. Qalāwūn, who held the throne, for his third reign, from 1310 to 1341. Muhammad's father, sultan Qalāwūn, had attempted to shift the state to a dynastic system, and he was one of the few Mamluk rulers to have his sons rule after him.

in seipsis. Sarraceni ergo humane dignitatis obliti, se ad illos effeminatos impudenter[d] inclinant, uel cum eisdem habitant sicut hic inter nos publice habitant uir
et uxor, sed et adhuc quid iniquitatis super iniquitatem addunt nostri catholici
inimici[e] iusticie, hoc uicium inesse Sarracenis animaduertunt, sciunt et consentiunt et uiam et incentiuum preparant[f] ad hoc scelus. Et cum aliquem puerum
aptum corpore inuenire possunt christianum uel tartarum ut premittitur ad uendendum, nullum pretium est eis carum dandum pro hiis quos uident ad huiusmodi complendam nequitiam aptiores. Quos postquam emerint, ut statuam,
ornant sericis et aureis indumentis, corpus eorum et facies lauant sepius balneis et
aliis lauamentis, et[g] eos pascunt lautis cibariis et potibus delicatis. Et hoc faciunt ut
pinguiores et rubicundiores et delicatiores, et per consequens magnis[h] apti et allec-
tiui ad Sarracenorum complendam libidinem uideantur. Quos ut uident libidi-
nosi, scelerosi et nefandi homines, Sarraceni uidelicet, humane nature peruersores,
statim in eorum concupiscentiam exardescunt, sed ut canes insani ad istos pueros,
diaboli laqueos, sibi emendos festinanter currere ut possint cum eis suam impu-
dititiam exercere.

Ecce, pater et domine, quanta mala faciunt hii nostri animarum hominum uen-
ditores, quantam ponunt maculam in gloriam fidei nostre, quantam confusionem
faciunt in domo Domini, quale exhibent sceleris incentiuum, quantam bonorum
morum destructionem procurant et excidium honestatis. Sed hoc flagitium non
perpetrant mercatores superius nominati ut plurimum, sed maxime Ianuenses, nec
omnes Ianuenses, sed potissime ille caput peccati Seguranus Saluatici et illi qui de
sua domo sunt et parentela, quos secum ad hec attraxit seruitia inimici Sathane
quosque secum in hoc diaboli ministerium[i] dedicauit, in tantum quod predictus
Seguranus, cum illis qui de parentela sua secum consentiunt, non ad aliud uidetur
intendere, nisi quomodo[k] possit[l] per hec opera Deo contraria ecclesiam confundere
et Sarracenos inimicos crucis et persecutores nostre fidei roborare. Ipse Seguranus frater soldani appellatur, Sarracenus esse creditur, et ut hostis, fidei Machomi-
starum fautor et promotor dicitur et defensor. In tantum est soldano coniunctus,
quod ipse soldanus eum fratrem suum in suis appellat litteris et amicum. In tantum
est sarracenus quod ipse permisit predicta peccata contra naturam in suis nauibus
perpetrari. Vexillum etiam Machometi et soldani Babilonie gestatum fuit in suis[m]

---

d impudentes C   e ecclesie *add. et eras.* B   f et *add.* C   g et *om.* C
h *recte* magis ?   i mysterium B   k quomodo *om.* C   l posset AC
m membris *add.* C

recompense of evil and *error*.[19] Unmindful of human dignity, therefore, the Saracens shamelessly turn to these effeminate men or live with them, just as a man and wife live publicly among us; and our catholics, the enemies of justice, piling iniquity on iniquity, observe, know, and consent to this vice among the Saracens and provide the means and incentive for this wickedness. And when they can find a Christian or Tartar boy who is physically suited for sale, as I said, they will give any price for those whom they regard as suitable for fulfilling this sort of evil. After buying them they decorate them like a statue with silken and golden clothes; they wash their bodies and faces frequently by bathing and other washings; and they feed them with sumptuous foods and delicate drinks. This is done in order that they may be fatter, rosier and more delicate and may consequently appear more suitable and enticing to satisfy the lust of the Saracens. The lustful, wicked, and evil Saracens, perverters of human nature, are immediately aroused by desire for these boys when they see them. Like mad dogs they hurry to buy them, the snares of the devil, for themselves, so that they can indulge their shamelessness with them.[20]

Behold, father and lord, how great are the evils done by these our sellers of the souls of men, how great a stain they impose on the glory of our faith, how great a confusion they make in the house of the Lord, how great an incentive for sin they offer, how great a destruction of good morals and downfall of honesty they furnish. The above-mentioned merchants do not commonly perpetrate this outrage, but most greatly the Genoese, nor all the Genoese but particularly Seguranus Salvago, the fount of sin, and the members of his house and family, whom he has attracted to serve with him the enemy Satan and whom he dedicated with himself so greatly to the service of the Devil that Seguranus and the members of his family who agree with him seem to devote themselves only to how, by these works, contrary to God, they can confound the church and strengthen the Saracens, the enemies of the cross and persecutors of our faith.[21] Seguranus is called the brother of the sultan, is believed to be a Saracen, and as an enemy is said to be a supporter, promoter, and defender of the faith of the Mohammedans. He is so closely allied with the sultan that the sultan himself in his letters calls him his brother and friend. He is a Saracen to such an extent that he allows the aforesaid sins against nature to be perpetrated in his ships. He himself and some members of his family have also carried the banner of Mohammed and of the sultan of Babylon in their

19 Rom. 1.27.
20 Claims of lust, hedonism, sexual deviance, and homosexuality were standard and persistent tropes among medieval European descriptions of Muslims. Remarks similar to William's were repeated in Latin Christian writings from the ninth century onward as, for instance, by Fidentius of Padua, *Liber*, 18, in Paviot (2008), 81–83.
21 William is substantially correct in the basic facts of his accusations against Seguranus Salvago, on whom see Kedar (1977), 75–91 and Epstein (2007), 162–66.

nauibus et galeis, per se et aliquos de parentela sua, sicut ego cum horrore et detestatione, oculis meis uidi. Quod fautor Sarracenorum existat manifeste apparet, quia cum soldanus aliquam legationem uellet mittere uel nuntios ad imperatorem Tartarorum aquilonis pro cultu sarracenico ampliando ipse huiusmodi legationem et nuntios transuehebat, sicut dicetur inferius magis clare.

Promotorem etiam se exhibuit eorumdem sic quod numquam aliquis fuit ante eum non sarracenus existens, qui tantam sectam illam pestiferam auxerit et promouerit, portando eis predictorum puerorum christianorum et aliorum multa milia ad exercendam malitiam uel alios actus[n] illicitos superius nominatos, portando etiam ferri et lignorum, ut predicitur, magnam copiam et aliarum rerum que portari per ecclesiam prohibentur. Non solum autem ipse et fratres eius et nepotes et propinqui per hunc modum Sarracenis talem fortitudinem prebuerunt, sed et multi alii Ianuenses, quos exemplo suo attraxit ad similia peragendum, quos ipse precedit et precellit iniquitatis huius dux et doctor nequitie contra Deum. Vnde hoc ueraciter est compertum, quod uix sit Ianue[o] aliqua nobilis parentela necque alicuius ualoris sit aliqua popularis cuius aliqui Alexandriam iuerint uel miserint quorum aliqui pueros aliqui alia prohibita portauerunt. Et cum solus predictus Seguranus decem milia pueros Sarracenis portasse dicatur, nec multitudo nec numerus sciri potest quos alii portauerunt.

Ad obuiandum autem ne tanta mala per nostros Christianos fiant, et ne Sarracenis tantum subsidium proueniat per eosdem, quadruplex remedium poterit adhiberi.

Primo quod preter sententiam excommunicationis que contra tales per dominum papam Clementem extitit promulgata, inducantur reges et communitates ut fiat per eos edictum generale et indispensabile ut quicumque in Alexandriam iuerit, uel ad terras soldano subiectas portando prohibita talis in exilium relegetur, et domus eius publicetur, et res eius in fiscum ueniant pro subsidio Terre Sancte, uel quod melius est curie seculari omni uolenti diripere concedatur.

Secundo modo ut quicumque Alexandrinum cepit[p] uel bona sua occupauerit, in terra uel in mari, ubicumque inuentus fuerit in actu eundi siue post, talem expolians numquam ad reddendum expoliato, uel loco eius alteri cuicumque,[q] per uim alicuius iuris uel consuetudinis astringatur; et quod rectores quicumque fecerint incurrant excommunicationis sententiam ipso facto, et

---

n actus alios B   o Ianue sit C   p cep[er]it R   q feceri̅ *add. et eras.* B

William of Adam | How to Defeat the Saracens

ships and galleys, as I have seen with my own eyes with horror and detestation. That he supports the Saracens is clearly shown by the fact that when the sultan wanted to send a legation or messengers to the emperor of the northern Tartars in order to propagate the cult of the Saracens they were carried by him, as will be related later in greater detail.

He has shown himself a greater supporter of these people than any predecessor who was not himself a Saracen, and he has greatly assisted and promoted that pestiferous sect by bringing them many thousands of Christian and other boys to engage in evil and the other illicit activities mentioned above and by transporting a great supply of iron, wood, and other things forbidden by the church. Not only have he and his brothers, grandsons, and relatives, however, provided such power to the Saracens in this way, but also many other Genoese, whom he has attracted by his example to do similar things, when he himself precedes and excels as the leader in this iniquity and teacher of evil against God. As a result it is truthfully proven that there is almost no noble family of Genoa or common family of some standing of which some members have not sent to Alexandria, some carrying boys and some other forbidden goods. And since Seguranus alone is said to have carried ten thousand boys to the Saracens, neither the multitude nor the number of those carried by others can be known.

A fourfold remedy can be applied, however, to prevent such evils being done by our Christians and such great support being given by them to the Saracens.

The first is that in addition to the sentence of excommunication promulgated by pope Clement against such men, the kings and communes should be persuaded to issue a general edict, with no possible dispensation, that anyone who carries prohibited goods to Alexandria or to lands subject to the sultan should be condemned to exile, his house should be confiscated, and his property should be given to the treasury for helping the Holy Land or, better, to a secular court for anyone who wants to take it.[22]

The second way is that anyone who captures a man from Alexandria or takes his goods, on land or on the sea, wherever he is found in the act of going or subsequently, will not be required by any law or custom to return what he has taken to him from whom it has been taken or to anyone in his place, and that any rectors who have done this will incur a sentence of excommunication for this deed and

---

22   Prohibitions against trading with Muslim states had been issued by the papacy, individual rulers, and urban governments since the twelfth century, but none had more than temporary effect, if even that. Traffic seems to have been especially active in the last decade of the thirteenth century and early fourteenth, despite prohibitions, with numerous treaties drawn up between Christian and Muslim states (see Holt [1986], 164) and routine absolution granted to merchants caught trafficking in illegal goods. Firmer rules imposed after 1323 seem to have been more effective, with a strict embargo lasting into the 1340s: Setton (1976), 167, citing the bulls of Clement V in 1308 and 1311; Ashtor (1983), 17–63; and n. 10 above.

castrum uel uilla uel ciuitas ubi presentes fuerint, ecclesiastico subiaceant inter-
dicto. Multi enim mercatores euntes in Alexandriam captiuassent, et eorum bona
omnia occupassent, nisi timuissent dominum temporalem.

Tercio si alique galee armate[r] tenerentur in mari cum quibus uiam illam facientes caperentur et in seruitutem redigerentur et bona eorum in sortem eos capi-
entium uel ecclesie deuenirent. Sed est aduertendum quod in armando istas galeas
exemplis quinque fuit hactenus ecclesia defraudata: primo quia illi qui eos arma-
bant[s] recipiebant stipendia pro sex galeis, et non tenebant nisi quatuor; secundo
quia si tenebant tot sicut recipiebant stipendia erant ita male munite de gentibus
et de armis quod non audebant tres inuadere; tertio quod dabantur stipendia pro
uno anno, et non stabant in mari ad hoc seruitium nisi per sex menses; quarto quia
solis illis sex mensibus insistebant pro custodia huius uic quibus non nauigant qui
faciunt uiam illam. Mercatores enim qui in Alexandriam uadunt non nauigant
nisi in hieme, quod faciunt uel quia uenti pro illa uia[t] maxime regnant in hieme
uel quia sciunt quod uia illa in estate solummodo custoditur; et ideo in estate refu-
giunt nauigare, uolentes sibi ab huiusmodi insidiis precauere; quinto etiam defrau-
dabatur[u] ecclesia quia ille qui preponebatur illis galeis ex parte ecclesie numquam
reddebat computum, si quid cepisset de predictis Alexandrinis, nec dabat aliquid
ecclesie de direptis. Oportet igitur ut ille prepositus galearum esset potens ex se,
et probus et fidelis, et quod ad dampnificandum Alexandrinis esset magis auidus
quam ad lucrum. Et sic posset cum tali[v] diligentia uia illa faciliter custodiri et utiliter impediri.

Quartum etiam remedium apponi debet, sine quo in uanum sunt omnia supradicta, et in uanum pro galeis ecclesie pecunia expenderetur. Quoddam enim officium habet commune Ianue quod contra Deum et bonum Christianitatis et contra
statuta ecclesie, militat in hac parte. Quod quidem officium uocatur officium Robarie. Est autem[w] huius una archa, scilicet in palatio communitatis Ianue, cum tribus
serraturis, super quam sunt tres prepositi ordinati, et quicumque christianus, iudeus
uel sarracenus undecumque si tamen de terra illa sit que contra Ianuam guerram non
habeat actualem, ubicumque per Ianuenses fuerit depredatus talis per se uel suum

---

r   ornate B, armati C   s   ornabant B   t   uia illa AR   u   defraudabitur B
v   reuerentia *add*. C   w   enim *pro* autem B

the castle, lands, or town where they are will be subject to ecclesiastical interdict. For many men would capture merchants going to Alexandria and take all their goods if they did not fear the temporal lord.

The third way is to maintain some armed galleys on the sea in order to capture and put in servitude those who are making that voyage and to give their goods to those who capture them or to the church. It should be noted, however, that the church was hitherto defrauded in five ways in arming these galleys: first, those who armed them received stipends for six galleys and maintained only four;[23] second, if they had as many as they received stipends for, they were so badly armed with men and arms that they did not dare attack three; third, they were given stipends for a year and stayed at sea for this service for only six months; fourth, they guarded this route for only the six months during which those who make the journey do not sail, for the merchants who go to Alexandria sail only in winter, either because the winds for that voyage prevail most greatly in winter or because they know that the route is guarded only in summer and therefore refuse to sail in summer in order to be on guard against such traps; fifth, the church is also defrauded because the man who was put in charge of these galleys on behalf of the church never rendered an account of anything he captured from the Alexandrians nor gave the church any of the spoils he took. The provost of the galleys should therefore be strong in himself, trustworthy, and faithful, and he should be more anxious to harm the Alexandrians than to gain money. With such diligence the route can be easily guarded and effectively blockaded.[24]

A fourth remedy should also be applied, without which all the others are useless and the money for the galleys of the church is spent in vain. The commune of Genoa has an office which in this respect militates against God and the good of Christianity and against the statutes of the church. This office is called the office of the Robaria.[25] It is a coffer with three locks in the palace of the commune of Genoa and is under the control of three provosts. Any Christian, Jew, or Saracen, whatever land he comes from provided it is not currently at war with Genoa, and wherever he has been robbed by the Genoese, may by himself or through his

23   On the six armed galleys referred to here, see Gatto (1956); Housley (1992), 32.

24   William was not alone in his call for a more effective blockade of shipping to and from Alexandria. In about 1307, the Hospitallers had urged the papacy to arm galleys in Rhodes and Cyprus to enforce a trade embargo (Edbury [1991], 106) and similar points were made in 1321 by the Venetian Marino Sanudo (1972) in his arguments for a new crusade to Egypt.

25   The Officium Robarie was established in Genoa, in about 1300, as an institution for compensating foreigners, including Muslims, who had been harmed by Genoese pirates. Its conception may stem from a treaty, negotiated in 1290, between Genoa and the Mamluk sultan Qalāwūn that guaranteed trade and peaceful relations between Genoa and Egypt. Starting in 1317, the same time that William was writing, the office seems to have disappeared for several decades, perhaps overwhelmed by increasing incidents of piracy and consequent claims for compensation. On the office, see Mas Latrie (1892); *Recueil*, cxcv and 527 n.a.; Kedar (1977), 23–24 and 29, and idem (1985); Epstein (1996), 180–81.

procuratorem in archam predictam nullo sciente unam cedulam intromittit de sua expoliatione querimoniam continentem. Prepositi igitur istius officii, astricti per iuramentum, certis anni temporibus archam illam aperiunt, et ibi inuentas cedulas perlegentes statim expoliatores uocant et ad reddendum expoliatis quicquid et quocumque modo rapuerant constringuntur. Si uero expoliatores comparere contempnant, bona eorum mobilia et immobilia arrestantur et expoliatis reddunt quod sufficit, raptores ob contumaciam prescribentes. Hoc autem officium est ita forte et ita stricte seruatur ut in eo dispensatio nulla cadat. Formidant ergo omnes Alexandrinos capere, cogitantes ex hoc iram sue communitatis debere incurrere, que debet eos constringere ad reddendum.

Ordinetur ergo quod hoc officium non ad illos qui Alexandrinos expoliant uel Sarracenos, sed ad alios tantummodo se extendat. Quod si fiat ad impediendum uiam illam maledictam sufficiet minor numerus galearum, et contra eam multi alii uiriliter et utiliter se opponent.[x]

II

Peregrini iterum qui uadunt in Ierusalem magnum adiutorium dant principi Babilonis in dispendium Terre Sancte, qui, sicut nec superioris excommunicationem metuunt, et quam habere debent reuerentiam ad[y] mandatum ecclesie non aduertunt nec cogitant quantum dampnum Christianitati inferant et quantum profectum exhibeant non attendunt. Soldanus enim circa triginta quinque turonensium grossos exigit et recipit a quolibet peregrino, et cum de diversis mundi partibus in Ierusalem confluant innumerabiles peregrini, uidebitur id quod dico cum multiplicatum fuerit hoc tributum. Ergo sub peregrinorum istorum pietate[z] celatur[a] iniquitas, et eorum deuotio inobedientiam parit, eorumque feruor indiscrete[b] iniustitiam operatur, dum, ex huiusmodi peregrinatione prohibita, comodum Sarracenis, persecutoribus crucis Christi, et incomodum ecclesie et Christianitati offensionis occasio ministratur.

Remedium autem contra ista facile erit ex quadruplici uia.

Primo ut detur excommunicationis sentencia contra istos et absolutio ad solum summum pontificem reseruetur. Hactenus enim cum in Ciprum ueniebant, post peregrinationem factam, uel in locum alium ubi esset patriarcha Ierusalem,

x   Quartum … opponent *om.* C   y   ad *om.* B; nec *pro* ad C   z   impietate C
a   colatur B   b   indiscretus C

procurator secretly place in the coffer a testimonial with a complaint about his loss. The provosts of this office, who are bound by an oath, open the coffer at certain times of the year and after reading the testimonials found there immediately summon the robbers and force them to restore to the victims whatever they took, however they took it. If the robbers refuse to settle, however, their moveable and immovable property is seized, adequate compensation is given to the victims, and the robbers are proscribed for contumacy. This office is so powerful and so strictly enforced that there is no exception. Everyone is therefore afraid to capture the men of Alexandria because they think that they may on this account incur the anger of their commune, which may force them to make restitution.

It should therefore be ordained that this office shall apply not to those who despoil the Alexandrians or Saracens but only to other men. If this were done a smaller number of galleys would be sufficient to blockade that evil route, and many other men would oppose it manfully and effectively.

II

The pilgrims who go to Jerusalem also greatly assist the prince of Babylon at the expense of the Holy Land. Just as they do not fear excommunication by their superior, they do not pay due attention to the mandate of the church, nor consider how great harm they do to Christendom, nor realize how great an effect they have. For the sultan exacts and receives about thirty-five pennies of Tours from each pilgrim, and since innumerable pilgrims flow to Jerusalem from various regions of the world, what I say will be clear when this tribute is multiplied.[26] Evil is concealed under the piety of those pilgrims, therefore: their devotion leads to disobedience; and their zeal indiscriminately produces injustice, since the Saracens, the persecutors of the cross of Christ, derive an advantage and the church derives a disadvantage and Christianity a reason for offense, from forbidden pilgrimage of this type.

A fourfold remedy against this will be easy.

First, a sentence of excommunication should be issued against these pilgrims, with absolution reserved to the supreme pontiff only. Hitherto, after pilgrims of this sort had made a pilgrimage, they came to Cyprus or to some other place where

---

26   Fidentius of Padua, *Liber*, 9, 20, 24, in Paviot (2008), 63, 85 (and n. 135), 95, said that each pilgrim paid 36 or 40 silver grossae "and with this money that the sultan receives from the Christians, the sultan can fight against the Christians." The necessity of paying tribute to Muslim authorities in order to visit Jerusalem appears in many western pilgrim narratives from the thirteenth to the fifteenth centuries. In 1346, the Italian friar Niccolo of Poggibonsi told of beatings and imprisonment for western travelers who were unable to pay the tribute: Niccolo of Poggibonsi (1945), 9–10. Likewise, the pilgrims Frescobaldi and Gucci mention payments for tribute and other costs in 1384: Frescobaldi and Gucci (1948), 38, 98–99, 150–51. See also Prescott (1954), 51–52; Allen (2004), 90–92.

huiusmodi peregrini statim temeritatem pecunia redimebant, faciliter absolutionis beneficium obtinentes, si tantum de pecunia dabant quantum dederant pro tributo; quod certe erat fraus et deceptio ex duobus. Ex uno quia dabatur intelligi peregrinis quod essent ab omni sententia plenarie absoluti, cum tamen littere eorum testimoniales quas eis absoluentes super hac materia concedebat, eos esse absolutos non a papali, sed patriarchali tantummodo testarentur. Erat etiam, ex alio, deceptio ecclesie, quia inimico ecclesie babilonico principi ex tali peregrinatione proueniebat talis fauor sciente, absoluente pariter et uidente; et sic, non solum peregrini Sarracenis prestabant comodum supradictum, sed eisdem etiam ipsemet patriarcha eisdem fauebat, tacite uel expresse, cum ex tali facilitate uenire multis aliis tribuebat materiam delinquendi. Et ego de hiis que dico in presenti scirem cxcmpli causam adducere, nisi timerem *ponere os in celum*.

Secundo adhibeatur[c] hoc remedium ut in rebus et personis omni uolenti eos capere et bona diripere exponantur, ut quos Dei timor uel ecclesie reuerentia a malis non retrahit, retrahat timor pene.

Tertio modo obuiari poterit si omnes transportantes eos in suis uasis, illuc euntes uel inde reuertentes, simili ut ipsi peregrini excommunicationis sententia innodentur.

Quarto quod excommunicentur illi qui dictos peregrinos ad sua hospitia scienter receperint, illuc euntes uel etiam redeuntes.

III

Imperator autem[d] iterum constantinopolitanus fauet soldano et eum adiuuat in omnibus quibus potest. Inuicem enim se fratres nominant et frequenter inique pacis et confederationis fedus ineunt, per internuntios[e] sepius muneribus et exeniis[f] se mutuo uisitantes. Et hoc predicto imperatori parum uidetur, nisi etiam mitteret dicto soldano pueros et puellas, quod est iam supradicti nefandi et horrendi sceleris incentiuum. Quando etiam Egiptus fame laborat, frumentum et alia que potest uite necessaria subministrat, sicut quando Christiani Accon et eius confinia perdiderunt, contigit ut Dominus Egiptum tanta percuteret plaga famis.[g] Non enim Nilus fluuius de tribus annis supereffluxerat, ut Sarraceni fame rabidi, hinc inde mortui, ruerent subsistere non ualentes. In tantum enim fames inualuerat ut,

---

c et *add.* C   d autem *om.* BR   e internuntios *om.* (*cum spatio*) B
f enceniis ABC   g flamis AB, flammis C

the patriarch of Jerusalem might be, and they immediately atoned for their temerity by a payment and easily obtained the benefit of absolution if they gave only the same amount of money as they had given in tribute. This is undoubtedly a fraud and a deception for two reasons: first, because the pilgrims were given to understand that they were fully absolved from all judgment, though the testimonial letters of absolution which he granted them regarding this matter showed that they were absolved not by the pope but only by the patriarch. Second, the church was deceived because with his [the patriarch's] knowledge, absolution, and awareness, the enemy of the church, the prince of Babylon, derived such support from this pilgrimage. Thus not only did the pilgrims provide the aforesaid support to the Saracens but the patriarch himself also tacitly or expressly supported them, since by giving such a possibility for coming he provided an opportunity of sinning to many others. And I could explain these things of which I speak now if I did not fear to set my *mouth against heaven*.[27]

Second, an additional remedy should be for the possessions and persons of such men to be liable to seizure by anyone wishing to take them and their goods, so that the fear of penalty may restrain those whom the fear of God and reverence for the church does not restrain from evil deeds.

A third remedy would be for all those transporting the pilgrims in their ships, both going and returning, to be bound by the same sentence of excommunication as the pilgrims themselves.

Fourth, those who knowingly receive the pilgrims in their hospices, both going and also returning, should be excommunicated.

III

The emperor of Constantinople also supports the sultan and assists him in every way he can. For they call each other brothers and often make treaties of iniquitous peace and confederation, and they frequently visit each other by ambassadors with gifts and offerings.[28] It is not enough for the emperor unless he also sends boys and girls to the sultan as an enticement to the aforesaid wicked and horrible evil.[29] When also Egypt suffers from famine he sends grain and whatever other necessities of life he can. When the Christians lost Acre and its surroundings it happened that the Lord afflicted Egypt with a great plague of famine, for the river Nile had not flooded for three years, so that the Saracens collapsed, wild with hunger, dead on every side, lacking the means to survive. The famine was so great that

27 Ps. 72.9.   28 Cutler (1996).
29   Cutler (1996) cites lists of gifts from Byzantium to the caliphate that include slaves (51, 54) but also notes that "Human beings . . . appear much less often [in lists of diplomatic gifts] than one might expect. . . ." (64).

non dico pro cibo, sed nec pro semine granum poterat inueniri. Quam quidem plagam Sarraceni imputabant miraculo, quod scilicet miraculo[h] Egiptum ideo Dominus taliter percussisset quod Christiani de Terra Sancta expulsi fuerant. Quam ob causam Terram Sanctam Christianis reddere cogitabant. Sed persecutor ecclesie romane et antiquus hostis imperator iste unam nauem fecit de maioribus mundi, quam onustam frumento in Alexandriam delegauit. Que quidem nauis habebat de frumento mulos ·xiv·m· oneratos, preter[i] arma et multa alia que portabat. Et sic iste imperator, perfidus Sarracenorum amicus et socius, et Romanorum hostis et stimulus, Babiloniorum inopiam releuauit, et breuiter quicquid potest cogitare et facere,[k] hoc acceptat et complet, quod potest cedere soldano Babilonie in beneplacitum et fauorem, et hoc tractat et facit quod esse potest in malum nostrorum Christianorum romane ecclesie, nolens eos habere in dominos nec socios nec uicinos.

Remedia autem contra hoc[l] sunt illa que contra Alexandrinos posita sunt. Et poterit et aliud adhiberi, quod uidelicet scribantur littere imperatori predicto per summum pontificem, pro sua reductione ad fidem et obedientiam romane ecclesie. Sed hoc ita fiat[m] secrete, sicut secretius poterit pertractari, ita quod nulla suspicio possit apud monachos grecos et alium clerum et milites aliqualiter suboriri. Si enim monachi doctissime de hoc aliquid presentirent,[n] opponendo se, possent negotium totaliter impedire. Monachi enim totum populum decipiunt et in erroris tenebris retinent, et ad perditionis laqueos secum trahunt. Magnam enim exterius simulant sanctitatem, et uulgus indiscretam[o] eos sequens et credens apparentem sanctitatis speciem admirando fidei deserit ueritatem, et ecclesie romane fugit

---

h miraculo *del.* A, *om.* C   i   alia *add. et expunc.* B   k   et facere *om.* C   l   hec BC
m fiat ita C   n   prescirent B   o   *recte* indiscrete *uel* indiscretum

grain could not be found I do not say for food but not even for seed.[30] The Saracens indeed attributed this plague to a miracle because through a miracle the Lord thus had afflicted Egypt because the Christians had been expelled from the Holy Land, and they therefore considered returning the Holy Land to the Christians. This emperor, however, the persecutor and ancient enemy of the Roman church, made one of the largest ships in the world and sent it loaded with grain to Alexandria. This ship carried fourteen thousand mule-loads of grain in addition to arms and many other things. Thus the emperor, the perfidious friend and ally of the Saracens and enemy and torment of the Romans, relieved the neediness of the Babylonians.[31] In short, he accepts whatever he can think of and do and he furnishes what he can give to the sultan of Babylon for his pleasure and favor and does what he can to harm our Christians of the Roman church, whom he does not want to have as lords, allies, or neighbors.

The remedies against this are the same as those against the Alexandrians. To those can be added that the supreme pontiff should write letters to the emperor in order to bring him back to the faith and obedience of the Roman church.[32] This should be done secretly, however, as secretly as possible,[33] to avoid any suspicion arising among the Greek monks and other clergy and the soldiers.[34] For if the monks most skillfully receive any hint of this, they can completely block the negotiation by their opposition, because they deceive all the people, keep them in the darkness of error, and draw them with themselves into the snares of perdition. For externally they simulate great sanctity, and the mob, admiring the appearance of sanctity, follows and believes them, leaves the truth of the faith, and deserts and

30   Egypt experienced severe famine in 1295–97, when the Nile failed to rise to normal levels, and this famine was quickly followed by an epidemic. These disasters are recorded by several contemporary Arab historians: Dols (1977), 34. In the west, the chronicle of Amadi commented under the year 1296 on the "grandissima carestia et fame in Babilonia" and the consequent deaths, and on the aid given by Sicily, Constantinople, and Rhodes: *Chronique d'Amadi* (1891–93), 1:233.

31   According to Laiou (1972), 73 "it is at least clear that Andronicus II controlled much of the sale of wheat to foreigners" around 1285–94. It seems unlikely, however, that Andronicus could have built "one of the largest ships in the world," given the state of Byzantine naval operations at this point (ibid., 74–76). See also Ashtor (1969), 283 n. h and idem (1983), 21.

32   William here proposes a papal letter following the model of letters from pope Clement IV (1265–68) to emperor Michael VIII (1259–82). These letters usually demanded acceptance of papal primacy, the right of any churchman to appeal to the papacy, and Latin doctrine and practice in matters such as the *filioque* and purgatory. For a summary of papal correspondence with Michael, see Roberg (1964), 29–64; Gill (1979a), 106–33. Clement's letter served as a model for many later letters: Tăutu (1953), doc. 23, 65–67. See also Geanakoplos (1959), 202–4; Gill (1979a), 113–17; Hussey (1990), 223–24, 238–39.

33   Barlaam the Calabrian said much the same thing when he traveled to Avignon and spoke to pope Benedict XII in 1339: Tăutu (1958), doc. 43, cited and translated in Gill (1979a), 197–98.

34   Monks spearheaded some of the opposition to reunion of the churches under Michael VIII, but they were not the only opponents: Evert-Kappesowa (1949); eadem (1952); Laiou (1972), 33; Nicol (1989); Hussey (1990), 227, 237.

et despicit unitatem. Et quamuis has litteras non credam ad^p multum posse proficere, non enim credo eos misericordia et dulcedine flecti posse sed gladio et terrore, tamen per has litteras duo bona sequi poterunt. Vnum quod, si monitis summi pontificis noluerit assentire et uenire noluerit^q ad unitatis gremium romane ecclesie matris sue sed^r elegerit in erroris et scismatis solitudine peruagari, remanebit sollicitudo et^s cura pastoralis regiminis excusata. Aliud bonum sequi poterit, quia si assentiat piis monitis patris sui et post longam dissimilitudinem uoluerit anulum et stolam suscipere a misericorde patre digno studio preparatam, filio reuertenti gaudebitis. Gaudebit et summus pontifex quod ad caulas matris ecclesie ouis et talis ouis perdita sit reducta, et paterna suscipiente clementia filius, et talis *filius* qui *mortuus* fuerat *reuiuixerit, et* qui *perierit* sit *inuentus*. Et simpliciter credo quod si per alios summos pontifices fuissent ad Grecos amicabiles legationes et dulces littere destinate, non fuissent sic implacabili odio a sua nutrice et matre et domina romana ecclesia elongati, unde ipsi Greci et maxime sapientiores eorum, illi uidelicet qui de prioribus temporibus recordantur, cum de fide nobiscum disceptant,^{t} quando uident se quod ueritati nostre fidei obiciant non habere cum suspiriis ita dicunt: "Heu, si quis recordetur de priori illo statu ecclesie romane quando nitebatur filios suos aliquando oberrantes dulcibus litteris et admonitoriis legationibus ad unitatis gremium reuocare, et reuocatos pietatis sinu colligere et recollectos uerbi pabulo enutrire. Nunc autem matrem non se exhibet, sed nouercam."

IV

Quomodo autem per imperatorem Tartarorum aquilonis soldano Babilonie emolumentum proueniat, sciendum est quod sunt quatuor imperia Tartarorum.

---

p   ad *om.* BC   q   noluerit uenire C   r   nostri sue se *pro* sue sed C   s   in *pro* et B
t   discrepant C

despises the unity of the Roman church. And although I do not believe that these letters can achieve much,[35] because I believe they can be influenced more by the sword and fear rather than by mercy and kindness, two advantages can nonetheless derive from these letters. One is that if he [the emperor] rejects the advice of the supreme pontiff and refuses to return to the bosom of the unity of his mother the Roman church but chooses to wander in the wilderness of error and schism, no blame will attach to the solicitude and care of the pastoral rule. The other possible advantage is that if he accepts the pious advice of his father and after his lengthy dissembling wishes to receive the ring and the scarf which the merciful father has prepared with due care,[36] you will rejoice in the returning son; and the supreme pontiff will rejoice that a lost sheep, and such a sheep, has returned to the fold of the mother church and that, received by paternal clemency, a *son*, and such a son, who *was dead, is come to life again*, and that he who *was lost is found*.[37] And I frankly believe that if other highest pontiffs had sent friendly legations and kind letters to the Greeks, they would not have been estranged from their nurse, mother, and mistress the Roman church by such implacable hate. For this reason when the Greeks themselves, and especially their more learned men, that is, those who remember previous times, debate with us concerning the faith, they see that they have no objections to the truth of our faith and say with sighs: "Alas, let us remember the previous state of the Roman church, when it tried to recall its wandering sons to the bosom of unity by sweet letters and admonitory legations and to gather the recalled to the bosom of piety and to nourish the gathered with the food of the word. Now, however, it shows itself not a mother but a stepmother."[38]

IV

To understand how the sultan of Babylon is benefited by the emperor of the northern Tartars, it should be known that there are four empires of the Tartars.

---

35   Such pessimism about the likelihood that Byzantines would agree to reunite their church with Rome was widespread by William's time.

36   Although he had repudiated the union of Lyons upon ascending the throne (see n. 74 below), later in his reign Andronicus periodically reopened negotiations for union. William expresses a common western opinion that such negotiations were insincere and used by Byzantine emperors merely to allay threats of crusade: Laiou (1972), 308–29; Hussey (1990), 255–56.

37   Luke 15.24.

38   Narrating a debate between himself and a representative of the Byzantine church in 1136, Anselm of Havelberg put a similar idea in the mouth of the Greek: "If the Roman pontiff, seated on the lofty throne of his glory, wishes to thunder at us and, so to speak, hurl his mandates at us from on high, and if he wishes to judge us and even to rule us and our churches, not by taking counsel with us but at his own arbitrary pleasure, what kind of brotherhood, or even what kind of parenthood can this be? We should be the slaves, not the sons, of such a church, and the Roman see would be not the pious mother of sons but a hard and imperious mistress of slaves." The translation is in Runciman (1955), 115–16.

Primum et maius est orientale, quod Catay dicitur. Secundum est aquilonare, quod Gazaria nominatur. Tertium est meridionale, quod Persidis appellatur. Quartum est medium inter istud meridionale et illud primum, quod Doa uel Caydo nuncupatur.

Iste igitur imperator Tartarorum aquilonis cum soldano Babilonie multo federe est coniunctus, et ex eo maxime inter hos duos amicitia est tam grandis ut fortius mutuo se contra tertium inuicem adiuuent et defendant. Imperator enim Tartarorum Persidis inter illos duos, soldanum uidelicet et aquilonarem imperatorem Tartarorum, medius terram habet, et cum utroque exercet inimicitias perpetuas et mortales, et ab utriusque dominio terras aliquas usurpauit et suo imperio subiugauit. Quapropter unus contra duo, et duo contra unum, modis quibus possunt nituntur se defendere et iuuare. Soldanus Babilonie ipsum dominum Persidis destruere et annichilare conatur, ut inimicum propinquum et uicinum sibi periculosum, quod quia per se complere[u] non ualet, alium imperatorem sibi coniungit et conciliat muneribus et promissis, et parentelas inter se faciunt et confirmationes firmissimas ineunt, ut unus hinc alius inde medium imperatorem predictum Persidis de terra exterminent et euellant. Ille etiam consimili modo imperator Tartarorum aquilonis soldanum Babilonis per munera et internuntios uisitat et salutat, mittendo sibi pueros et puellas ad supradictum facinus perpetrandum. Sarracenos etiam[v] facarios,

u complacere C   v eius *pro* etiam AC

The first and greatest is the eastern, which is called Cathay. The second is the northern, which is called Khazaria. The third is the southern, which is called Persia. The fourth, which is called Duwa or Qaidu, is in the middle, between the southern and eastern empires.[39]

The emperor of the northern Tartars is allied with the sultan of Babylon by many treaties, which create so great a friendship between them that they strongly assist and defend each other against a third party. For, the land between them, that is, between the sultan and the emperor of the northern Tartars, is held by the emperor of the Tartars of Persia, who wages constant and deadly hostilities against them both and who has usurped and subjected to his power lands from the dominions of both. For this reason, one against two and two against one, they try to defend and help each other as best they can.[40] The sultan of Babylon tries to destroy and abolish the lord of Persia as a nearby and neighboring enemy dangerous to him, but since he cannot do this alone he has allied with the other emperor and won him over by gifts and promises. They make alliances between themselves and enter into very firm assurances so that one here, the other there, will exterminate and root out the emperor of Persia, who is in the middle. The emperor of the northern Tartars likewise visits and greets the sultan of Babylon with gifts and envoys and by sending him boys and girls to perpetrate the aforesaid crime. He receives into his domains and promotes and protects Saracen fakirs,

39   William identifies the four main branches of the Mongols (Tartars) in the early fourteenth century. The first, the Great Khans (later the Yüan dynasty in China), ruled from Mongolia and China (hence William's designation "eastern") after the conquests of their founder Chinggis (Ghengis) Khan, who died in 1226. The second "northern" Mongol group, which William locates in Khazaria (Khwarazim, perhaps Crimea), was the khans of the Golden Horde, descended from Chinggis's eldest son, Jochi (d. 1227). This Mongol dynasty controlled regions north of the Black sea, western Siberia, southern Russia, and the Qïpchaq steppe. The third or "southern" group, ruling in Persia, was the Ilkhānids, descended from Hülegü (d. 1265), a brother of the Great Khan, Möngke. The fourth or "middle" group was the Chaghatayids, who held control of eastern Turkestan and Transoxania and were descended from Chinggis's son, Chaghatay. Qaydu (or Qaidu), who died in 1301, was a great-grandson of Chinggis, who also had influence in the same region in the late thirteenth century (see *Recueil*, clxxviii n. 8). William mentions Du'a (or Duwa), who led this group in the early 1280s and died in 1307, and whose sons dominated the dynasty into the 1320s. On Mongol dynasties, see Bosworth (1996), 246–54, and on the collaboration between Christians and Mongols, Heyd (1885–86), 2:68–69, 122–23; Allsen (1987), 74–75, 82–83, 204–5.

40   The khans of the Golden Horde ("northern" Mongols) were heavily Islamized by the early fourteenth century and had strong economic connections with the Mediterranean world by way of the Black sea. The Mamluks established trade contacts with the Golden Horde, who were the principal source of northern slaves, who were transported to Egypt on Greek and Turkish and later Genoese ships. Because of this traffic, many Mamluks originally came from the region of the Qïpchaq steppe, a factor which aided further connections and alliances between Egypt and the Golden Horde. In contrast, the Ilkhānids ("southern" Mongols) were often in conflict with the Mamluks: Amitai (1995) and idem (2005), esp. 359–66 on the troubled years from 1260 to 1323, when peace was finally concluded.

id est monachos, et alios quoscumque in suo dominio recipit, promouet et tue-
tur, per quos tandem ipsemet cum multis aliis Tartaris Sarracenus pessimus
et Christianorum inimicus et persecutor est effectus.[w] Nam ad preces soldani,
omnes campanas ammouit de Christianorum ecclesiis sui dominii et edictum
fecit ut nullas ammodo haberentur.[x] Quod quidem cedit in Christianorum non
modicum scandalum et grauamen. Has uero societates predicti duo imperatores
per se tractant et firmant, scientibus et cooperantibus Ianuensibus, sine quibus
has colligationes inter se minime facere possent, nec soldanus ille tartaro imperatori facarios, id est monachos sarracenos, et alios nuntios ad peruertendum eum et
suum populum, nec Tartarus soldano posset mittere pueros et huiusmodi exenia[y]
prauitatis. Quicquid enim isti duo, uidelicet Tartarus et soldanus, sibi mutuo uolunt mittere, hoc Ianuenses transuehunt in suis nauibus et galeis, et talis iniquitatis
ministri et cooperatores effecti, exardescentes ad lucrum et ad pecunias iniantes,[z]
ad omne quod contra Deum et ecclesiam est, et ad omnium Sarracenorum et Tartarorum crimina fautores et promotores se exhibent et actores. Et tamen cum
Ianuenses dico, Alexandrinos illos solum intelligo quos Deus deberet et ecclesia
detestari tamquam ueritatis et fidei inimicos. Nam sunt multo plures incompara-
biliter alii Ianuenses qui talium crimina detestantur, nec pro omni auro[a] ad talia
consentirent.

Insuper sunt aliqui qui ad talem uiam euntibus uiriliter se opponunt, et multos Alexandrinos in rebus dampnificant et personis, inter quos sunt quidam
qui sunt filii domini Paleologi, filii quondam domini[b] Benedicti Zacharie,
cuius adhuc fama bona et celebre nomen uiuit. Qui quamdam habent insulam
in uia media sitam de Tartaria imperii aquilonaris et Constantinopolis, de quibus imperiis predicti pueri[c] extrahuntur in Alexandriam, ut predicitur,[d] depor-
tandi. De ista igitur insula per predictos Ianuenses qui in ea dominantur euntibus

w est effectus et persecutor C   x *recte* haberent   y encenia AC, encenie B
z iniantes *om.* (*cum spatio*) B, iuuantes C   a caro ACR   b domini *om.* C
c pueri predicti *corr.* predicti pueri C   d premittitur C

that is, monks, and any others by whom at length with many other Tartars he has become the worst Saracen and the enemy and persecutor of Christians. For at the request of the sultan he took away all the bells from the Christian churches in his dominions and decreed that henceforth they should have none, which created a great scandal and grievance among the Christians. These two emperors made and strengthened the alliances between themselves with the knowledge and cooperation of the Genoese, without whom these links between them would be impossible and the sultan could not send fakirs, that is, Saracen monks, and other messengers to the Tartar emperor in order to pervert him and his people, and the Tartar could not send to the sultan boys and offerings for this sort of depravity. The Genoese transport in their ships and galleys whatever these two, that is, the Tartar and the sultan, want to send to each other. They become agents and associates in such iniquity, eager for profit and avid for money, and show themselves supporters, promoters, and agents of all that is against God and the church and of the crimes of all the Saracens and Tartars. When I say the Genoese, however, I mean only those Alexandrians whom God and the church ought to detest as enemies of truth and the faith. For there are incomparably more other Genoese who detest the crimes of such men and would not for any price agree to such things.

Furthermore, there are others who vigorously oppose those who make such a journey and condemn many Alexandrians in their goods and persons. Among these are some who are the sons of the lord Paleologus, son of the late Benedetto Zaccaria, whose good reputation and famous name still live.[41] They have a certain island midway between the northern Tartar empire and Constantinople,[42] from which empire the aforesaid boys are taken to be carried, as said above, to Alexandria.[43] From this island, therefore, the Genoese who rule it prepare and

---

41   In 1275 or slightly earlier Michael VIII granted jurisdiction over the port of Phocaea, on a peninsula at the entrance to the gulf of Smyrna, to the Genoese merchant-adventurers Benedetto (d. 1307) and Manuele Zaccaria. Phocaea was rich in alum, crucial in the dyeing process, and the Zaccaria brothers, already from a prominent family, became wealthy and powerful figures in the eastern Mediterranean. Benedetto even served as a Byzantine imperial envoy in some crucial situations (as to the king of Aragon immediately before the Sicilian Vespers). They developed their own fleet to protect their interests: Miller (1911); Lopez (1933); Gatto (1956); Argenti (1958), 1:52–60; Geanakoplos (1959), 210–13, 251, 347–48, 357–58, 375–77; Laiou (1972), 152–53, 261, 319; Balard (1978); Kazhdan (1991a); Talbot (1991d); Trapp (1996), nos. 6490–96.

42   In 1305 Benedetto Zaccaria used the family's fleet to occupy the island of Chios, defending it against the Turkish advance and the Catalan company when the empire was unable to do so. The emperor granted him the island in fief—a further source of wealth because Chios was the only source of the aromatic herb mastic, a luxury product. In addition to references in n. 41 see Laiou (1972), 91, 152–53; Balard (1978), 308–10, 467–69; Gregory (1991).

43   Benedetto was famous for attacking and seizing Egyptian shipping, but William is more interested here in his sons and grandsons, whom he later identifies as Martino, Benedetto II, and Bartolomeo, who held Chios from 1307 and attempted to turn the island into a Christian military and naval outpost against Islam. This effort had the support of the papacy, but not of the Byz-

in Alexandriam cum predictis dampnabilibus mercibus multa dampna et offensiones et insidie preparantur et inferuntur, et adhuc plura facerent si manus ecclesie secum esset.[e] Nam nunc absque aliquo fauore ecclesie fere mille pedites et centum equites et duas galeas bene paratas et electe armatas, omni tempore, secum habent propriis sumptibus et expensis, cum quibus contra Turcos sarracenos eis uicinos, et contra illos qui uiam illam[f] faciunt maledictam, inimicitias et insidias[g] exercent grauissimas et mortales. Qua ex re inimici eis proueniunt capitales. Ad obuiandum autem ne tantum subsidium Sarracenis proueniat per imperatorem Tartarorum[h] aquilonis, quadruplex adhibeatur remedium.

Primo ut, sicut supra de aliis tactum est, contra omnes talia exennia portantes uel nuntios huiusmodi, uel Sarracenos facarios, uel quoscumque alios transuehentes in suis nauibus uel galeis que[i] mittuntur imperatori Tartarorum aquilonis per soldanum, uel econuerso, excommunicationis sententia promulgetur.

Secundo quia sunt aliqui qui nuntios, exennia[k] et pueros non portant in Alexandriam, uel aliquam terram soldano subiectam, sed portant in Turciam ad aliquem Babilonem[l] turcum, soldano amicitia obligatum, et ille postea curat[m] soldano cum diligenti sollicitudine delegare, quod ordinetur et declaretur uel statuatur, quatinus omnes simulationes huiusmodi facientes excommunicationis sententia innodentur, cum ut manifeste apparet per huiusmodi umquam mediationem soldano adiutorium prebeant et fauorem.

Tercio ut, quia sunt aliqui sue salutis obliti qui excommunicationem non metuunt, ordinentur alique galee per ecclesiam, que istum impediant transitum et defendant, et constituantur super illas domini supradicte insule que, ut predicitur, in medio uie de Tartaria in Egiptum sita est, utpote magis deuoti et uoluntarii et fideles ad hoc negotium peragendum. Vel, si forte ecclesia pecuniam pro galeis expendere nollet, quod saltem daretur predictis dominis et omnibus eos de persona iuuare uolentibus in hoc facto, uel pro certo numero hominum indulgentia que dari consueuit transfretantibus in subsidium Terre Sancte. Et si hoc fieret

---

e esset secum B   f illam uiam C   g et insidias *om.* B
h Tartarorum imperatorem B   i qui AC   k exemi B, encenia C
l balonem A, Babilonem *om.* C   m curat postea C

carry out many injuries, raids, and ambushes against the men going to Alexandria with their damnable cargoes, and they would do still more if the hand of the church supported them. For now, without any support from the church, they keep ready at all times at their own cost and expense almost a thousand foot-soldiers, a hundred horsemen, and two well-prepared and fully armed galleys, with which they inflict serious and deadly hostilities and attacks on the neighboring Saracen Turks[44] and the men who make that perfidious journey. From this they emerge as their mortal enemies. A four-fold remedy should be applied, however, to prevent such help coming to the Saracens from the emperor of the northern Tartars.

First, as has been said above, with regard to others, a sentence of excommunication should be promulgated against anyone carrying such offerings, messengers of this type, or Saracen fakirs, or any others transporting in their ships or galleys what is sent by the sultan to the emperor of the northern Tartars, or the reverse.

Second, since there are others who do not carry messengers, offerings, and boys to Alexandria or any land subject to the sultan but who carry them into Turkey to some Turk of Babylon who is bound to the sultan by friendship and who undertakes to send them afterward with diligent care to the sultan, it should be ordained, declared, and established that all those who cheat in this way should be bound by the sentence of excommunication, since, as is manifestly clear, they furnish aid and support to the sultan by this kind of mediation at any point.

Third, since some men are not mindful of their salvation and do not fear excommunication, the church should establish some galleys to hinder and prevent this traffic, and there should be established over them the lords of the island which is midway between Tartary and Egypt, since they are more dedicated, willing, and faithful in carrying out this mission. Or, if the church is unwilling to pay for the galleys, the indulgence customarily granted to those traveling to support the Holy Land should at least be given to the aforesaid lords and to all or some of the men who want to assist them in person in this activity.[45] If this were done

---

antine emperor, Andronicus II, or the Greek population of the island. In 1329, the Genoese were expelled from Chios. In addition to references in nn. 41 and 42, see Heyd (1885–86), 2:28–29; Balard (1989), 162.

44   When William was writing the Ottoman Turks controlled the northern part of Asia Minor, but the neighboring enemies of whom he speaks were the coastal emirates of Aydin, Menteshe, and Saruhan, which sponsored piracy in the Aegean and raids on neighboring islands and coastal areas: Zachariadou (1983, 1991a, 1991b, 1991c).

45   William suggests indulgences and other help for the Zaccaria family of Chios, on which see Heyd (1885–86), passim; Brătianu (1929), 138–44; Doehaerd (1941), 140, 225; Gatto (1956). By the time William wrote, the Zaccaria family had become legendary for their stand against the Turks, which was in fact motivated probably as much by self-interest as by Christian loyalty. It may have been this reputation that led the popes to grant them an exemption from the papal prohibition of trade with Egypt. They were allowed to sell mastic in Alexandria by explicit papal permission in

tria bona possent sequi: unum impeditio predicte uie; secundum quia omnes uadunt in Alexandriam de Constantinopoli, uel de alio loco huius imperii, uel de Tartaria predicta aquilonem, habent facere transitum per insulam illam, uel prope, in qua iam dicti domini principantur, et ideo uia[n] illa posset per hunc modum faciliter impediri. Tertium bonum indubitanter sequeretur ex hoc, si dominis predictis[o] hec indulgentia donaretur, quod uidelicet Ephesus et tota Minor Asia faciliter caperetur. Non enim ista insula est solummodo pro insidiis contra Alexandrinos disposita, sed etiam contra Turcos sarracenos mirabiliter ordinata. Vix enim ab Asia Minori, quam Turci possident fere totam, quinque miliaribus distat, et ideo quanto Turcis propinquior, tanto eiusdem[p] dampnabiliora irrogat nocumenta. Non enim Turci uicini predicte insule de duodecim miliaribus ad[q] maris litora appropinquant, timentes manum ualidam et audacem illorum qui in dicta insula dominantur, quam manum eos fortiter atterentem iam multipliciter sunt experti. Domini[r] dicte insule Turcos terre[s] marique uiriliter persequuntur et quotquot inueniunt uel gladio cedunt uel subiciunt seruituti, in tantum quod, mihi siue multi siue pauci sint, in terra uel in mari, cum dictorum dominorum uexillum conspiciunt, statim animo consternantur et mente deficiunt, non in defensionem, sed in fugam presidium affretantes.[t] Vnde anno presenti predicti domini, postquam octodecim[u] uasa piratica Turcorum et plus in mari cepissent, cum magna gloria et triumpho ad terras eorum descenderunt, et uillas multas magna cede uastantes, captiuos multos christianos, qui per dictos Turcos capti fuerant et seruituti subacti,[v] libertati pristine reddiderunt, eos cum armorum potentia et uirtute de manu sarracenica liberantes. Et hanc uictoriam non semel, sed pluries habuerunt, non in sua uirtute sed in Dei potentia confidentes, qui eos direxit in hiis et ab iniquorum Sarracenorum crudelitate protexit, sue solite medicine gratiam largiendo. Et per hunc modum a dextris et a sinistris inimicos Christi cedendo, captiuando et ad nichilum redigendo, aliorum Christianorum uicinorum suorum qui in aliis multis insulis commorantur, defensionis clipeus sunt effecti. Vnde conscientia mea est et omnium illorum qui de probitate istorum dominorum et de feritate Turcorum et de pusillanimitate[w] habitantium in insulis Romanie aliquid cognouerunt, quod, in nulla insula Turcis uicina homo, nec mulier, nec canis, nec cattus, nec aliquod uiuum animal remansisset, nisi dictorum dominorum uirtus et potentia obstitisset. Videte,[x] domine, quantum prodesset si eis concederetur fauor ecclesie, in hoc facto, et

---

n uilla *corr.* uia A, uilla C   o dictis dominis *pro* dominis predictis C
p huiusmodi *pro* eiusdem C   q litoris *add.* C   r Deinde *pro* Domini B
s *recte* terra   t afferentes C   u decem octo B   v subiecti B
w pusillamitate AC   x enim *add.* C

three advantages could follow: one, the blockade of the aforesaid route; second, this route could easily be blockaded in this way because anyone going to Alexandria from Constantinople, or from another port of this empire, or from northern Tartary has to go by or close to this island, where the said lords rule. A third advantage that would certainly follow if this indulgence were granted to the lords is that Ephesus and all of Asia Minor would be easily conquered. For this island is not only well situated for attacks against the Alexandrians but is also marvelously ordained against the Saracen Turks.[46] It is barely five miles from Asia Minor, which the Turks hold almost entirely, and the closer it is to the Turks the greater the damages inflicted on them. For the Turks who are neighbors to this island do not come closer than twelve miles to the shores of the sea out of fear of the strength and bravery of the rulers of the island, from whose attacks on them they have already suffered many times. The lords of this island vigorously persecute the Turks by land and sea, and they kill by the sword or subject to servitude as many as they find, so that, whether they are many or few, on land or on sea, for me, when the Turks see the banner of the said lords, they are at once frightened out of their wits and load soldiers not for defense but for flight. Whence in the present year the aforesaid lords, after capturing eighteen and more piratical ships of the Turks on the sea, attacked their lands with great glory and triumph, laid waste many estates with great slaughter, and set free many Christian captives who had been taken and put in servitude by the Turks, freeing them from the hands of the Saracens by the force and strength of arms. They had this victory not once but many times, relying not on their own strength but on the power of God, Who directed them in these matters and protected them from the cruelty of the iniquitous Saracens by granting the grace of His customary medicine. In this way, by killing, capturing, and reducing to nothing the enemies of Christ on the right and on the left, they became the defensive shield of their other Christian neighbors who live on many other islands. It is well known to me, therefore, and to everyone who knows anything about the trustworthiness of those lords, the ferocity of the Turks, and the cowardliness of the inhabitants of the islands of Romania[47] that no man, woman, dog, cat, or any living creature has remained on any island close to the Turks without the resistance of the strength and power of the said lords. See, o lord, how advantageous it would be if they were granted the support of the church for these exploits and

---

1320, 1322, and 1325. In 1323 and 1329 the popes granted crusading indulgences to all Christians who were mortally wounded in battles against Turks in or near Chios: Argenti (1958), 55–59.

46   Mas Latrie (*Recueil*, 532 n. a) identifies these "Saracen Turks" as the emirate of Aydin. The family of Aydïn Oghlu Muhammad Beg (d. 1308) held territory on the coast of western Anatolia from the early fourteenth century and was often allied with Byzantium against the early Ottoman states. On this dynasty, see Bosworth (1996), 221.

47   A commonplace in western references to Greeks before, during, and after the crusades: cf. below at n. 57 and Setton (1976), 166 n. 17.

quam facile esset illis dominis cum aliquali manu ecclesie, et uiam illam maledictam Alexandrie^y impedire, et Turcos illos Minoris Asie subiugare, cum ipsi
per se sine alicuius adiutorio nisi Dei tantum negotium inceperint tam laudabili-
ter et tam strenue atque continuauerint, semper de celo uictoria eis data. Istorum
nomina, si quis scire uelit, Martinus Zacharie, Benedictus Zacharie, Bartholemeus Zacharie, fratres germani, sic per ordinem geniti nominantur, quamuis sint
alii eorum fratres in numero copioso.

Quartum remedium adhiberi posset quod omnibus malis suprapositis obui-
aret, uidelicet si Dominus nostrorum regum cordi infunderet ut ipsi interdum
zelarent partem Domini, et eos moueret aliquando honor crucis, ut sicut frequenter pro caducis et miseris rebus mundi pro honore proprio uago et fragili,
mortibus et stragibus se opponunt pluribus^z et diuersis, suos gladios fidelium
Christianorum suorum fratrum sanguine mirabiliter^a sauciantes, non sine deco-
ris fidei scandalo et ruina, ita^b aduersus Babilonios conuenirent, qui hereditatem
Domini cum iniustitia detinent, et de eadem quod est flebile dicere cultum et
nomen Christianitatis penitus deleuerunt. Meo autem iudicio [et]^c omnium illorum qui morantur in partibus orientis, numquam fuit nobis sic paratum, si corda
regum adessent et principum, generale passagium, sicut modo.

Primo ex parte illorum contra quos habet passagium fieri; secundo ex parte
illorum cum quibus habent transire nostri reges, si passagium ordinetur; tertio ex
parte illorum qui christiani non sunt, qui possunt et uolunt passagium adiuuare;
quarto ex parte domini pape cuius auctoritate habet passagium ordinari.

Quia soldanus Babilonie, ut satis uestris auribus innotuit, prout credo, omnes
admiratos et principes et pugnatores strenuos qui de bellis aliquid nouerant de suo
dominio expulit uel occidit, propter quod ad repugnandum redditur minus fortis.
Iterum Sarraceni habent multas suas prophetias, quibus fidem adhibent sicut nos
euuangelio, quod in breui debet eorum secta pestifera terminari et per nostros
totaliter annullari, et ex hoc tantam formidinem in suis cordibus conceperunt
ut statim audito passagio non uidetur ut ad pugnam se preparent, sed ad fugam.
Vnde tempore felicis recordationis Clementis pape ·v·, cum ego^d essem in partibus
Indie et Persidis, cum de passagio uox insonuit, non uidebatur Sarracenis ad

---

y Allexandrie maledictam C   z   plurimis C   a *pro* miserabiliter (?)   b et *add.* C
c [et] *add.* R   d   ego *om.* C

how easily those lords with some help from the church could both blockade the accursed route to Alexandria and subdue the Turks of Asia Minor, since they have by themselves, with no help except that of God, so laudably and vigorously begun and prosecuted such an undertaking, always with victory granted them by heaven. Their names, if anyone wants to know, are the brothers Martino Zaccaria, Benedetto Zaccaria, and Bartolomeo Zaccaria, so named in order of birth, though they have many other brothers.

A fourth remedy that could be applied and would obviate all the aforesaid troubles is for the Lord to inspire the hearts of our kings zealously meanwhile to take the part of the Lord and for the honor of the cross finally to move them. Rather than, to the scandal and ruin of the good name of the faith, frequently exposing themselves to death and destruction and wonderfully shedding with their swords the blood of their faithful Christian brothers for the sake of perishable and miserable worldly things and their own inconstant and fragile honor, they should join together against the Babylonians who unjustly hold the inheritance of the Lord and lamentably have entirely destroyed the cult and name of Christianity from this [inheritance]. In my judgment, however, and that of all those who live in the east, the time has never been so ready as now for us to go on a general crusade, if the hearts of kings and princes would help.

First, on the part of those against whom the crusade ought to be directed; second, on the part of those with whom our kings must travel if a crusade were ordained; third, on the part of those who are not Christians but who can and want to assist a crusade; fourth, on the part of the lord pope, by whose authority a crusade has to be ordained.

Since the sultan of Babylon, as is I believe well known to you, has expelled from his dominions or killed all his admirals, generals, and vigorous warriors who know anything about fighting, he is rendered less able to resist.[48] The Saracens, furthermore, have many prophecies,[49] which they use for their faith as we do the Gospel, that their pestiferous sect will soon be terminated and entirely abolished by our men, and from this they have conceived so great a fear in their hearts that as soon as they hear of a crusade they seem to prepare not for war but for flight. In the time of pope Clement V of happy memory, when I was in the regions of India and Persia and there was word of a crusade,[50] it seemed to the Saracens that they

---

48   William is probably referring to the second attempted usurpation of the sultan Muhammad I b. Qalāwūn in 1309–10, after which he purged the old guard of *amirs* associated with his rival Baybars II, of whom he had a number arrested, imprisoned, or killed: Holt (1986), 111–13.

49   There is a reference to these prophecies in the *Directorium* (1906), 513.

50   The Templars and Hospitallers had drawn up a proposal for a new crusade in 1306, at the request of Clement V, and the possibility of a new crusade had also been discussed at the council of Vienne in 1311–12.

abscondendum se satis, pro tempore, latibula^e inuenire. Iterum Sarraceni Egipti usum armorum totaliter perdiderunt.

Ex parte uero illorum cum quibus nostri reges passagium habent facere, ut sunt barones, milites et populares, quantum sit bene paratum per eorum deuota suspiria satis patet. Desiderat enim passagium omnis hominum conditio, gradus, sexus et etas, ita ut non uideantur Sarracenos uelle inuadere, sed eos uiuos et integros deglutire. Sed et si quis est quem transfretare uel etatis grauitas, uel corporis debilitas, uel carnis infirmitas, uel sexus fragilitas non permittat, dolent, suspirant et gemunt, uel quia Deus non prolongat eis uitam ut uideant, uel quia fortitudinem et uirtutem non reformat ut pugnare ualeant, uel quia Deus eos tales fecit ut non pro armis idonei habeantur ad mortem Domini uindicandam. Omnium hominum denique multitudo desiderat ut in diebus suis nostra preclara hereditas recuperetur, quam nobis Dominus^f preelegit, quam sua presentia benedixit, in qua nasci, conuersari, uiuere et mori uoluit homo Deus, ut inibi Christianitas augmentetur, et cultus ecclesie uigeat, et nomen Domini libere predicetur, glorificetur et digne et simpliciter adoretur. Tanti desiderii stimulus, tanti amoris flamma corda nostrorum Christianorum stimulat et succendit pro passagio Terre Sancte, quod, si nunc fieret, mihi apparet certissime ante posse naues quam gentes deficere, nec posse omnia mundi uasa recipere transeuntes. Videtis ergo quomodo, contra naturam, precessor manet immobilis, et sequens uelociter currit; membra, sensus et uite germina preferunt, et caput manet emortuum; cessat motus in uita, et uiuit et uiget quod per motum uiuere consueuit. Quod ergo peccatum in regibus, que iniquitas nostri temporis, que infelicitas Christianitatis, quod uidemus hostes fragiles, nostros pugiles audaces et fortes, gloriam triumphi dispositam et coronam nobis uictorie preparatam, et accipere rennuamus immo etiam fugiamus.

Illi uero qui parati sunt passagium adiuuare est imperator Persidis, qui quantum et quare illud cupiat et affectet breuiter uideamus. Imperator enim iste inter supradictos imperatorem Tartarorum aquilonis et soldanum Babilonie medius terram habet, et ob causam superius memoratam contra illos duos guerram habet perpetuam et^g inimicitias capitales. Et quia non habet alios reges sibi uicinos quos possit in suum adiutorium inuitare, et in Sarracenorum Babilonis odium prouocare, nostrorum Romanorum querit sibi^h amicitiam uendicare, et contra dictos Sarracenos nostros Christianos concitare nititur quantum potest, ut nostri ex una parte uersus meridiem, et ipse cum suis ab aquilone ex altera, medium soldanum opprimerent, submitterent et calcarent. Et hoc est ad quod ipse laborat pro uiribus, et quod toto suo spiritu desiderat et affectat, et ut Sarracenorum destructio expeditius et ualidius compleretur, in promotionem passagii multa promittit subsidia uictualium et hominum armatorum,

e latabilia C   f Deus C   g ob causam … perpetuam et *om.* B   h sibi querit C

could not find enough hiding places in which to hide themselves for the time. Furthermore, the Saracens of Egypt have entirely lost the use of arms.

With regard to those with whom our kings must make a crusade, such as the barons, soldiers, and commoners, their devout sighs show clearly enough how ready they are. Every condition, rank, sex, and age of men desires a crusade, so that they seem to want less to invade the Saracens than to eat them alive and whole. Anyone who is unable to cross the sea owing to the burden of age, weakness of body, infirmity of flesh, or fragility of sex grieves, sighs, and groans, either because God does not prolong their lives so that they may see, because He does not restore their strength and manliness so that they are strong enough to fight, or because God created them such that they are unsuited for arms to vindicate the death of the Lord. All men, finally, want our magnificent inheritance, which the Lord predestined for us, which His presence blessed, and where the God-man wished to be born, abide, live, and die, to be recovered in our time so that Christianity may increase there, the discipline of the church may flourish, and the name of the Lord may be freely preached, glorified, and worthily and straightforwardly adored. The stimulus of such great desire and the flame of such great love stimulates and inflames the hearts of our Christians for a crusade to the Holy Land, for which, in my view, if it is made now, ships would certainly be lacking before people and all the ships in the world could not take the men who were crossing the sea. You see therefore how, against nature, the leader remains unmoving and the follower runs swiftly; the limbs, senses, and signs of life are in front and the head is lifeless; the movement in life ceases and that which is accustomed to live by movement lives and flourishes. What a sin it is in our kings, therefore, what an iniquity of our time, and what a misfortune for Christianity that we see our enemies weak and our warriors brave and strong and that we refuse to accept and even flee from the glory arranged for our triumph and the crown of victory prepared for us.

Among those who are ready to help a crusade is the emperor of Persia, and we shall briefly see how much and why he wants and strives for this. For this emperor holds the land between the emperor of the northern Tartars and the sultan of Babylon, against whom, for the reason explained above, he wages constant war and deadly hostilities. And since there are no other nearby kings whom he can ask for help, and provoke to hate the Saracens of Babylon, he tries to win the friendship of our Romans and to arouse our Christians as much as he can against the Saracens so that with us on one side, to the south, and he himself with his men on the other side, from the north, they may oppress, subjugate, and crush the sultan in the middle. He strives for this with all his strength and wants and pursues it with his whole spirit; and in order that the Saracens may be more quickly and effectively destroyed he promises great supplies of food and armed men to promote a crusade,

ob hoc etiam frequenter ad curiam romanam solemnes nuntios mittere attemptauit, et hoc anno potissime, nisi quod per mortem imperatoris predicti et alias per uacationem curie fuerunt eius nuntii impediti.

Vt autem uideatur quam facile[i] sit promittere omne quod uelit et attendere quod promittit, ex hoc patet. Nam preter Tartaros sui dominii posset habere de terris sibi subditis plus quam ·l·m· equitum christianorum, et plus quam[k] ·cc·m· peditum, qui eum, pro hoc negotio, omnes uno et prompto animo sequerentur. Inter quos est quoddam magnum[l] regnum quod uocatur uulgato nomine[m] Georgianorum, sed greco nomine Hiberorum, quia[n] de Hiberia, hoc est de Hispania, originem habuerunt. Isti ergo Georgiani regem habent quem semper David uocant, et super omnes orientales sunt strenui bellatores, insatiabiliter sanguinem Sarracenorum sitientes, et supra modum passagium affectantes. Tales sunt ut numquam imperator Persidis uictoriam de Sarracenis habuit, nisi istorum potenti gladio mediante. Vnde quando Tartari Baldacum obsederant numquam ante ingredi presumpserunt quam Georgianorum exercitus precessisset. Cumque, post cedem innumerabilem Sarracenorum ibi factam, galifa eorum, id est papa, solus quasi superstes fuisset, et contra Tartarum in modum maledictionis excommunicationis maledicta congereret, et ex hoc in eum manus mittere Tartari formidassent, Georgianus[o] unus princeps audacior ceteris manu ualida ensem uibrans, trinitatis prius nomine inuocato uno solo ictu caput cum dextro humero amputauit, sicque ictus ille tale discrimen Sarracenis[p] contulit et iacturam, quam ex tunc nullus galifa alius resurrexit.

Nec[q] hoc uideatur[r] extraneum, quia suadeo esse de hoc negotio in Tartaris confidendum. Nam, tempore quo sanctus Ludouicus rex passagium fecit, opus simile actum est ut Tartari qui tunc nouiter Persidem occuparant

i facilis C   k et plus quam *om.* B   l magnum *om.* B   m nomine uulgato C
n qui C   o autem *add.* C   p Sarracenis discriminem C   q Ne B
r uidetur C

and for this he has often tried to send solemn messengers to the Roman curia, and especially this year except that some of his messengers were held up by the death of the emperor and others by the vacancy at the curia.[51]

It will be clear from the following, however, how easy it is to promise everything he wants and to give heed to what he promises. For in addition to the Tartars from his dominions, he can raise from the lands subject to him more than fifty thousand Christian horsemen and more than two hundred thousand foot soldiers, all of whom would follow him for this purpose with a single and ready spirit. Among these lands is a large kingdom called of the Georgians in the vulgar tongue and of the Iberians in Greek, since they had their origins in Iberia, that is, Spain. These Georgians have a king whom they always call David, and of all the men of the east they are the most vigorous warriors, thirsting insatiably for the blood of the Saracens and striving beyond measure for a crusade.[52] They are such that without the help of their powerful sword, the emperor of Persia never has had a victory over the Saracens. When the Tartars besieged Baghdad they did not presume to enter unless the army of Georgians went first; and when, after innumerable Saracens were killed, their caliph, that is, pope, was almost the only survivor and heaped up curses against the Tartars like an excommunication and the Tartars on this account were afraid to raise their hands against him, a Georgian prince, braver than the others, brandished his sword with a strong hand, invoked the name of the Trinity, and with a single blow cut off the caliph's head and his right shoulder, and that blow marked such a turning point and loss for the Saracens that afterward no other caliph has arisen.[53]

This is not irrelevant, because on the basis of this event I urge that confidence should be put in the Tartars. It likewise happened that when the king St. Louis went on crusade the Tartars who had at that time recently occupied Persia

51   There were several contacts between the Ilkhānids and Europe from the middle of the thirteenth century into the early fourteenth century, and there is some evidence of hope for an alliance against the Mamluks. Among other evidence, this is suggested in a letter written by khan Hülegü to the French king Louis IX in 1262, and the expatriate Armenian prince Haython (Het'um) urged a Mongol-European alliance in a treatise on crusading written in 1307 at the behest of Clement V: Jackson (2005), 119–20, 184–86. The Ilkhānid ruler, Muhammad Khudābanda Öljeytü, died in 1316, and when pope Clement V died in 1314, there was an interregnum of two years until the election of John XXII in 1316.

52   On the warlike qualities of the Georgians, see Fidentius of Padua, *Liber*, 92, in Paviot (2008), 163; also Heyd (1885–86), 1:68; Von den Brinken (1973), 118; Allsen (1987), 74, 205.

53   In 1258, Mongol forces led by Hülegü had captured Baghdad and killed the last undisputed Abbasid caliph, al-Mustansir. Although there were Christian Georgian forces traveling with the Mongol armies, there is no evidence that al-Mustansir met his death at their hands: Allsen (1987), 83–85. In 1250, two Georgian kings—both called David—had been set in place by the Mongols, and these two men ruled simultaneously in Georgia until one, Narin David, revolted and broke with the Mongols in 1259: see *Recueil*, 535 n.a.; Suny (1994), 41. On the caliph "whom the Saracens consider pope" and the death of the last caliph, see William of Tripoli, chaps. 11, 23 (1883), 581, 589.

ex una parte Sarracenos hostes premerent, de consensu et conniuentia predicti regis, ut ipse rex ex altera eosdem hostes fortiter cohartarent,[s] unde et tunc Tartari totam Chaldeam et Baldacum eiusque confinia suo dominio subiugarunt. Si igitur reges nostri cum dicto imperatore uelint, ut predicitur, conuenire, hinc inde obpugnantibus nostris et Tartaris taliter medius inter istos inimicos crucis, princeps babilonicus prosternetur,[t] quod *non adiciet ut resurgat.*

Quomodo uero passagium sit dispositum ex parte domini pape, cuius habet auctoritas ordinare, posset quilibet ex diuersis signis et operibus similibus comprobare. Quamuis enim ego et mei similes non possumus scire, nec decet, eius ordinationis profunditatem, nec eius alti consilii plene cognoscere ueritatem, tamen possumus utrumque perpendere quod eius mens tota ad exaltationem fidei, ad dilatationem nominis christiani, ad consolationem fidelium et ad gloriam domus Domini sit intenta. Cognoscere possumus quod tota eius intentio occupetur, totum eius desiderium inardescat, tota eius anima feratur in hoc, ut in[u] diebus suis dilatetur ecclesia, cultus christianus fulgeat, populus Deo seruiens merito et numero augeatur, et nomen Domini Iesu, ut dignum est, suscipiat incrementum. Cognoscere possumus quia eius in tempore omnis uiperarum *abhortiua plantatio quam pater* omnium *non plantauit*, omnisque structura quam manus Domini non fundauit, excisionem patitur et iacturam, omnisque nouella seminaria gratie et uirtutis dant folia et[v] flores et fructus utiles et producunt, et omnis celestis fundatio sumit ortum, erigitur et proficit et firmatur. Cognoscere possumus quod, more diligentis opificis, incessanter eius animus occupetur qualiter materia celesti patrocinio disponatur, ut cum disposita fuerit forma debita materie perfectio imprimatur. Quia materia uitiata et nimis idonea comprobatur, et perfectionis formam suscipere non modo negligit, sed recusat. Inde est quod passagium differtur totaliter uel aufertur, unde non est defectus capitis nutrimentum debitum subministrans, si membra emortua uita carent. Culpa est rei mobilis, non motoris, si[w] res mouenda motum non recipit, si[x] per motorem motui modus debitus adhibetur. Si ergo summus noster pontifex preuenit admonendo, disponit indulgentias conferendo, perficit decimas ecclesie largiendo, nutrit in hiis perseuerando, mouet exempla saluberrima ostendendo, que culpa eius est si reges et principes christiani non obtemperant ut imperfecti, non sentiunt ut infirmi, non mouentur ut indeuoti, non obediunt ut elati? Vnde satis patet ex hiis[y] quantum sit summus pontifex ad passagium uoluntarius et deuotus, quantum sint inimici debiles et infirmi, quantum sint nostri

---

s   *recte* cohartaret   t   prosterneretur BR   u   in *om.* C   v   et *om.* C
w   sed motoris non est *pro* non motoris si C   x   sed *pro* si B   y   ex hiis *om.* B

attacked the Saracen enemies on one side, with the consent and agreement of the king, who strongly pressed the same enemies from the other side.[54] For this reason the Tartars also at that time brought all of Chaldea and Baghdad and the surrounding lands under their rule. If therefore our kings want to make an agreement with this emperor, as has been said, when our men and the Tartars attack on this side and that, in such a way, the Babylonian prince, as if caught in the middle of the enemies of the cross, *shall fall and* furthermore *not rise again.*[55]

Anyone can show from various signs and similar works how a crusade may be arranged on the part of the lord pope, by whose authority it must be ordained. For although I and others like me cannot and should not know the depth of his ordinance nor fully understand the truth of his lofty counsel, we can however consider that his mind is fully devoted to the exaltation of the faith, the spread of Christianity, the consolation of the faithful, and the glory of the house of the Lord. We can know that his entire intent is occupied, his entire desire burns, and his entire spirit is driven by his desire that the church should be expanded in his days, Christian worship may shine, the people serving God may increase in merit and number, and the name of the Lord Jesus, as is proper, may grow. We can know this because in his time *every untimely plant* of vipers *which the Father* of all things *hath not planted*[56] and every structure which the hand of the Lord did not establish suffers excision and loss, and every new seed bed of grace and virtue gives and produces leaves, flowers, and useful fruits, and every heavenly foundation is born, rises, prospers, and is confirmed. We can know that like a diligent craftsman his spirit is ceaselessly concerned with how the matter is arranged under heavenly protection so that perfection may be imprinted when the due form of the matter has been arranged. Since faulty material is both proven very unsuitable and not only disregards but refuses to receive the form of perfection, it is for this reason that a crusade is totally put off or cancelled. It is therefore not the defect of the head ministering the proper nourishment if the dying limbs lack life. If the proper method of motion is applied by the mover [the pope] and the thing to be moved [the kings and princes] does not move, the fault lies not with the mover but with the thing to be moved. If therefore our supreme pontiff acts by advising, arranges by confirming indulgences, executes by granting tithes of the church, nourishes by persevering in these things, and moves by showing most salubrious examples, what fault of his is it if the Christian kings and princes, being imperfect fail to submit, being weak fail to feel, lacking devotion fail to move, and being proud fail to obey? These things show clearly how willing and devoted the pope is for a crusade, how weak and infirm are the enemies, how willing and ready are our

---

54   On communications between Hülegü and Louis IX, see Amitai (1995), 94–102.

55   Is. 24.20.   56   Matt. 15.13; cf. Matt. 23.33; Job 3.16.

pugiles uoluntarii et parati, quantum sint potentes et prompti qui debent et uolunt[z] passagium adiuuare. In solis ergo regibus et principibus remanet et deperit tantum bonum.

Vbi[a] uero passagium istud[b] incipi debeat dicendum existimo et dico quod qui uult ut[c] passagium prosperetur a Constantinopoli illud debere incipi iudicabit. Et hoc septem rationibus sic[d] ostendo.

Prima ratio est quia nunc peccatis exigentibus populi[e] Christiani, ab Alexandria Egipti usque in Constantinopolim Christiani catholici non tenent passum unum, sed totam terram illam uel Sarracenorum Egipti uel Turcorum Minoris Asie hostilis gladius occupauit. Vnde nec castrum est, nec uilla, nec ciuitas, nec portus aliquis, maxime ad maritimam, infra predictum spatium, que non sint Sarracenorum uel Turcorum ditioni[f] subiecta. Inter alia uero que passagio necessaria sunt est ut habeant equi et homines ubi, post maris tedia et labores, possint aliqualiter recreari. Si enim debilitati et maris tempestatibus et lassati haberent, statim hostes inuadere possent in descensu ad terram de nauibus, ab hostibus iaculorum et arcuum et balistarum obstaculis multa incomoda substinere, uel certe pati diuersas insidias et insultus, sicut possumus in multis exempli causam inducere, quos insperata aduersitas in casu simili occupauit. Et hoc non debet aliquis credere, cum hostes illi crucis et Christi castra Dei aduersus se moueri senserint, quin castra sua maritima fortiter muniant, portus defendant, littora armatis operiant, ut pro posse exercitum Domini ueri Dei[g] a se[h] reiciant et repellant. Sed ut concilium[i] malignantium Sarracenorum in sua nequitia pereat, et ad impediendum Dei partem locum non habeant malignandi penitus uel nocendi, cogitanda et eligenda uia est per quam cura maiori nostrorum consolatione et comodo et aduersariorum periculo et iactura passagium maturius et salubrius principium assequatur, quod erit si incipiat ubi dico. Ad quod aduertendum quod quamuis uterque[k] sint hostes romane ecclesie et fidei inimici Sarraceni, uidelicet et Greci, inter quos distinctionem non facio in hac parte, atque[l] uterque ad resistendum nostris, si hoc contingeret, se fortiter prepararent, et ex hoc nostri in Grecia ut in Egipto resistentiam inuenirent, tamen, quia Greci minus quam Sarraceni habent de audacia et uirtute, ex quo potissime a romana ecclesia discesserunt, et ex hoc possent facilius subiugari. Tamen[m] nullus credat quod de istis et de illis subiugandis et conterendis faciliter diffidentiam[n] habeam, quia scio quod Dominus iam descendit et contra eos irascitur furor eius, nempe iam clamorem opere compleuerunt.

---

z   uolunt et debent C   a   ergo *add.* C   b   istud passagium C   c   quod *pro* ut C
d   sic *om.* C   e   populi *om.* C   f   inditioni B   g   et *add.* C   h   a se *om.* B
i   consilium C, uia *add.* AC   k   utrique C   l   et *pro* atque C   m   cum *pro* tamen C
n   diffidendum C

warriors, and how strong and keen are the men who should and want to assist the crusade. Such good remains unmoved and perishes, therefore, only in the kings and princes.

I think it should be stated, however, where a crusade should start, and in my view anyone who wants a crusade to prosper will think that it ought to start at Constantinople, as I shall show by seven reasons.

The first reason is that owing to the sins of the Christian people, the catholic Christians do not now hold a single foot between Alexandria in Egypt and Constantinople and that the entire region is occupied by the hostile sword of either the Saracens of Egypt or the Turks of Asia Minor. Within that region there is no fort, estate, town, or port, especially on the coast, that is not subject to the rule of the Saracens or the Turks. Among other requirements for a crusade is that the horses and men have a place where they can somewhat recover after the weariness and labors of the sea. For if they are worn out by weakness and the storms of the sea, and the enemy can attack as soon as they land from the ships, they will sustain many injuries from the spears, bows, and balisters of the enemies and will certainly suffer various ambushes and attacks, as we can show from many examples of men seized by unexpected adversity in such circumstances. No one should believe that when the enemies of the cross and Christ feel the armies of God moving against them they will not strongly fortify their coastal fortresses, defend the ports, and fill the shores with armed men in order to repulse and repel as much as they can the army of the Lord the true God. But in order that the counsel of the malignant Saracens may perish in its iniquity and that they should have no chance to impede the side of God by inflicting serious harm and damage, a route should be planned and selected by which the crusade will begin more wisely and advantageously with greater care, consolation, and advantage for our men and greater damage and loss to our enemies, as will be the case if it begins where I say. It should be noted in this regard that although both the Saracens and the Greeks, between whom I make no distinction in this respect, are enemies of the Roman church and of the faith, and both would be prepared to resist our men strongly if necessary and would mount resistance to our men in Greece as in Egypt, the Greeks nevertheless are less brave and manly than the Saracens,[57] especially now that they have separated from the Roman church and can therefore be more easily subjugated. No one should believe, however, that I lack confidence that both the latter and the former can be easily subjugated and defeated, since I know that the Lord has already come down and His anger is aroused against them, and they have certainly already carried out His word in deeds.

57   See p. 53 and n. 47 above.

Est etiam alia causa quare Grecia haberetur facilius quam Egiptus, quia sunt iam ibi multa loca, castra et insule que nunc a filiis obedientibus et deuotis romane ecclesie possidentur.

Est enim una insula quorumdam dominorum Ianuensium de Zachariis, de quibus feci superius[o] mentionem, habundans in portibus optimis et quietis, riuis, fontibus irrigua et amena, planis, montibus et nemoribus est iocunda, aere sana, fructibus copiosa, que quantum esset passagio comoda scio ego, sciunt et multi qui ibi fuerunt, maxime si nostri principes in Grecia principium passagii dirigi iudicarent. Habet enim hec insula ante se ad tria miliaria locum quemdam in Turcia, que apud nos Asia Minor dicitur, qui quidem locus est lingua terre in mare protensa, que est angusta in principio uersus Turcos et uersus mare et uersus dictam insulam rotunda, et in modum circuli dilatatur. Habet autem in circuitu miliaria ·clxxx·, et ubi angustior est tria tantum. Est etiam uersus partem illam magis stricta, hinc Smirna, inde ciuitas Ephesina. In ista lingua que caput uocatur sunt uineta pulcerrima, oliueta iocundiora et maiora de toto imperio romano, pascua, fruges pingues, aque preterfluentes, uenatica nemora et umbrosa. In isto capite Turci habitare non audent, nec etiam aliquando apparere, quia dicti domini dicte insule ibi eos quiescere non permittunt, et[p] domini insule illud nequeunt possidere, quia non habent secum alicuius potentis uel ecclesie manum fortem. Istud caput posset sine scuto et lancea, et fere sine sanguine, occupari. Quo habito totum generale passagium posset in eo recreari consolabiliter et secure, et in portibus qui circa sunt totum mundi nauigium reparari, nec oporteret timere Turcorum per terram insidias uel insultus, quia per partem illam in qua angustius est, nullus nisi per passum strictum posset accedere. Quem passum possent contra omnium Sarracenorum et Turcorum impetum pauci homines custodire. Sunt etiam castra circumquaque pulcerrima et fortia, cum fossatis magnis et turribus, sed omni habitatore carentia. Per istud caput non dubito quin tota Minor Asia caperetur. Est etiam quoddam castrum in terra firma Turcorum, a latere predicte lingue uel capitis, uersus aquilonem, quod quidem castrum munitissimum est per Ianuenses et per eosdem habitatur, cuius dominium

o   superius feci C   p   et domini insule ibi eos quietem non permittunt et *add.* A

Another reason why Greece would be held more easily than Egypt is that there are many places, forts, and islands there which are already held by obedient and devout sons of the Roman church.

There is one island of the Genoese lords Zaccaria,[58] of whom I spoke above, which has many excellent and quiet ports, is well watered and pleasant with rivers and springs, is agreeable with plains, mountains, and woods, and abundant in clean air and fruits. I and many others who have been there know how suitable it would be for a crusade, especially if our princes decide to begin a crusade in Greece. Opposite this island, three miles away, in Turkey, which we call Asia Minor, is a promontory extending into the sea, narrow at the beginning toward the Turks and round and like a circle towards the sea and the island.[59] It is a hundred and eighty miles in circumference and only three where it is narrower. In that direction it is narrower, with Smyrna on one side and the town of Ephesus on the other. On this promontory, which is called a cape, there are excellent vines, the largest and most delicious olives in the entire Roman empire, pastures, rich crops, abundant water, and shady hunting forests. The Turks do not dare to live on or even ever to visit this cape, because the lords of the island do not allow them to be at peace there, and the lords of the island cannot hold it because they lack the power of any ruler or of the church. This cape could be occupied without a shield or lance and almost without bloodshed. After it is held the whole crusade could be comfortably and securely refreshed there, and the whole fleet of the world could be refitted in the surrounding ports. There would be no need to fear ambushes or attacks from the Turks by land, since on the narrow side no one could come except by a narrow pass which a few men could guard against the attack of all the Saracens and Turks. There are around it, furthermore, excellent and strong forts, with great moats and towers but without any inhabitants. I do not doubt that all of Asia Minor could be taken from this cape. On the Turkish mainland, to the north from the side of the peninsula or cape, there is a fort which has been fortified by the Genoese and is inhabited by the same men.[60] Its lordship belongs in

58   On Chios, see nn. 42–43 above.

59   The peninsula extends from the Asian mainland to the west and north, forming the gulf of Smyrna/Izmir. Chios is immediately to the west of this peninsula. This region has been known since antiquity for the wealth of its resources, including grain, olives, and fish: Heyd (1885–86), 1:463–64, 486, 491, etc.; Ahrweiler (1965), 17–19; Setton (1976), 166.

60   Mas Latrie (*Recueil*, 537 n. c) takes this as a reference to the fortifications built by John III Vatatzes (1221–54) above and northeast of the city of Smyrna to protect that city from the Turks. By the terms of the treaty of Nymphaeum in 1261, Michael VIII granted the Genoese some of the "fiscal revenue of the city and of the port of Smyrna," as well as the usual amenities of a merchant colony: loggia, church, bath, market stalls, etc.: Ahrweiler (1965), 8–9, 40–41. The fate of the fortress after 1304 is uncertain (details ibid., 41). It was taken by the Turks of Aydin in 1317, then recaptured by Latins (Hospitallers, Venetians, Cypriots, and Latin rulers of other Aegean islands) in 1344, and finally fell to Timur in 1402. But this "new fort" at Smyrna was never controlled by

partim est predictorum dominorum qui in supradicta insula dominantur, partim quorumdam aliorum Ianuensium, et uix uel numquam est quin Turci contra istud^q castrum et castrum contra Turcos guerram habeant actualem. Vnde frequenter ad bellum conueniunt manuale. Habet etiam portum tutum et bonum, per que omnia utile passagium esse posset. Quamdam etiam ciuitatem Ianuenses possident, quam et nouiter construxerunt, nobilem et omnibus bonis et diuitiis habundantem, refectam populi^r multitudine numerosa. Quam quidem ciuitatem et Constantinopolim solus portus diuidit, habens in latitudine uix quartum miliaris unius, in longitudine uero sex miliaria continet; portus securus, tranquillus et bonus, meo iudicio maior mundi et pulcrior, profundus modo debito, ita ut in medio eius super octo uel decem passibus corde ubi altior fundus est, ancora figi possit et ad litus ad unum passum uel medium appropinquare, et ad anulos portarum ligari et firmari ualeant naues magne, uacue et honuste. Que ciuitas, si per nostros haberetur, nullus dubitet quin per illam possemus non dico Constantinopoli sed etiam toti imperio dominari. Preter illa que dicta sunt, habent iam nostri Lombardi, Veneti et Ianuenses et Hospitalarii insulas multas et ciuitates, uillas et castra, adiacentia Grecorum et Turcorum terris, per que omnia pro passagio comodius, facilius et utilius principium haberetur.

Hoc autem quod dico, quod uidelicet in Grecia, deinde in Turcia, passagium incipi debeat, nulli nouum uel extraneum uideatur, nam quoddam passagium ibi incepit quo nullum umquam aliud^s de quo legatur, fuit melius prosperatum, nam fuerunt infra trium uel quatuor annorum spatium regna tredecim acquisita.

Secunda ratio est quare in Constantinopoli passagium incipi debeat, ut uidelicet uictualium sufficienter copia habeatur. Expedit siquidem ut uictualia nec nimis effluant, nec nimis deficiant, ne superhabundantia lasciuiam pariat, et egestas nimia in bellantium cordibus inducat formidinem et pauorem. Qualiter autem hec mediocritas et temperantia in exercitu Domini ualeat obseruari, non est dicere presentis opusculi, sed solum ostendere quomodo, habundantius et melius, et cum minoribus laboribus et expensis, exercitus uictualia sufficienter habere ualeat de imperio Romanie.

q illud B   r populi *om*. C   s aliud *om*. C

part to the lords who rule the aforesaid island and in part to some other Genoese, and the Turks never or almost never attack this fort, or the fort actually attacks the Turks, but they often meet in hand-to-hand fighting. It also has a safe and good port, through all of which there can be a profitable crusade. The Genoese also have a noble city which they recently built and which has an abundance of all good things and wealth and is strengthened by many people.[61] Indeed, this city is separated from Constantinople only by the port, which is barely a quarter of a mile wide but six miles long. It is a safe, tranquil, and good port, in my view the greatest and finest port in the world, suitably deep, so that an anchor can be fixed in the middle, where it is deeper, by a cord of more than eight or ten paces, and at the shore big ships, empty or loaded, can approach to a pace or a half and be tied and firmly attached to rings in the piers. If this town were held by our men no one would doubt that we could rule through it not only Constantinople, I say, but also the entire empire. In addition to what has already been said, our men, Lombards, Venetians, and Genoese, and the Hospitallers already hold many islands, towns, estates, and forts adjacent to the lands of the Greeks and Turks, through all of which a convenient, easy, and efficient beginning for a crusade can be obtained.

There is nothing new or strange, however, in my saying that a crusade should begin in Greece and then go into Turkey, for the [first] crusade started from that place and prospered better, we have read, than any other crusade, since thirteen kingdoms were acquired within the space of three or four years.

The second reason that a crusade should begin in Constantinople is that sufficient supplies of food can be obtained. It is proper that there should be neither too much nor too little food, because an excess promotes lasciviousness and a deficiency creates fear and terror in the hearts of the fighters. The present work, however, is concerned not with how moderation and temperance should be observed in the army of the Lord but only with how the army may have enough food more abundantly and better, and with less work and expense, from the empire of Romania.[62]

---

the Zaccaria, "the lords who rule the aforesaid island." It makes more sense to think that William is speaking of Phocaea: n. 41 above; Geanakoplos (1959), 88; Ahrweiler (1965), esp. 40–42; Laiou (1972), 149, 314; Foss (1991); Kazhdan (1991b).

61   William shifts at this point from considering Smyrna and Chios to Constantinople and Pera, which was a suburb of Constantinople, across the Golden Horn from the city, and was known as Galata to the Greeks and Pera to the Latins. On the Genoese colony there and its status, see Geanakoplos (1959), 206–9, 248–51; Laiou (1972), 68–69, 104–5, 113, 148–52, 154–57, 174–75, 183–85, 261–63, 276, 301–2; Balard (1978), esp. 1:105–14, 179–98, 359–68.

62   The need to supply crusading armies with food, fodder, and other necessities was a constant source of stress between the inhabitants of the Byzantine empire and the crusaders. Most crusades saw repeated skirmishes between crusaders and indigenous people, who strove sometimes merely to protect their own staples and sometimes to profit from the crusaders' need, while the crusaders sometimes offered fair recompense and sometimes took what they needed without compensation: Odo of Deuil (1948), 40–45, 72–85, 96–99, 106–9, with a relatively evenhanded account of

Ad quod attendere debemus quod imperium Grecie, quantum scilicet nunc tenet presens imperator, in tribus habundat egregie, uidelicet in frumento, uino et carnibus, in tali uidelicet habundantia ut non sit annus uix quo de Romania tantum de frumento non exeat quod possent plus quam quinquaginta naues maxime onerari. Gentes enim grece militiam perdiderunt, usum armorum nesciunt, artes alias[t] mechanicas comuniter non exercent, litterarum studia non sequuntur, sed inertiam sectantes et otiosas fabulas amplectentes, habitare in terris ubi plus bladi nascitur solum ut habeant panis habundantiam, sunt contenti, et ideo terris colendis insistunt, et quomodo de segetibus uitam habeant elaborant. Et quia sunt pingues terre et fertiles, eorum pigritie satisfaciunt et uentri, dum non oportet eos terram uomere frequenter scindere, uel stercoribus impinguare, et dum pro paruo semine recipiunt amplas fruges. De uineis autem, prout conuenit, parum curant, specialiter ubi terra est pro frugibus magis apta; quod quidem contingit, uel quia uineas colere nesciunt, uel quia uinum quod ibi nascitur non plene ad maturitatem producitur, uel quia maius[u] lucrum acquirunt de segetibus quam de uineis, uel quia, sicut gentes que quietem sectantur et otium, et plus laboris est in uineis quam in campis, contenti sunt ut[v] quilibet tantum de uino habeat quod possit domui sue sufficere transitorie in habundantia aliquali. Quamuis sint loca multa[w] non sic pro frugibus apta in quibus uinum nascitur colore fulgidum, gustu suaue, sapore amicabile,[x] nutrimento placidum, effectu uirtuosum, sicut potest inueniri in aliqua mundi parte, et hoc non mediocriter sed habundanter. De carnibus uero habent habundantiam in excessu, quia pascua habet illa regio magis[y] uiridia et iocunda, equis et bobus forte nutrimentum prebentia et pecoribus uirtuosum. Habere igitur poterit totum passagium plene et complete de dictis tribus, maxime de blado et carnibus et uino,[z] et hoc pro leui foro, et absque periculo et labore. Terra ergo illa sufficienter nobis carnes[a] ad nutriendum, panem ad fortitudinem, uinum ad letitiam ministrabit, si primo ditioni ecclesie submittatur.

Tercia ratio est ut uia facilior[b] pateat castris Dei. Sunt enim multi qui maris motum et aerem tempestatesque tam moleste substineant, ut motu et fere[c] sensu carentes, nec cibum sumere nec immissum stomacho nisi cum difficultate ualeant retinere, ita quod magis uideantur uicini[d] morti quam uite, et magis uideantur apti esse ad feretrum quam ad bellum. Qua[e] quidem causa multos retrahit a nauigio uel retardat, uel in multis infirmitates inducit[f] multas et graues, uel certe

t   illas B   u   magis C   v   quod *pro* ut C   w   multa loca C   x   amabile C
y   magis *om.* C   z   et uino *om.* AC   a   carnes nobis sufficienter C   b   faciliter C
c   fere et B   d   uicini *om.* C   e   Que BC   f   inducit infirmitates B

For this we should know that the empire of Greece, as the present emperor holds it, abounds particularly in three things, that is, grain, wine, and meat, in such abundance that almost every year as much grain as could completely fill more than fifty ships is exported from Romania. For the Greek peoples have lost their army, do not know how to use arms, do not commonly exercise the mechanical arts, and do not follow the study of letters, but seeking inactivity and embracing idle stories, they are content to live in lands where more grain is produced only in order to have an abundance of bread, and they therefore persist in cultivating lands and strive to live from the crops.[63] And since the lands are rich and fertile they are satisfied in their laziness and stomach so long as they do not need to till the soil with a plow frequently or to enrich it with manure and so long as they receive ample crops from a little seed. They care correspondingly little for vines, however, especially where the land is better fitted for crops. So it happens that they are content that every man should have only enough wine for the passing needs of his own house in sufficient abundance, either because they do not know how to cultivate vines, or because the wine which is produced there is not brought fully to maturity, or because they gain more profit from crops than from vines, or because they seek quiet and rest and there is more work in vines than in crops. There are many places which are unsuitable for crops, however, where wine is produced that is as bright in color, smooth in taste, pleasant in flavor, gentle in nourishment, and powerful in effect as can be found in any part of the world, and produced abundantly, not moderately. They have an excess of meat, since that region has green and pleasant pastures, providing invigorating food for horses and cows and good food for flocks. An entire crusade could therefore be fully and completely supplied with these three things, especially grain, meat, and wine at a low price and without danger and exertion. After that land has been subjected to the church, therefore, it will supply us sufficiently with meat for nourishment, bread for strength, and wine for joy.

The third reason is that an easier way will be open to the armies of God. For there are many men who suffer the motion of the sea, air, and storms so badly that they cannot move or almost feel and cannot eat or keep down except with difficulty anything put in their stomachs, so that they seem to be closer to death than life and to be more suited for the bier than for war. This prevents or delays many men traveling by sea and is the cause of many serious infirmities or at least

crusader pillaging and Greek profiteering. Instructed by the experience of earlier crusaders, later planners of crusades tried to ensure adequate supplies from the beginning: Housley (2003).

63   The plentiful food available to armies crossing the Balkans, Thessaly, and Thrace, were it not for the treachery of the Greeks, is a theme of several western crusading chronicles, while others see the area as barren and desolate. No doubt it depended on the time of year: Odo of Deuil (1948), 40–41; Robert the Monk (2005), 95–96. The most recent synthetic treatments of Byzantine agriculture are by Lefort (2002) and Laiou (2002a).

debilitat, uel morte aliquando absorbentur. Quod ne contingat exercitui Domini cauendum pro posse est cum magna diligentia et cautela. Ad quod manifeste scitur quod hii qui transitum desiderant, et qui habent passagium promouere, et sine quibus nec capi potuit nec prosperitatem habuit Terra Sancta sunt Gallici, quibus iuncti Almani et Anglici, non dico Terram Sanctam posse capere, sed uniuersas terras,[g] linguas, tribus et populos obruere, conterere et calcare. Et ideo quanto magis sunt uoluntarii et ardentes, quanto magis sunt probitate pollentes, et potentia excellentes, et zelo utiles et uirtute, tanto magis diligendi et dirigendi sunt, et eis uia tutior et facilior ostendenda. Predictas[h] igitur marinas angustias magis timent et eas odiunt et subterfugiunt quantum possunt, quod est uel quia non habent consuetudinem nauigandi, uel quia eorum naturalis corporis dispositio hoc abhorret. Sunt enim complexionis humide, uel quia sunt delicate nutriti[i] et a molestiis penurie elongati, lectisterniorum, cibariorum et potus et aeris subita mutatio eos terret pariter et affligit. Per terram est[k] ergo eis uia potius eligenda, et quia per terram non est alia uia breuior, facilior, tutior et consolabilior quam per Greciam, illam eligere et ad illam dirigere nos debemus.

Videatur ergo possibilitas huius uie. Pro omnibus igitur predictis qui transire habeant, processus unus erit,[l] ut scilicet tam Gallici quam Almani[m] et Anglici uiam faciant per Vngariam, et inde transitis montibus qui Vngariam diuidunt et Ratiam[n] in plana Bulgarie descendentes, post hec plano pede Constantinopolim properabunt, uel per flumen uel per ripam fluminis, iuxta Constantinopolim ad paucas dietas uenient et inde reliquo exercitui se coniungent. Per mare etiam necessarius erit certus numerus galearum, que portabunt reliquum populum qui per terram uenire nequiuerunt, uel per mare[o] uenire elegerint[p] potius quam per terram. Poterunt etiam haberi naues ad equos et arma portandum, et uulgus promiscuum et alia que exercitui necessaria esse possunt. Cum uero iam in Constantinopolim uenerint hii uel illi uidebunt econtra hostes Dei inimicos crucis et interfectores populi christiani, Turcos uidelicet, quos a Constantinopoli trium uel quatuor miliarium[q] diuidit strictum maris.

Capta igitur nec dubium faciliter ciuitate, reliquum imperium[r] faciliter obtinetur. De resistentia enim quam Greci facere ualeant uel audeant, nullam penitus facio mentionem. Tanta enim est eorum uirtutis audacia, tanta armorum experientia, tanta probitas animorum, ut non milites nostros uel pedites necessarios esse iudicem, sed nostras, ut ita dicam, mulieres posse sufficere non[s] eorum non dico potentiam sed pusillanimitatem spiritus conterendam. Superat enim eos et suppeditat uilior populus orientis, Turci uidelicet,

g   terras *om.* AB   h   Prcdict A, predictas *om.* (*cum spatio*) C   i   nutrite AC
k   est *om.* B   l   est *pro* erit C   m   Alamanni AB   n   Rassiam C
o   eligere *add.* C   p   eligerint AC   q   miliariorum AC   r   imperii C
s   ad *pro* non R

weakness in many men, and sometimes they are swallowed by death. All possible care and caution should be exercised to prevent this happening to the army of the Lord. It should therefore be known that those who want to cross the sea and ought to promote a crusade, and without whom the Holy Land cannot be taken or prosper, are the French together with the Germans and English. I do not say they can only take the Holy Land but also overwhelm, crush, and trample on all lands, tongues, tribes, and peoples. The more they are willing and eager, strong in worth, excellent in power, and fit in zeal and manliness, therefore, the more they should be loved, directed, and shown a safer and easier route. Either because they are unaccustomed to sailing or because the natural disposition of their bodies abhors it, they are more afraid of the difficulties of the sea and hate and avoid them as much as they can. For they are of a moist complexion, or because they are delicately nourished and untroubled by poverty, a sudden change in their usual bed, food, drink, or air terrifies and likewise afflicts them. They therefore prefer the route by land, and since there is no land route that is shorter, easier, safer, and more reassuring than that by Greece, we should choose and recommend it.[64]

The practicality of this route is therefore obvious. For all the aforesaid people who have to make the trip there will be one route, so that the French, Germans, and English will all go by way of Hungary and then, after crossing the mountains which divide Hungary and Raetia and descending into the plain of Bulgaria, they will afterward go rapidly on level ground to Constantinople either by river or on the bank of the river. In a few days they will reach Constantinople and will then join the rest of the army. By sea a certain number of galleys will also be needed to carry the other men who cannot come by land or who would choose to come by sea rather than by land. There will also be ships to carry horses and arms, and the common crowd and other things needed by the army. When they reach Constantinople both these men [who came by sea] and those [who came by land] will face the enemies of God, the foes of the cross, and the killers of the Christian people, that is, the Turks, who are separated from Constantinople by a channel of three or four miles.

When the city has been captured, without doubt easily, the rest of the empire will be easily taken. I make utterly no reference to the resistance which the Greeks can or will dare to make. The bravery of their strength, experience of arms, and worth of spirit are such that I consider our women, so to speak, rather than our knights or soldiers, would suffice to conquer I do not say their strength but their cowardliness of spirit.[65] They are defeated and crushed by the baser people of the east, that is, the Turks,

---

64   On the difficulties of the crusaders on the second crusade (including problems of travel and differences in food and climate) see the references in G. Constable (2008), 288. On the routes across the Balkans see Jiraček (1877), 69–112. Cf. Dubois (1956), 86 n. 41.

65   Another commonplace in western sources writing about the Byzantines: they cannot fight themselves and must pay others to fight for them, as in *Itinerarium* (1997), 57.

qui suppeditantur ab omni alia natione. Vnde Turci nec contra Tartaros, nec Cumanos, nec Georgianos, audent arma capere, uel coram eis aliqualiter apparere. Ergo ex consequenti apparet[t] liquide quid in Grecorum cordibus remansit prudentie et uirtutis, ex quo maxime a romana ecclesia et fide catholica decesserunt. Reducto ad manum ecclesie predicto imperio, non remanet transeundum nisi unus paruissimus maris alueus, longus et strictus, qui quidem durat in longum in modum fluminis ·cc·xx· miliaribus, et in latum uix sex miliaribus, quantum uidelicet est predicti aluei latitudo. In isto stricto alueo est brachium sancti Georgii, quod est quedam pars huius[u] stricti, in quo fuit quoddam passagium simile, sicut dico, cui Deus pietatis sue potentiam manifestans et prosperitatem condonans manifeste ostendit quod eis fuit ipse misericors dux et rector. Cum uero transito alueo predicto in Turciam transierint, non spero quod resistentiam faciant inimici, Deo pro nostris pugnante et uoluntates et actus et itinera dirigente.

Quarta ratio est ut caveatur populo christiano ne cum ante se inimicum ferire cupit, ipse a tergo ab inimicis aliis irruentibus uel insidiis latentibus feriatur, et hinc inde conuersis contra se hostibus medius opprimatur. Dispositio igitur Terre Sancte talis est, ut sit inter Egiptum et Turciam, ita quod qui Terram Sanctam inuadere et occupare desiderat si statim descenderit ad terram cautela non adhibita, de qua loquor, non sit aliud quam imprudenter se ingerere inter hostes. Sarraceni enim Egipti optime norunt quod non possunt se defendere contra nostros, et ideo quod ex se minus possunt minusque sufficiunt ab aliis suppleri cupiunt et laborant. Prece igitur et pretio Turcos uicinos sibi[v] uniunt et inducunt in defensionem sui, et obligant pretio contra exercitum Domini preliari, et illi sicut inopes, ut sunt, ad stipendia iniant, et sicut crudeles et inimici Dei, sitiunt sanguinem christianum, et sicut dolosi et pauidi, timent ne cum ignis gladii nostrorum Sarracenos oppresserit, ita postea eos deuoret et consumat, et ideo, propter predicta, se Sarracenis libenter associant, ut, si castra Dei extirpare et a suis finibus non ualent excludere, saltem dampnificent, uel certe uideantur aliqualiter impedire. Tantus enim[w] est autem[x] nostrorum zelus ad Terram Sanctam capiendam et desiderium possidendi quod dispositionis obliuiscitur ducis belli, tantusque[y] est amor tamque impatiens et affectus[z] quod circa hoc aliquando non deliberat quid agendum, more glutonis qui cum suo discrimine ante cibum comedit quam frigescat.

Sarraceni uero non possunt Turcis tale adiutorium exhibere quale eis exhibetur a Turcis. Quod est ex causa duplici, uel quia Sarraceni Egipti non consueuerunt ad terras longinquas egredi, quia parum in terra propria et in extranea minus ualent, uel quia non est talis dispositio quod ita possint Sarraceni Turcos defendere uel iuuare, sicut est possibile. E conuerso, quia Turci qui sunt iuxta

---

t patet C   u huius *om.* C   v sibi uicinos C   w enim *om.* AB   x autem *om.* C
y tantusquoque C   z astrictus *pro* affectus C

who are crushed by all other nations and who do not dare to take arms, therefore, against the Tartars, Cumans, or Georgians or to appear in any way before them. It is consequently clear how much prudence and strength remain in the hearts of the Greeks, especially after they left the Roman church and catholic faith. After the said empire has been returned to the hand of the church, nothing remains to be crossed except one small, long, and narrow channel of the sea, which extends in length like a river two hundred and twenty miles long and barely six miles broad, which is the breadth of the channel. In this narrow channel is the arm of St. George, which is part of this channel, in which there was a similar crusade, as I say, to which God manifested the power of His piety, granted success, and clearly showed that for them He was a merciful leader and rector. When they have crossed this channel and entered Turkey, I expect that the enemy will not resist and that God will fight for our men and direct their wills, acts, and routes.

The fourth reason is the fear that, although the Christian people want to fight the enemy in front, they may be struck from behind by other attacking enemies or by hidden ambushes and thus be caught in the middle by enemies who have turned here and there against them. The disposition of the Holy Land is such that it is between Egypt and Turkey, so that anyone who wants to invade and occupy the Holy Land has imprudently placed himself between enemies unless he exercises as soon as he lands the caution of which I speak. For the Saracens of Egypt know very well that they cannot defend themselves against us and therefore want and try to have others do what they are unable or inadequate to do themselves. By requests and rewards therefore they unify the neighboring Turks, whom they persuade to defend them, and whom they pay to fight against the army of the Lord. These men, being poor, long for money; being cruel men and enemies of God, they thirst for Christian blood; and being deceitful and fearful, they are afraid that after conquering the Saracens the fire of the sword of our men will subsequently devour and consume them. For these reasons, therefore, they willingly ally with the Saracens so that they at least hurt and certainly hinder somewhat the armies of God even if they lack the strength to extirpate and drive them out of their boundaries. The zeal of our men to capture, however, and their desire to possess the Holy Land are so great that they forget the plan of the leader of the war, and their love is so great and their desire so impatient that they sometimes do not consider what should be done, like a glutton who to his own disadvantage eats his food before it is cool.

The Saracens cannot help the Turks in the same way the Turks help them, however, for two reasons, either because the Saracens of Egypt are unaccustomed to go to distant lands, since they are of little use in their own land and less in foreign lands, or, as is possible, because the Saracens are not inclined to defend or help the Turks in this way. On the contrary, since the Turks who are next to

Constantinopolim, quos capta Constantinopoli[a] prius moneo inuadendos, distant ab Egipto plus quam quadraginta dietas, et si Sarraceni uellent illos Turcos defendere, haberent transire per uias inimicorum suorum, per dominium scilicet imperatoris Persidis, eiusque gladium non euaderent, Sarracenorum Egipti, ut supradictum est, sanguinem sitientis. Imperator enim predictus in Turcie medio dominatur, et si sciret[b] Sarracenos inimicos suos fines sui dominii ingressuros, eos curialiter reciperet cum eos deuorantibus gladiis et sagittis. Relinquentur[c] ergo Turci qui iuxta Constantinopolim sunt si in Grecia passagium incipiat sine adiutore et sine aliquo defensore. Ergo ibi passagium incipiat ubi dico, ubi uidelicet sit nostri exercitus maior securitas, et ubi melius et facilius nostrorum inimicorum audacia ualeat deprimi et confundi. Attendendum igitur est quia numquam passagium legitur factum esse in quo exercitus noster a Turcis insidias non sit passus. Vnde qui legit historiam quando sanctus Ludouicus transiit, et in multis aliis passagiis inuenitur, quod Turcorum exercitus nostris intulerit multa dampna, sicut in transitu Antiochie legitur specialiter et expresse quod Antiochia prius capta et possessa a nostris, postea a Turcis conductis a rege Persarum obsessa fere fuisset, fame destructa et inedia et consumpta,[d] nisi Dei potentia affuisset. Hoc etiam obmittendum non est quia numquam legi quod a Sarracenis exercitus Domini sit deuictus nisi quando nos peccata propria[e] expugnabant, uel quando exercitui deerat dispositionis diligentia et cautela. Disponatur ergo in illo et per illum cuius sapientia disponit et ordinat uniuersa, a quo et per quem omnis meritorius actus initium debitum et omnis perfectionis intentio suscipit incrementum.

Quinta ratio est ut possit sibi exercitus Domini precauere a fraudulentiis et insidiis quas imperator Grecie cum gente sua contra filios romane ecclesie moliri et componere consueuit. Quia enim imperator predictus non est potentia fretus, nec militum probitate munitus, uidensque quod[f] contra nostros non est sibi defensio nec adest euasio, ad fraudes et malitias se conuertit, et quicquid potest malitie machinatur, ut possit nostris in quibuscumque subdola calliditate nocere, et ut inuidus contra nos et ueneno odii plenus non uult pro nobis prospera, sed cupit aduersa, plusque

a quos capta Constantinopoli *om.* C   b sciret *om.* B
c relinquuntur C, relinqu[er]entur R   d combusta B   e nostra *pro* propria B
f quod *om.* B

Constantinople and who I advise should be first invaded after Constantinople has been taken are more than forty days [journey] from Egypt, the Saracens, if they wanted to defend the Turks, would have to cross by the routes of the enemies, that is, through the domain of the emperor of Persia and would not escape the sword of him who thirsts, as I said above, for the blood of the Saracens of Egypt. For this emperor rules the middle of Turkey, and if he knew that his Saracen enemies were about to enter the boundaries of his domain he would receive them courteously with swords and arrows devouring them. The Turks who are next to Constantinople will be deserted, therefore, without assistance or any defense, if a crusade starts in Greece. A crusade should therefore start where I say, that is, where our army will be safest and where the audacity of our enemies may best and most easily be defeated and confounded. It should be noted from reading that no crusade has ever been made in which the Turks did not attack our army. Whoever reads history finds that when St. Louis crossed the sea and in many other crusades the army of the Turks inflicted great damage on our men. On the journey to Antioch,[66] for instance, it is read specially and expressly that after our men first captured and held Antioch it was subsequently besieged by the Turks, led by the king of the Persians, and would have been destroyed by famine, starvation, and exhaustion if the power of God had not been at hand. It should also not be omitted that I have read that the army of the Lord was defeated by the Saracens only when our own sins defeated us or when the army lacked diligence of arrangement and caution. Let it therefore be arranged in Him and by Him Whose wisdom arranges and ordains all things, by Whom and through Whom every meritorious act duly begins and every intention of perfection is increased.

The fifth reason is that the army of the Lord can protect itself against the frauds and plots which the emperor of Greece and his people are accustomed to make and devise against the sons of the Roman church.[67] For since this emperor lacks confidence in his own power and is not armed with the prowess of soldiers and seeing that he has no defense against our men and no escape is possible, he turns to frauds and malicious deeds, and he devises any malice he can to harm us by some treacherous cunning. Being envious of us and full of the venom of hate, he does not want things to go well for us but wants bad things, and he wants and

66   During the first crusade.
67   Complaints that the Byzantine emperor was more enemy than friend of the crusade date to the earliest crusading chronicles. The *Gesta Francorum*, probably used as part of Bohemond's attempt to launch a crusade against the Byzantines (1105–6), stands at the beginning of a series of histories of crusade that blame the emperor in Constantinople for plotting against the crusaders, not supplying them adequately, fearing them more than he fears the Turks, hating them more than he hates the Saracens, and so on: Odo of Deuil (1948); *Gesta Francorum* (1962); Raymond of Aguilers (1968), 18–19, 21–24, 26–27; Robert the Monk (2005), chaps. 6–9, 14–19 (trans. 93–94, 96–100).

pro Sarracenis quam Christianis nostris bona desiderat et affectat. Et hoc quasi naturale fel amaritudinis contra nos ab eis semper habuit originem, et adhuc hic malus thesaurus in eorum cordibus perseuerat. Iste igitur imperator, qui patribus suis non est melior, immo peior, tanto magis ardet furibundus in nos, tanto magis nequitie animo feruet, tantoque magis si posset uellet[g] in nos toto malignitatis spiritu debacchari, quanto magis tempus adesse considerat, quod ueretur quo scilicet[h] suis demeritis in se suscipiat dignam penam. Igitur attendendum est quod ex tribus imperator predictus potest nostris inferre periculosas insidias et nociuas. Primo quia si alibi passagium fieret uel inciperet, cum in toto mundo tanta uictualium habundantia nequeat inueniri, sicut in Grecia et in terris sibi conuicinis, ut aliqualiter est pertractum, et passagio expediat ut non ab una parte uel prouincia sed ab omni loco undique confluant uictualia ut habundent, posset esse dampnum non modicum castris Dei, si inde nutrimentum corporalis uite haberi non posset, hoc est de Grecia, que, quando fertilitatem habet, consueuit alimenta bladi propinquis et remotis regionibus ministrare, uel etiam si speratur quod ab imperatore Grecie, non prius subiugato, pro passagio uictualia haberentur. Hoc nouum est; hoc sperandum non est quod ille alimenta prebeat, uel etiam substentamentum[i] aliquod administrat, qui nostros fraudulenter consueuit occidere, non nutrire.

Vnde legitur in historia de passagio Antiocheno quod, cum nostri partim per Vngariam, partim per Rutheniam, processissent in Constantinopolim, ut sicut ego moneo nunc fiendum, brachio sancti Georgii transito superius nominato, subiugando Turcos, ad Terram Sanctam ultimo deuenirent, imperator Grecorum tunc mala machinatus[k] contra nostros et multa. Item legitur quod alia uice non audentes se opponere contra nostros, hanc malitiam cogitarunt ut scilicet calcem uiuam cum[l] farina apponerent et sic panes conficerent, quos quidem nulli uenderent nisi nostris. Quod et factum est. Vnde cum ex hac causa multi ex populo uel morte caderent uel infirmitate percussi uiribus deperirent, infirmitates uidentes et mortes, et causam penitus ignorantes, ceperunt inuestigare quid esset. Quo cognito manum quam contra Sarracenos uoluerant extendere, iam contra Christianos illos Grecos perfidos conuerterunt. Iterum legitur quod classem que nostros transueherat in portu Constantinopolitano incendere[m] disponebant, ut postea liberius possent dolorem quem contra nostros conceperant cum iniquitatibus parturire. Quod et factum fuisset

g   in nos tanto ... uellet *om.* B   h   sicut C   i   sustamentum C   k   [est] *add.* R
l   ut *pro* cum B   m   intendere AR

strives for good things for the Saracens more than for our Christians. This almost natural venom of bitterness against us has always originated with them, and this evil store still perseveres in their hearts. This emperor, therefore, who is no better, indeed worse, than his fathers, burns the more with rage against us, is roused the more by the spirit of evil, and would want the more to rave against us, if he could; in a total spirit of malignity, the more he thinks that the time is at hand for him to fear that he may himself be duly punished for his failings. It should therefore be noted that this emperor can inflict dangerous and harmful plots against us in three ways. First, since if a crusade were to be made or start elsewhere, although Greece and the neighboring lands have a greater abundance of food than anywhere else in the whole world, as is discussed elsewhere, and it would promote a crusade for plentiful provisions to be gathered not from one place or province but from everywhere, it could do great damage to the armies of God if nourishment for bodily life could not be had from Greece, which when it is fertile customarily furnishes supplies of grain far and wide, and also to hope that the emperor of Greece would provide supplies for a crusade if he were not first subjugated. This is new: there is no hope that he who is accustomed not to feed but to kill our men fraudulently will supply food or even furnish any assistance.

In the history of the crusade of Antioch one reads that when our men had traveled to Constantinople,[68] in part through Hungary and in part through Ruthenia, just as I advise should be done now, crossed the aforementioned arm of St. George, conquered the Turks, and finally came to the Holy Land, the emperor of the Greeks then devised many and evil plots against us. One reads furthermore that on another occasion they [the Greeks], not daring to fight against us themselves, planned an evil deed by mixing quicklime with flour and making bread which they sold only to our men.[69] This was done. When on this account many people either died or were weakened and lost their strength, they saw the weakened and dead and being entirely ignorant of the cause, began to investigate what it was. When it was known they turned the hand which they wanted to raise against the Saracens against those perfidious Greek Christians.[70] One likewise reads that they arranged to burn the fleet which had carried our men into the port of Constantinople, so that they could later carry out more easily the trouble which they planned with evil deeds against our men. This would have been done if the

68   See *Recueil*, 541 n. a, and 1036. Any number of western histories of the first crusade and its aftermath, including Norman control of Antioch, include details about "the emperor of the Greeks" plotting against the crusaders and their principalities.

69   See Ricaldus of Monte Croce (1997), 78–79, and the comment of Monneret de Villard (1948), 33, calling this "tardo riflesso di quell'accusa che ai byzantini fu fatta durante la disastrosa crociata dell'imperatore Corrado III nel 1147," with further references in n. 112.

70   Crusaders regularly decided to attack "perfidious" Greeks rather than (or at least before) Saracens. For example, see passages cited in n. 62 above.

nisi Dominus consilium malignantium detexisset. Sed et si uellem omnia enarrare, et superbias eorum describere, et quam sit inimicus ille populus semper malignatus in sanctos, enarrante me uel scribente, penna deficeret, et[n] libellum huiusmodi[o] excederet quod promisi. Secundo potest a Grecis exercitui nostro dampnum contingere si passagium in Grecia non inciperet, ut premisi. Posset enim imperator cum suo populo se Turcis coniungere contra nostros, et esset eis in maximum firmamentum et[p] nobis non[q] inmodicum[r] detrimentum, ut cum nostri Terram Sanctam inuaderent Turci hinc et inde Sarraceni Egipti medium opprimerent populum christianum. Tercio quia imperator qui nunc est inuasor est non iustus possessor, predo non dominus, quantoque magis est sibi conscius imperium iniuste usurpasse quod habet et indebite possidere quod tenet, et contra uoluntatem romane ecclesie illud se detinere considerat, quod non decet, tanto magis ardentius aspirabit et quomodocumque diligentius laborabit ne talem populum in dominum habeat uel uicinum, qui eum expellere uelit et ualeat de throno imperii, cui preest indebite et quod iniuste possidet et indigne. Sibi enim[s] uel suis illud imperium iure successionis uel hereditario non debetur, quia pater suus illud interfecto per eum suo domino usurpauit. Iste etiam adhuc illud retinet, iure proditorio patris sui.

Sexta[t] ratio quare in Constantinopoli passagium incipi debeat est et hoc propter maiorem utilitatem Christianitatis. Turcorum enim populus, quamuis in se uilis sit, nec armorum peritiam habeat nec uirtutem, tamen terras multas[u] prouincias suo dominio subiugauit. Et in tantum pestifer ille turbo[v] inualuit contra christianos Grecos sibi uicinos, ut non dicam ciuitates et castra munitissima absque habitatore reliquerint,[w] non dicam quod aliquas ciuitates pro sua ditione sub capitali tributo possederint, sed[x] in tantum creuit scabies illa morbida quod tota Minor Asia deuastata crudeliter et possessa usque in Constantinopolim ad tria uel quatuor miliaria suum dominium extenderunt. Nec hoc contenta est insatiabilis eorum crudelitas et ineffrenata rabies et audacia fastuosa, sed insuper naues piraticas facere ausi sunt, cum quibus insulas multas et pulcras desertas fecerunt, earum incolas necantes atrociter, uel in seruitutem durissimam redigentes,[y] nec eos inibi dimittentes ut saltem naturalis soli et aeris possessio[z] iugum seruitutis plenum amaritudine subleuaret, sed eorum uniuersos et singulos ad uniuersas mundi plagas[a] et uentos, terras et prouincias uentilantes, uenduntur Greci miseri et serui omnium nationum effecti, Sarracenorum uidelicet et Tartarorum et Iudeorum, eorum quilibet sectam illam sequitur quam eius dominus profitetur. Adhuc etiam in habendo

---

n   uel *pro* et C   o   huiusmodum A   p   a *pro* et C   q   non *om.* C   r   modicum B
s   autem *pro* enim C   t   [T]ertia B   u   [et] *add.* R   v   tumbo AB, bubo C
w   relinquerint BC   x   quod *pro* sed C   y   redegentes AB   z   passagio C
a   plagas *om.* C

William of Adam | How to Defeat the Saracens

Lord had not detected the plan of the evil men. But if I wanted to narrate every-thing and describe their pride and the constant hostility of that people against the saints, my pen would not suffice for my narrative and writing and would exceed a book of the type I promised. Second, the Greeks might damage our army if the crusade does not start in Greece, as I said above. For the emperor and his people could ally with the Turks against us,[71] and they would be greatly strengthened and we would suffer no small loss, so that when our men invaded the Holy Land the Turks on one side and the Saracens of Egypt on the other would crush the Christian people in the middle. Third, since the present emperor is a usurper and not a just possessor,[72] a robber not a lord, and the more he is aware that he usurped his empire unjustly and possesses what he holds improperly and considers that he keeps it against the wish of the Roman church, which is wrong, the more ardently he will aspire and diligently endeavor in any way he can not to have such a people as lord or neighbor who want and have the power to expel him from the throne of the empire over which he rules improperly and which he holds unjustly and unworthily. For the empire does not belong to him or his family by the law of succession or by heredity, since his father usurped it after killing his lord. This man also still holds it owing to the treachery of his father.

The sixth reason why a crusade ought to begin at Constantinople is the greater benefit of Christianity. For the people of the Turks, though low in themselves and without skill in arms or strength, have nonetheless subjected many lands and provinces to their rule. And as much as that pestiferous storm grows stronger against their neighbors, the Christian Greeks, I shall not say that they have left towns and strongly fortified forts without inhabitants, I shall not say that they have imposed capital tribute on some towns by virtue of their power, but rather that the deadly disease has grown so much that with all of Asia Minor cruelly devastated and under their control, they have extended their rule to within three or four miles of Constantinople. Their insatiable cruelty, unbridled rage, and haughty audacity are not content with this, and they have also dared to build pirate ships with which they make many fine islands into deserts, barbarously killing the inhabitants or reducing them to the harshest servitude, and not leaving them in that place, so that the possession of their natural sun and air might at least relieve the bitter yoke of servitude, but scattering all and each of them to every quarter of the world, winds, lands, and provinces. The miserable Greeks are sold and become slaves of every nation, that is, of the Saracens, the Tartars, and the Jews, and each of them follows the sect professed by his master. They still continue to have

---

71 See intro., p. 11.

72 Emperor Andronicus II Paleologus (1282–1328), whose father Michael VIII Paleologus (1259–82) had usurped the throne by means duplicitous enough to require no western exaggeration: Geanakoplos (1959), 16–46; Laiou (1972), 17–21.

naues piraticas perseuerant; et plura mala, quamque dicta sunt, facerent, alias insulas que adhuc Christianorum subsunt dominio deuastantes, nisi quod Martinus Zacharie et Benedictus frater eius, de quibus feci superius mentionem, resistunt uiriliter cum galeis quas semper in mari tenent ad hoc seruitium preparatas. Videritis miserandum spectaculum, et omni luctu et compassione plenum, greges magnos ut ciuium[b] duci captiuos de Grecis Asie in Tauricium Persidis ad uendendum, quorum numerus est aliquando[c] duo[d] milium, aliquando plurium, ut ego uidi et mei consocii,[e] pluries et frequenter; uideritis matres cum filiis, quorum alter collo pendebat, alter ad ubera, alter in uentre latebat, alter manu non[f] ducebatur, sed potius trahebatur. Desiderabant femine matres non esse, et filios natos non fore oblite desiderii feminei affectabant, genuisseque prolem obligatam tante miserie penitebant, angebanturque angustiis, dum se liberare nequibant, nec filios, nec etiam consolari. Nati econtra[g] matri, et si loqui non nouerant, rugienti gemitu et queruloso suspirio annuebant: "Quo nos ducis, mater? Quid de nobis agit?" Et sic mater, bellum uidens angustum, in corde femineo latens pietas in filiis, diluuium miseriarum inundans, in Turcis subactoribus patens crudelitas, nesciebat quid agere, quia dolorem suum multiplicem delinire, nec filiorum placare[h] querimonias flebiles et uagitus, nec illorum qui eam cum filiis tali seruituti subegerant crudelitatem poterat mitigare; ducebantur interim, et si quis esset[i] qui uel senio pregrauatus uel infirmitate confectus, uel nature, uel etatis conditione, decenter ambulare nequiret, talis uerberabatur, uel in uasta heremo relinquebatur uel immisericorditer et mortaliter cedebatur.[k]

Ego quod uidi narro: mulierem quamdam talibus angustiis pressam ductam fuisse magis ad aborsum quam partum, que filium editum amare conspiciens: "Heu me," inquit nato, "fili, quid in hanc lucem uenisti, ut te hic tenebrosus turbo[l] possideat? Quid te genui que ante te[m] habui seruum quam natum, de te et ex te coartor e duobus unum eligere, aut te necare, ut hostis non mater, et tibi ante mortem dare quam mammas, ne si uixeris et Deum deseras, et te ad dampnationem eternam sarracenicus error adducat, aut certe te uite seruare ut Dei pietas te illuminans ab erroris tenebris te defendat, et ab offensionis fidei macula te preseruet?" Sicque dum in materno pectore pugnarent fides et pietas, fides uincebat, et flens et eiulans, iam deliberabat filio magis[n] mortem dare quam uitam. Et subito circumspiciens et me cum meo socio uidens exultauit in gaudio, et occulte nobis filium intulit baptizandum. Non enim audebat palam facere, timens Sarraceni domini sui offensam incurrere, et ex hoc sui

b *recte* ouium   c aliquando est C   d duorum C   e quam *add.* C
f non *om.* C   g eius *pro* econtra B   h placare filiorum C   i aliquis *add.* C
k occidibatur C   l trabo B   m te *om.* C   n magis filio C

pirate ships, and they would do more evil deeds than have been mentioned and devastate other islands which have hitherto been subject to Christian rule except that Martino Zaccaria and his brother Benedetto, of whom I have spoken, vigorously resist them with the galleys which they always keep in the sea ready for this service. You can see, as I and my companions have often seen, the miserable spectacle, full of grief and compassion, of large bands of captive Greeks from Asia, numbering sometimes two thousand and sometimes more, led like flocks of sheep into the Taurus of Persia to be sold. You can see mothers with children, one hanging to the neck, another on her breast, another hidden in her stomach, and another not led but rather dragged by the hand. The women did not want to be mothers, and forgetting their feminine desire, they strove not to have sons. They regretted having produced offspring condemned to such misery and were afflicted with distress that they could not free or even comfort themselves or their sons. The children on the other hand [said] to the mother, or if they did not know how to speak, indicated by a screaming groan and plaintive sigh: "Where do you take us, mother? What will become of us?" And thus the mother, seeing the troubled strife—her piety for her children lying hidden in her heart, a flood of miseries overflowing, the manifest cruelty in the debauching Turks—did not know what to do, since she could not soothe her many griefs, nor placate the feeble complaints or cries of her sons, nor mitigate the cruelty of the men who subjected herself and her children to such servitude. Meanwhile they were led away, and anyone who was unable to walk properly for reasons either of affliction, weakness, nature, or age was beaten, or left in the vast desert, or mercilessly and mortally killed.

A certain woman, oppressed by such afflictions, as I myself saw, was driven to an abortion rather than a birth and when she saw with bitterness the boy to whom she had given birth, she said to the newborn:

> Alas for me, son, why have you come out into this light that this dark
> storm may possess you? Why have I given birth to you who are a slave
> rather than a child? Why am I forced by you and from you to choose one
> of two things, either as an enemy rather than a mother to kill you and to
> give you death rather than my breasts, in order that you may not live and
> desert God and the error of the Saracens may not bring you to eternal
> damnation, or to keep you alive so that the piety of God may enlighten you
> and protect you from the darkness of error and keep you from the stain of
> loss of faith?

And while faith and love thus fought in the maternal breast, faith conquered, and with tears and wails she finally decided to give her son death rather than life. And suddenly looking around and seeing me and my companion, she exulted with joy and secretly brought the boy to us for baptism. For she did not dare to do this openly, fearing to offend her Saracen master, and she was afraid that in this way

et filii sui[o] mortem non posse euadere formidabat. Nos e contra cogitantes nobis imminere periculum matri et filio mortem cepimus dubitare quid facere, et tandem elegimus puerum baptizare, scientes et sperantes quod Deus de altitudine diuitiarum suarum diuersis diuersas uias et occultas[p] preparat ad salutem, et quantum in se est omnes homines uult saluos fieri et neminem uult perire. De istis autem qui sic captiui ducti sunt et uenditi et Sarraceni effecti in solo imperio Persidis plus esse quam ·cc·m· extimantur.

Et ego, sic dico et assero, qui totum predictum imperium quantum in longum extenditur peragraui, nec in uita mea fui in aliqua regione, quantumcumque extranea et remota, in qua Grecos captiuos Sarracenos effectos non uiderim, etiam in Indie regione, sic sunt disperditi et dispersi. In sola uero una ciuitate, que Tauricium[q] Persidis appellatur, et in uillis eius certissime plus quam ·c·xx·m· de predictis captiuis grecis nunc uiui esse dicuntur. Et si habet una sola ciuitas tot captiuos nunc uiuos, quot habent[r] alie prouincie et ciuitates innumere omnis terre, et quot sunt illi qui mortui sunt uel gladio interfecti?

Tantum autem hos postquam Sarraceni effecti sunt diabolus dementauit, tantum in eis infixit perfidie uestigia et impressit, ut omnis fidei et christianitatis obliti nos fratres et alios christianos, plus quam illi qui a Sarracenis originem habuerunt, et acrius persequuntur. Hoc autem, ut dicunt, faciunt ut crudeles effici possint[s] apud crudeles dominos suos ampliorem gratiam promereri. Vnde,[t] cum essem in India, causa fidei predicande, et unus ex illis mihi quippiam iniurie[u] irrogasset; et cum, captata hora, inter me et ipsum solum[v] dure sed caritatiue, reprehendissem quod sic Dominum postposuisset, eiusque fidem negasset, legemque Christi fidei et ueritati et saluti contrariam suscepisset, et insuper Christum in suis seruis impudenter et imprudenter persequi presumpsisset, ille deponens oculos et suspirans ait: "Heu, nos infelices quos Deus posuit in obprobrium omnis terre. Ostendit nobis Dominus dorsum et non faciem et calce reiecto percussit nos et destruxit[w] radicitus et euulsit, et sic stipitem inutilem deputatam incendio nos reliquit, et, ut apparet, a[x] sua memoria nos deleuit. Nos autem," addens, "quid faciemus? quibus Deus pietatis sue oculos clausit, nec propugnatorem mittit qui liberet nos, cum inter istos canes[y] mori et uiuere habeamus. Si enim eis non consentimus, ut, lege Christi abiecta et oblita eos sequentes salutem nostram totaliter preponamus, afficient nos ludibriis, uerberibus et tormentis, aut certe, sicut sunt omni pietate priuati, crudeli et pestifere morti tradent. Et quamuis credam et sciam melius esse hanc carnis sarcinam deponere quam uitam perdere sempiternam, tamen non est mihi datum desuper morte fidem quam corde teneo confirmare. Sed, si benignus et misericors ille Deus nobis concedere dignaretur brachium aliquod cui possemus inniti, non

---

o et filii sui *om.* B   p et occultas uias C   q turicium C
r sunt *pro* habent B   s [et] *add.* R   t tamen *pro* Vnde B   u iniuriam C
v solum *om.* non *add. in marg.* B   w destruxissit AB   x in *pro* a B   y et *add.* B

she could not escape death for herself and her son. We on the other hand, think-ing to ourselves that danger threatened the mother and death the child, began to doubt about what to do and finally chose to baptize the boy, knowing and hoping that God from the depth of His treasures prepares diverse and hidden ways to sal-vation for diverse people and wants all men to be saved and none to perish. But it is estimated that more than two hundred thousand of those who were thus enslaved, sold, and became Saracens are in the empire of Persia alone.

I, as I say and assert, have traversed the entire empire for as far as it extends and was never in my life in any region, however foreign and remote, even India, where I did not see ruined and scattered Greek captives forced to be Saracens. In one city alone, which is called Tabriz in Persia, and its estates there are said to be most cer-tainly over a hundred and twenty thousand living Greek captives. And if one city alone has at present so many living captives, how many are in the innumerable other provinces and towns of the whole world, and how many are there who are dead or who have been killed by the sword?

The more, however, the Devil made these men mad after they became Sara-cens the more he fixed and imprinted in them the marks of perfidy, so that they forget all faith and Christianity and, more than those who were born Saracens, they persecute us, their brothers, and other Christians even more sharply. They say that they do this, however, so as to become cruel and merit more favor among their cruel lords. Whence when I was in India in order to preach the faith one of them did me an injury, and when we were at a suitable time between ourselves, I rebuked him, firmly but lovingly, for neglecting the Lord in this way, denying his faith, receiving a law contrary to the faith, truth, and salvation of Christ, and moreover presuming impudently and imprudently to persecute Christ in His ser-vants. He lowered his eyes and said, sighing,

Alas, we unhappy men whom God has placed in the opprobrium of every land! The Lord has turned His back to us, not His face; He has stricken us with His heel, utterly destroyed, and uprooted, and deserted us as use-less logs cut for burning and has apparently deleted us from His memory. What shall we do? (he added) We to whom God has closed the eyes of His piety and to whom He does not send a champion to free us, since we have to live and die among these dogs. For if we do not join with them and fol-lowing them totally abandon our salvation, rejecting and forgetting the law of Christ, they will assail us with derisions, blows, and torments or cer-tainly, being pitiless men, deliver us to a cruel and pernicious death. And although I believe and know that it is better to put down the burden of the flesh than to lose eternal life, I have not been granted by heaven the gift of dying for the faith which I hold in my heart. But if the benign and merci-ful God would deign to grant us some arm on which we could lean, there

est seruus qui non statim manus suas sui Domini sanguine consecraret." Et idem dicunt qui in Perside et Chaldea, quod scilicet non sperant aliud nisi ut habito tempore possent[z] suam seruitutem durissimam uindicare, et dampna que patiuntur in suos dominos retorquere. Ecce quantum dampnum Christianitatis est differre passagium, quantum dedecus Christi[a] nominis, quantum[b] fidei detrimentum. Puto quod, nisi subueniatur citius Grecie pereunti, non relinquetur in eo non dico qui fidem Christi habeat,[c] sed nec nomen. Videtis ergo quanta sit necessitas ut in Grecia passagium incipiat, et quantum nostrorum profectus et fidei utilitas acquiratur. Quia quamuis ab unitate matris ecclesie sint recisi, et filii illegitimi censeantur, tamen Sarraceni eos odio christiani nominis[d] persequuntur, scisma quod inter nos et Grecos est penitus non curantes, uel etiam ignorantes. Ipsi etiam,[e] licet fidei lumen amiserint, palpitantes tamen, utcumque in tenebris gaudent se christianos esse, et nomen Domini[f] deuote in necessitatibus inuocant et dulciter[g] profitentur.

Septima ratio est quia non dico tantum sed plus tenemur Grecos quam Sarracenos expugnare, et hoc ex causa duplici[h] uel amoris stimulo uel uindicte zelo et odio prouocati.[i] Amore quidem, quia plus tenetur pater filium castigare, quam seruum reducere domesticum aberrantem, quam extraneum, et si quem uidet pater filium sua monita non seruantem, sed uelut freneticum et insanum contra se rebellem uiderit et proteruum, apponit remedia ut constrictis flagellis et uinculis obediat et obtemperet, uel inuitus, quia uexatio dat auditui intellectum. Item zelo uindicte plus tenemur Grecos inuadere quam Sarracenos. Quanto enim plus grauant a filio, a propinquo, ab amico et noto offense et iniurie irrogate, tanto quilibet contra offendentem se spirat acrius ad uindictam, maxime si rogatus ad pacem ut obdurat, pacem rennuat, et beneficiis obligatus multiplicare offensas et grauamina non desistat. Qui autem antiquas historias mente retinet romana ecclesia, ecclesiarum omnium mater, inter omnes alias ecclesias et super omnes alias ecclesias[k] exaltauit Grecorum ecclesiam et promouit, etiam cum quarumdam aliarum ecclesiarum grauamine non modica et offensa. Ita ut alie ecclesie aut inuidebant ut emule, aut certe detrahebant romane ecclesie, ut grauate. Romana ergo ecclesia grecam optatis dignitatibus demulcebat, beneficiis uariis attrahebat, errantem reducere satagebat, reductam dulciter confirmabat dulcibus monitis et exemplis. Sed illa tumida et superba in matrem proterua et effrenata

z   audire *add. et expunc.* B   a   nos quantum dedecus Christi *add.* C

b   dedecus Christi nominis quantum *add.* (*rep.*) A   c   habeant C   d   nomine C

e   tamen *pro* etiam C   f   non Dominum *pro* nomen Domini AB   g   dulce C

h   duplici causa C   i   prouocat C   k   et super ... ecclesias *om.* B, ecclesias *om.* C

is not a slave who would not immediately consecrate his hands with the blood of the Lord.

The men in Persia and Chaldea likewise say that their only hope is that at the right time they might avenge their harsh servitude and inflict upon their masters the injuries they themselves suffer. See how great an injury to Christianity it is to delay a crusade, what a disgrace to the name of Christ, what a loss to the faith. I think that no one will be left there I do not say who has the faith of Christ, but rather not even the name unless help is rapidly given to Greece, which is dying. You see therefore how necessary it is for a crusade to start in Greece and how great an advantage for our men and benefit for the faith will be acquired. For although they have been cut off from the unity of the mother church and are considered illegitimate sons, they are persecuted out of hate of the Christian name by the Saracens who do not care or even know anything about the schism between us and the Greeks. Also, although they have lost the light of the faith, trembling nonetheless, as in darkness, they rejoice in being Christians and when in need, they devoutly invoke and sweetly profess the name of the Lord.

The seventh reason, roused by the double cause of the stimulus of love and the zeal for revenge and hate, is that we have to fight the Greeks I do not say as much as but even more than the Saracens. By love, indeed, because a father should chastise his son rather than subdue an erring domestic servant or a stranger, and if a father sees a son who is not following his instructions but is, like an uncontrolled and insane man, a rebel against him and reckless, he applies remedies so that restrained by rods and chains he obeys and submits, even if unwillingly, because pain gives understanding to the hearing.[73] Zeal for revenge likewise binds us to attack the Greeks more than the Saracens. For the more someone is offended and injured by a son, relation, friend, or acquaintance, the more bitterly he wants revenge against the offender, especially if he persists after being invited to make peace, rejects peace, and does not refrain from repeating the offenses and injuries after receiving favors. He who recalls ancient history [knows that] the Roman church, the mother of all churches, exalted and promoted the church of the Greeks among other churches and above all other churches, even when it was very displeased by the injury of some other churches which either as rivals envied or as victims disparaged the Roman church. The Roman church therefore soothed the Greek church with desired dignities, attracted it with various kindnesses, tried to bring the errant one back and confirmed the returned one sweetly by kindly advice and examples; but it was presumptuous and proud, shameless and unbridled toward its mother, and

73   This passage resembles Augustine's remarks on the obligation of a father to punish a son in spite (or because) of his love: see Augustine, *Epp.* 138.14, 153.17, 185.21 (*Corpus scriptorum ecclesiasticorum latinorum*, 44:140, 415–16; 57:19, 20).

in dominam semper diuisiones et scismata adinuenit pariter et nutriuit, et paci et unitati impatiens, elegit singularis incedere, et nouitatum et presumptionum inuentrix que sanam doctrinam non sapiunt, incrassata, inpinguata, dilatata, fidem orthodoxam romane ecclesie diuersis erroribus maculauit et obedientiam dereliquit. Si uero ingratitudines et malitias et iniurias per Grecos romane ecclesie irrogatas enumerem, libelli modum excederet quod, ut premisi, uitare cupio, quantum possum.

Quedam tamen et pauca de multis que uos ignorare non decet, immo scire expedit, que contra fidem et cultores fidei in Grecia per grecorum dominum nouiter contigerunt,[1] breuiter ennarrabo.

Imperator enim Grecie qui nunc est a principio sui regiminis fautor et nutritor errorum, cui semper fuit fidei ueritas et ecclesie unitas odiosa, a principio inquam sui regiminis fidem reliquit, ecclesiam romanam[m] in multis offendit, et a se et ab aliis sui dominii nostre Christianitatis cultum quantum potuit eneruauit, nolentesque fidem deserere, uel a suo imperio expulit uel carceribus mancipauit. Hic patrem habuit nomine Paleologum, quod idem sonat sicut antiquum uerbum, qui licet imperium uiolenti et infideli usurpatione habuerit, tamen romane ecclesie humilis et deuotus eius suscepit obedientiam et fidem, quam et tenuit uiriliter et defendit usque ad terminum uite sue. Conuocato enim suorum concilio[n] monachorum, ab illis qui inter eos auctoritatis maioris et scientie uidebantur sollicite requisiuit cui fidei, romane scilicet ecclesie uel grece esset potius adherendum.

Altercatione autem quadam prehabita, omnium fuit una et ista sententia quod extra fidem et obedientiam romane ecclesie non sit salus. Et cum eis adhuc diceret, ne precipitarent sententiam in hoc facto, sed post dies decem deliberationis firmiter responderent, et de hoc talem sententiam promulgarent quod non oporteret nec liceret eis modo aliquo reuocare, similem ut prius sententiam protulerunt. Quibus cum adhuc adderet minas mortis, si eos contingeret reuocare,

---

l contingerunt AC   m romanam ecclesiam C   n concilio suorum C

always discovered and nourished divisions and schisms against its mistress. It had no patience for peace and unity and chose to go its own way, and the fattened, swollen, and puffed up inventor of novelties and presumptions, ignorant of wholesome doctrine, stained the orthodox faith of the Roman church with many errors and left its obedience. But if I were to enumerate the ingratitudes, evils, and injuries done by the Greeks to the Roman church I should exceed the scope of a small book, which I want to avoid as much as possible, as I said before.

I shall relate briefly, however, a few of the many things of which you should not be ignorant, which you should indeed know, and which the lord of the Greeks recently inflicted on the faith and cultivators of the faith in Greece.

For the present emperor of Greece has been from the beginning of his reign a promoter and cultivator of errors. The truth of the faith and the unity of the church have always been hateful to him. From the beginning of his reign he left the faith and offended the Roman church in many ways.[74] He himself and others under his rule weakened the practice of our Christianity as much as they could, and he either expelled from his empire or imprisoned those who were unwilling to desert the faith.[75] He had a father named Paleologus,[76] which says the same as ancient word,[77] who although he held the empire by violent and faithless usurpation[78] was nonetheless humble and devout to the Roman church and received its obedience and faith, which he both held strongly and defended to the end of his life. For he summoned a council of his monks and earnestly asked those who were of greater authority and learning among them to which faith, that is, of the Roman church or of the Greek, they should adhere.[79]

After some debate they all unanimously decided that there was no salvation outside the faith and obedience of the Roman church. And when he said to them that they should not issue a decision on this matter in a hurry but after ten days of deliberation they should firmly reply and promulgate a decision on this, which they neither should nor could in any way revoke, they produced a sentence like the previous one. When he added threats of death to this if they revoked it,

---

74   Andronicus II began his reign by repudiating the church union negotiated by his father and ratified at the second council of Lyons (1274): Laiou (1972), 21, 32–37; Gill (1979a), 182–83; Hussey (1990), 243.

75   There were few unionists who did not recant, but among those who retained their unionist convictions were the deposed patriarch John Bekkos, George Metochites, and Theodore Meliteiniotes: Laiou (1972), 35.

76   Michael VIII. See p. 79 n. 72 above.

77   In Greek *palaios* means "ancient," *logos* means "word."

78   See n. 72 above.

79   William is probably referring to the synodal document issued 24 December 1273. This was a meeting of the standing synod in Constantinople—that is, not of monks only: see the document edited with introduction and commentary in Darrouzès and Laurent (1976), 24–27, 320–23; English trans. Gill (1974), 18–21; reprinted in idem (1979b), art. V.

iterum dicentes idem quod prius et unanimiter asserentes[o] se cuicumque pene uel morti quam uellet eis imperator infligere subdiderunt, si huic sententie uerbo uel facto aliqualiter contrairent. Ad petitionem igitur predicti imperatoris Paleologi humilem et deuotum summus pontifex in Constantinopolim legatum misit abbatem, scilicet tunc Montis Casinensis, quem legatum ipse Paleologus idcirco petiuerat, ut ex parte summi pontificis ipsum uniret fidei orthodoxe ad gremium matris ecclesie redeuntem. Cumque legatus in ecclesia Sancte Sophie conuocata multitudine innumerabili solemniter celebraret, collatione uerbi per eum premissa ad populum, imperator accedens, obedientiam promisit romane ecclesie et fidem coram astante[p] multitudine est professus solemniter et constanter, et sic more nostro de manu legati ibidem sacra communione ab imperatore recepta cum exultatione fidelium, sacra misteria terminantur[q] celebrantur. Cum uero tempus institit quo debeat Lugdunense generale concilium[r] celebrari, Paleologus imperator fidelem et deuotum patriarcham suum ad illud uenire precepit, ut ordinationes et consuetudines romane ecclesie in Greciam secum ferret, cupiens secundum illas[s] subiectum[t] sibi clerum et populum informare. Sed cum patriarcha ad hoc[u] deuotus insisteret et fideliter laboraret, et ex hoc et[v] propter mortem pape oporteret eum in hiis partibus aliquamdiu commorari, monachi qui salutem uite imperatori suaserant penitere ceperunt, et submurmurantes, errores et noua scismata seminantes, totum populum accepto salubri proposito peruerterunt. Quo comperto, imperator iussit

o [quod] add. R   p astante coram corr. coram astante C   q [et] add. R
r concilium generale C   s illam C   t subiectam AC   u adhuc B, ad hoc om. C
v et om. B

they again said and asserted unanimously the same as before and subjected themselves to whatever penalty or death the emperor wanted to inflict on them if they in any way by word or deed went against this decision. At the request of this emperor Paleologus, therefore, the pope sent as a humble and devout legate to Constantinople the abbot of Monte Cassino,[80] for whom Paleologus asked in order on behalf of the pope to unite to the orthodox faith him who was returning to the bosom of the mother church. And when the legate solemnly celebrated in the church of Sta. Sophia,[81] where an innumerable crowd was gathered, and gave a speech to the people, the emperor entered and promised obedience to the Roman church,[82] and in the presence of the attending crowd he solemnly and firmly professed his faith. And thus, according to our custom, the holy mysteries were completed and celebrated with the joy of the faithful after the emperor received holy communion from the hand of the legate.[83] But since the time for the meeting of the general council of Lyons was drawing near,[84] the emperor Paleologus ordered his faithful and devout patriarch to come to it so that he could bring the ordinations and customs of the Roman church with him into Greece and wishing to instruct in accordance with them the clergy and people subject to him.[85] But when the devout patriarch set about and faithfully worked for this, and for this and owing to the death of the pope had to stay for some time in these parts, the monks who had advised the salvation of life to the emperor began to repent and complain, and sowing new errors and new schisms they perverted the entire people after the salutary proposition had been accepted.[86] After the emperor discovered this he ordered

---

80   William seems to have transposed certain events from the period after the second council of Lyons to the period before the council. The abbot of Monte Cassino was part of the legation that went to Constantinople from Lyons in the autumn of 1274: Gill (1979a), 161.

81   Again, nothing like this happened before the council of Lyons. After the ambassadors who had been sent to Lyons returned to Constantinople (autumn 1274), with John Parastron and the abbot of Monte Cassino in their party, a liturgy of reconciliation was scheduled. On 16 January 1275, a solemn liturgy was celebrated in the Blachernai palace chapel. The Latins were present, and the pope was commemorated, but the celebrant was an eastern bishop, Nicholas of Chalcedon, not the abbot of Monte Cassino: Gill (1974), 163.

82   Michael VIII "promised to obey the Roman church" many times in the course of union negotiations.

83   I know of no evidence that Michael VIII "received holy communion from the hand of the legate."

84   Second council of Lyons, 1274.

85   The Byzantine embassy to the council of Lyons did not include the incumbent patriarch, Joseph I, who had withdrawn to a monastery to protest the proposed terms of union. It did include a former patriarch, Germanos III (1265–66): Roberg (1964), 108, 228; Gill (1979a), 132–41.

86   The Greek delegation returned from Lyons at the end of the council, arriving in Constantinople in the autumn of 1274. Gregory X (1271–76) lived until 10 January 1276. William seems to be saying here that Germanos stayed in the west until after the death of Gregory, but I have been unable to find any confirmation of this.

omnes monachos, ubicumque inueniri possent sine spe uenie et absque interrogatione submergi. Hac ergo causa multa milia consumpsit monachorum. Illos autem quibus sub attestatione imperator[w] minas intulerat si id quod de fide asseruerant reuocarent, ligatos super singulos asinos, uersis ad caudas uultibus, uisceribus animalium ad colla appensis clamante precone per totam Constantinopolim duci precepit nasibus amputatis. Hos autem occidere noluit,[x] sed sic permisit[y] cum hac ignominia uiuere, ut semper in eorum facie signum sue perfidie appareret.

Post mortem uero huius Paleologi, monachi, qui diu eo uiuente latuerant, sunt unanimiter congregati, et seditione commota in populo istum qui nunc est noluerunt in imperatorem modo aliquo consecrare, nisi sex conditionibus interiectis, quos imperator iuramento prestito promisit et firmiter se inuiolabiliter et in perpetuum seruaturum. Prima conditio fuit quod fidem et obedientiam romane ecclesie abnegaret et insuper anathematizaret et malediceret omnes communionem et[z] obedientiam et fidem romane ecclesie[a] profitentes. Secunda quod numquam uerbo uel opere Grecorum fidei immo perfidie in aliquo contrairet. Tertia quod, quia pater eius fidem catholicam susceperat et mortuus fuerat in eodem,[b] ipsum malediceret et excommunicaret et anathematizaret aut[c] anathemati perpetuo obligaret. Quarta quod, quia[d] idem pater suus multos monachos piscibus maris et uolucribus celi et terre bestiis tradiderat deuorandos, numquam in perpetuum eundem permitteret sepeliri. Quinta quia monachi illi timebant ut cum iste esset in imperio[e] confirmatus contra eos, sicut pater eius fecerat, dampnis et iniuriis anhelaret, quod numquam

w   imperator *om.* B   x   *pro* uoluit (?)   y   promisit AC   z   et *om.* B
a   romane ecclesie et fidem *pro* et . . . ecclesie C   b   in eodem *om.* C
c   anathematizaret aut *om.* AB   d   quia *om.* C   e   in imperio esset C (in *ss.*)

that all the monks who could be found should be drowned without any hope of forgiveness and without questioning.[87] For this reason he destroyed many thousands of monks. The emperor ordered, however, that those whom he had threatened under oath if they went back on what they affirmed concerning the faith should have their noses cut off and be led with a shouting herald through all Constantinople tied backwards on single donkeys with their faces toward the tails and with the inner organs of animals hung around their necks.[88] He did not want to kill them, however, but allowed them to live with this ignominy so that the mark of their perfidy would always be visible on their faces.

After the death of this Paleologus, however, the monks who had long been hidden during his lifetime were all gathered, and after rebellion had been aroused among the people, they refused to consecrate the present emperor in any manner except on six conditions which the emperor solemnly and firmly swore he would preserve inviolably and forever.[89] The first condition was that he would renounce the faith and obedience to the Roman church and in addition would anathematize and curse anyone who professed communion, obedience, and fidelity to the Roman church. Second, that he would never in any way in word or deed go against the faith or rather the faithlessness of the Greeks. Third, that since his father had received the catholic faith and died in the same, he would curse, excommunicate, and anathematize him or bind him by perpetual anathema. Fourth, that since his father had delivered many monks to be eaten by the fish of the sea, the birds of the sky, and the beasts of the land, he would in perpetuity never allow him to be buried. Fifth, since the monks feared that after he had been confirmed as emperor he would breathe against them with punishments and injuries, as had his father, that he would never in his whole empire, either by himself or through another, decree a

---

87   Drowning was not a common method of capital punishment in Byzantium, and I know of no reference to Michael VIII drowning monks. He did have opponents, including monks, blinded, tortured, and exiled. In at least one case he had a monastic opponent's tongue cut out: Pachymeres, bk. 6, chap. 24 (1984–2000), 2:611–21.

88   In discussions of church union before the second council of Lyons, emperor Michael VIII became especially frustrated with Manuel Holobolos, who had originally been a supporter of union but then changed his stance. In October 1273 he had Holobolos brought to Constantinople in chains, along with nine other men and Holobolos's niece. Pachymeres reports that the emperor then organized a "novel triumph." He had the ten men tied together by their necks: Holobolos first, then the others, with Holobolos's niece at the end. They were all denounced for magic. The first two men were loaded down with sheep guts filled with excrement. Holobolos was struck repeatedly with a sheep's liver. All were led around the city in procession. This helped considerably to persuade the clergy to go along with the synodal statement of union discussed above, pp. 86–88. It is interesting that William includes this episode in events after the council of Lyons because Pachymeres also inserts it into his narrative with events after the council. Pachymeres clearly states, however, that the event actually happened some years earlier: Pachymeres, bk. 5, chap. 18 (1984–2000), 2:495–99.

89   In fact, he lists only five. On these oaths see *Directorium* (1906), 434 and the notes in *Recueil*, 546 n. b and cxcvii.

mortis uel sanguinis, nec per se nec per alium in toto suo imperio iudicium pro-
mulgaret. Prima conditio[f] et secunda eum Deo reddidit odiosum, quia sine fide
impossibile est placere Deo. Tertia eum peccato contra naturam, iniquitate et
scelere, maculauit, quia patrem maledicere contra preceptum legis nature est que
parentes precipit honorare. Quarta conditio eum omni etiam[g] communi caritate
et pietate priuauit, quia de misericordie operibus est mortuos sepelire. Quinta conditio eum omni iniquitate repleuit, quia ad principem pertinet penis et morte peccata corrigere, quia iusticia cum iudicio dicitur preparatio sedis regni. Has autem
conditiones iniquas ita stricte et cum tanta diligentia obseruauit usque ad hanc
diem, ut in hiis dispensatio nulla cadat.

Ipse quos potest a fide nostra abducit, et ad suam inducit perfidiam muneribus et promissis, sicut de uxore sua que fuerat[h] filia marchionis Montis Ferrati,
que greca per eum effecta, greca uixit, et greca mortua est, et a grecis more ipso-
rum sacramentis susceptis in Grecorum ecclesia est sepulta. Vxor etiam filii sui
que nuper in dedecus romane ecclesie de quodam sororum nostrarum monas-
terio, in quo oblata a parentibus per aliquos annos fuerat, reclamante puella, et
illuc de Alamannia est traducta, per eum Greca perfida est effecta. Filium etiam
fratris regis Cipri qui dicebatur dominus de Sur, cum ad ipsum imperatorem de
Armenia confugisset, dando sibi neptem suam in uxorem suam,[i] ad suam perfidiam inclinauit. Quemdam etiam Ianuensem spurium et male natum, ut posset eum ad suam sectam attrahere, admiratum galearum fecit, et eidem quamdam
suam consanguineam in coniugium copulauit. Quemdam etiam apostatam
duorum ordinum, Predicatorum uidelicet primo et secundo Templariorum,

f   est *add*. AC, conditione B   g etiam omni C   h fuit C   i   suam *om*. B

judgment of death or blood. The first and second conditions rendered him hateful to God, since without faith it is impossible to please God. The third stained him with a sin against nature and with iniquity and crime, since to curse a father is against a precept of natural law, which requires people to honor their parents. The fourth condition also deprived him of all common love and piety, since to bury the dead is one of the works of mercy. The fifth condition filled him with all iniquity, since it is the duty of a prince to correct sins with punishments and death, and justice with judgment is called the preparation for a seat in the kingdom. He has observed these evil conditions up to the present day so strictly and with such diligence that there are no exceptions.

By rewards and promises he leads those whom he can away from our faith and brings them into his faithlessness, as he did his wife, who was a daughter of the marquis of Montferrat and was made a Greek by him, lived as a Greek, died as a Greek, and was buried by the Greeks in a church of the Greeks after receiving the sacraments according to their custom.[90] The wife of his son, to the disgrace of the Roman church and in spite of her protests, was recently removed from a certain monastery of our sisters to which she had been presented some years ago by her parents and was also taken by him from Germany to Greece and made a perfidious Greek.[91] He also turned to his perfidy the son of a brother of the king of Cyprus, who is called the lord of Sur, when he fled to the emperor from Armenia, by giving him his niece for his wife.[92] He also made a certain Genoese of unknown father and low birth admiral of the galleys in order to attract him to his sect and married him to one of his female relations.[93] He also attracted and promoted a certain apostate from two orders, first the Dominicans and second the Templars,

90   Yolanda of Montferrat, born 1273 or 1274, renamed Irene and married to Andronicus II (his second marriage) in 1284, died 1317. She was the granddaughter of king Alfonso X of Castile and daughter of marquis William VII of Montferrat. The marriage was "a diplomatic triumph," according to Laiou (1972), 48, for the Paleologus family for two reasons: first, it strengthened the Byzantine alliance with Castile and the house of Montferrat against Charles of Anjou, who was planning to launch a crusade against Constantinople; second, the Montferrat family had claims to the "kingdom of Thessalonica" stemming from the partition of the empire after the fourth crusade. Yolanda took these claims as her dowry into the marriage, thus ending a source of tension between the Greeks and the Montferrat: Constantinidi-Bibikou (1950); Laiou (1972), 44–48, 229–32; Talbot (1991b).

91   None of Andronicus II's sons married a woman from a convent in Germany. His grandson, Andronicus III, married Adelheid of Brunswick-Grubenhagen, who was renamed Irene, 23 October 1317. The marriage was part of Andronicus II's attempts to ally himself with anti-papal forces in Germany, of which Adelheid/Irene's brother, duke Henry II of Brunswick-Grubenhagen, was one. Adelheid/Irene died 16 August 1324; her only son had predeceased her: Laiou (1972), 252.

92   Guy of Lusignan: *Recueil*, 533 n. c (Mas Latrie) and cxcviii and 1036 (Kohler).

93   Andrea Morisco: *Recueil*, cxcviii and 1036. There were not many galleys for an admiral to command in this period. Laiou (1972), 74–76, reports that Andronicus inherited only the remnants of a navy from his father and, in 1285, had even that remnant scrapped.

uirum nequissimum, moribus et uita et genere sordidum, sic attraxit et subli-
mauit, quod eum primo magnum ducem dehinc cesarem fecit, et eidem filiam
sororis sue in coniugium sociauit. Insuper illum patriarcham quem olim pater
istius ad concilium Lugdunense transmiserat, pro causa superius memorata, cum
in[k] Constantinopolim peruenisset cum ordinationibus et decretis romane curie
et apostolicis litteris graciosis et imperatorem Paleologum mortuum inuenisset,
statim per istum imperatorem qui nunc est capitur et, nolens fidem quam susceperat abnegare terroribus uel promissis, cum multis de suo genere carceri mancipa-
tur, et in illa confessione perdurans gloriose in carcere obdormiuit.

Multos etiam adhuc idem imperator in carcere detinet, et a tempore mortis
patris sui, quia fidem nostram quam susceperat tenere et in ea et pro ea mori potius
elegerunt quam[l] promoueri et extolli denariis, dignitatibus et promissis. Vnde
adhuc uiuunt aliqui de illis incarceratis, fide feruentes et in penis constantes, obedientiam profitentes romane ecclesie et amantes. De quibus iniustum mihi uidetur quia, pro liberatione[m] eorum a carcere ab ecclesia romana numquam littera
aliqua emanauit, quod[n] forte contigit quia hoc ad ecclesie notitiam non peruenit,
uel forte non fuit qui has litteras procuraret, quia etiam pertimescebat ne populus ad sanam doctrinam et uite exemplum fratrum nostrorum, Predicatorum scilicet et Minorum, conuertentur,[o] eis de ciuitate constantinopolitana expulit, et
iurauit in manibus monachorum quod numquam aliquem de predictis fratribus
infra Constantinopolim permitteret habitare. Et in hoc uult[p] Tartarorum et Sarracenorum malitiam et perfidiam superare, qui fratres ad predicandum uerbum
Dei ad eos declinantes permittunt habitare inter se pacifice et quiete, nec uidetur aliud uersari in eius mente perfida[q] nisi quomodo posset sui et commissi sibi
populi saluti obstaculum inuenire.

Pater etiam eius ut iste imperator iurauerat adhuc[r] non est traditus sepulture.
Corpus autem eiusdem patris sui tanta integritate perdurat, et tanta est usque
nunc incolumitate seruatum,[s] ut consumptionis alicuius uel fetoris in eodem

k in *om.* C   l   non *add.* AC   m deliberatione AC   n hoc *pro* quod C
o confitentur C, conuerterentur R (*recte*)   p quod *add.* C   q perfidia C
r adhuc *om.* C   s   conseruatum C

a very evil man, sordid in his ways, his life, and his birth, and made him first grand duke and then Caesar and married him to the daughter of his sister.[94] Furthermore, when the patriarch whom his father had formerly sent to the council of Lyons for the business mentioned above came to Constantinople with the ordinations and decrees of the Roman curia and gracious apostolic letters and found that the emperor Paleologus was dead, he was at once arrested by the present emperor and, when in spite of threats and promises he refused to deny the faith which he had received, he was imprisoned with many of his family and persisted gloriously in that confession until he died in prison.[95]

The emperor since the time of his father's death has kept many men in prison because they have chosen to keep the faith which he had received and to die in and for it rather than be promoted and exalted by money, dignities, and promises. Some of these prisoners are still alive, fervent in faith and constant in punishments, and profess and love obedience to the Roman church. It seems to me unjust that no letter concerning these men has ever come from the church of Rome asking for their delivery from prison. This may be because it has not come to the attention of the church or perhaps because there was no one to procure these letters. The emperor also expelled the [Dominican] Preachers and [Franciscan] Minors from the city of Constantinople because he feared that the people might be converted by the sound doctrine and example of life of our friars,[96] and he swore in the hands of the monks that he would never allow any of these brothers to live in Constantinople. In doing this he wants to exceed the malice and perfidy of the Tartars and Saracens, who allow the friars who come to them to preach the word of God to them and to live peacefully and quietly among them. His only object in his perfidious mind seems to be to find an obstruction to the salvation of himself and of the people entrusted to him.

His father, too, as the present emperor swore, has not yet been buried.[97] The body survives in such integrity, however, and is so well preserved up to now that no

---

94   Roger de Flor (ca. 1267–1305) had been a Templar and had left that order in disgrace (1291). For Frederick II of Sicily he commanded a company of Catalans and Aragonese fighting the Angevins in Italy. When peace was made in 1302, he offered his services to Andronicus II, who accepted, gave Roger the title of *megas dux*, and married him to his niece Maria, the daughter of king Ivan III Asen of Bulgaria. He and his army, known as the Catalan Grand Company, arrived in Constantinople in 1303. The subsequent problems they caused played a role in the disintegration of the empire in Andronicus's time and beyond: *Receuil*, 547 n. e; Setton (1975); Laiou (1972), 1:131–229; Talbot (1991a, 1991c).

95   See p. 89 above. Mas-Latrie (*Recueil*, 547 n. f) takes this to refer to the patriarch John Bekkos, but Bekkos had not attended the council of Lyons, was not imprisoned, and did not die in prison. I can find no references to Germanos doing so, but it is more likely that he is referred to here.

96   The friars were expelled from Constantinople in 1307.

97   Stories about how, when, and where Michael VIII was buried and claims that his body remained incorrupt circulated in both the east and the west. William is representative of western

---

aliquod uestigium nequeat inueniri. Immo contigit ut candela que sui matris studio circa corpus eius ardet die noctuque casu caderet, et cum omnia que circa corpus illud erant ignis ex candela accensus penitus consumpsisset, tantum de archa in qua integrum seruabatur remansit illesum, tantumque de panno serico quod illud tegebat fuit intactum quantum mensura corporis contingebat. Ita quod nec[t] in corpus, nec in aliquod aliud quod corpus contingeret, ardor incendii preualeret, sed cum ad fines corporis ignis pertigit, sine omni humano studio est extinctus.

Ex hiis autem paucis de multis que dicta sunt potestis aduertere quantum tenetur ecclesia istum imperatorem perdere, qui, tot contra nos nequitiis perpetratis et dolis inuentis et iniuriis irrogatis, in malis perdurans, non desistit cogitare et facere quicquid sperat posse contingere in malum romane ecclesie et in[u] detrimentum nostre fidei et iacturam. Quem ergo pietatis affectus et longanimitatis benignitas ecclesie non inclinant et emoliunt sed indurant, exemplo[v] secundo Domini seruato potenti[w] ecclesie gladio feriatur, ut sic eius amplius non regnet iniquitas sed impietas destruatur,[x] tranquillusque status pro nostris inde proueniat et securus, et passagio prosperitas optata arrideat, ut hinc inde prostratis et deletis hostibus crucis Christi in sancta Ierusalem affectatum finem et[y] beatum exitum assequamur. Iam ergo ad partem ultimam huius opusculi redeamus.

V

Emolumentum[z] ergo quale et quantum Sarracenis Egipti proueniat de partibus Indiarum hoc nullus dubitet quin incidenter sit causa potissima omnium transgressionum et peccatorum que per nostros eundo in Egiptum contra reuerenciam romane[a] ecclesie perpetrantur, et hoc ut melius cognoscatur presciendum est quod unum brachium maris occeani uersus meridiem terram diuidit, quod innumerabiles prouincias et ciuitates in suis littoribus habet et infra sinum suum ambit et continet paruas et magnas, mirabiles et miserabiles insulas infinitas. Et istud brachium mare Indicum appellatur.

t non *add. supra* C   u in *om.* B   v exempto ABC
w secundo … potenti *om.* B (*cum longo spatio*)   x deseruatur C   y in *pro* et C
z Emolimentum A   a Romae C

vestige of any corruption or foul smell can be detected in it. Indeed when a candle which by the care of his mother burns night and day around his body accidentally fell over and the fire from the candle completely consumed everything around the body, only the part of the chest in which he was preserved intact remained unharmed and the part of the silken cloth which covered it was untouched up to the point where it touched the outline of the body, so that the heat of the fire did not consume either the body or anything touching the body but went out without any human effort when it came to the edges of the body.

These few examples, chosen from many that have been reported, will show you how greatly the church is bound to destroy this emperor who persists in evil deeds against us by so many contrived plots and inflicted injuries and who does not cease from planning and doing whatever he hopes can damage the Roman church and harm and diminish our faith. Let the strong sword of the church therefore strike him whom the feeling of piety and kindness of patience harden rather than turn to the church or soften, keeping the second example of the Lord,[98] in order that his iniquity may rule no more but his impiety be destroyed, and a peaceful and just state may thus come for our men, and the desired success smile favorably upon the crusade, and hence when the enemies of the cross of Christ have been defeated and destroyed on both sides we may secure in holy Jerusalem the desired end and blessed conclusion. Let us therefore now return to the last part of this little work.

<h1 style="text-align:center">V</h1>

No one questions how great a profit the Saracens of Egypt derive from India,[99] because this is incidentally the greatest of all transgressions and sins which our men perpetrate against the reverence for the Roman church by going to Egypt. For this to be better understood it should be known that one branch of the sea of the ocean toward the south divides the land and has innumerable provinces and cities on its shores and clasps within its breast and contains an infinite number of islands, small and great, marvelous and miserable. This branch is called the Indian sea,

---

accounts, which tended both to exaggerate how long Michael remained unburied and to claim that his incorruptibility was proof of his sanctity. Eastern sources, in contrast, claimed that the body was bloated and black but whole, indicating his damnation for heresy: Geanakoplos (1959), 370 and n. 13.

98   This may be a reference to Christ's statement in the New Testament that He came to bring not peace but the sword (Matt. 10.34; Luke 12.51): cf. the interpretation of Christian of Stavelot, *Liber generationis*, bk. 10, chaps. 34–42 (*Corpus Christianorum: Continuatio medievalis*, 224:229–33), who distinguished between good and bad peace.

99   The author shows a remarkable understanding of the contemporary commercial scenario as he is fully aware that the bulk of this trade between India and Egypt (known as Misr/Masr in Islamic texts) was overseas in nature. On the Indian ocean maritime scene see Chaudhuri (1985 and 1990); Ghosh (1992); Hourani (1999); Pearson (2004); Sidebotham (2011); Habicht (2012).

Quod maius esse quam istud nostrum Mediterraneum[b] comprobatur. Brachium uero[c] istud diuiditur in[d] gulfos et portus plurimos et anfractus.

De quo inter alios unus magnus gulfus uersus occidentem regionis illius[e] protenditur, qui ex uno latere uersus meridiem Arabie partem et Idumeam et ex altera montes maximos, preter multa que omitto in parte inaccessibiles. Vltra quos montes ueram Ethiopiam habet et in fine sinus sui est quedam ciuitas situata que Eden nuncupatur, que illa esse dicitur quam in Genesi Chaym[f] legitur construxisse. Hec ciuitas ex una[g] parte habet[h] gulfum maris Indici et[i] ex altera mare Rubrum, ad quod itur de predicta ciuitate per quoddam strictum quod est quasi alueus fluuius. Quod quidem strictum fluxu maris impletur et refluxu euacuatur et ex[k] hoc bis in die naturali. Per hunc ergo modum, mare Indicum est contiguum mari Rubro. Hoc mare Rubrum et Nilum fluuium qui in Egiptum currit paruum terre spatium diuidit, ita de mari Rubro in Egiptum breuis et facilis sit ingressus. Habita igitur ista dispositione preambula, quilibet potest aduertere quod premisi, scilicet quod[l] India omnium malorum que supra posui materia sit, non casualiter nec[m] occasionaliter sed ueraciter effectiue.

b   m . . . terraneum A (francum?) BC   c   uero om. C   d   in om. C   e   illius regionis C
f   chayn B, cayn C   g   una om. C   h   habet ex parte C   i   et om. C
k   ex om. B   l   quod om. C   m   uel pro nec B, non casualiter nec om. C

and is acknowledged to be larger than our Mediterranean. But this arm of the sea is divided into many gulfs, ports, and branches.[100]

Of these, among others, one great gulf extends toward the west of this region and has on one side toward the south part of Arabia and Idumea and on the other, in addition to many things which I omit, some great and partially inaccessible mountains, beyond which is true Ethiopia.[101] At the end of the gulf is the city called Aden [Eden], which is said to be that which in Genesis Cain is read to have built and which has on one side a gulf of the Indian sea and on the other the Red sea, to which one goes from Aden by a strait that is like the channel of a river.[102] This strait is twice a day filled by the flow of the sea and emptied by the reverse flow. In this way the Indian sea is contiguous to the Red sea. A small space of land divides the Red sea from the river Nile, which flows in Egypt, so that the way from the Red sea into Egypt is short and easy. Bearing in mind this disposition, therefore, anyone can observe, as I said before, that India is truly and effectively, and not casually or occasionally, the source of all the evils which I described above.

100   The significant expression here is *mare Indicum* (literally meaning the Indian sea or Indian ocean), of which the earliest known use is in Pliny's *Naturalis historia*, bk. 10, chap. 21.56: Wright (1925), 279–81; Beckingham (1980), 297. *Mare Indicum* does not correspond to the modern Indian ocean, which covers about a fifth of the total maritime space in the earth, but seems to correspond to the western sector of the Indian ocean, including the Arabian sea. In the voluminous geographical and travel literature in Arabic and Persian, the expression is *al bahr al Hindi*, the sea of India: Chakravarti (2007a). William shows his awareness of the Indian ocean by stating that it was much larger than "our Mediterranean." The expression "our Mediterranean" is significant because since the days of the Roman empire, the Latin world viewed the Mediterranean as our sea (*mare nostrum*): Wright (1925), 307. The Indian ocean did not belong to any political power before the arrival of the Europeans in the early sixteenth century. It was in a way an open sea (*mare liberum*), an arena of seafarers, shippers, travelers, and merchants.

101   Many crusading treatises referred to Ethiopia in their search for the legendary Christian king Prester John, but they invariably associated Ethiopia with India: Beckingham (1980). William never confused Ethiopia with India. See also Richard (1960), 328; Von den Brinken (1973), 295–96, 312 n.140.

102   William here differentiates the Red sea from the gulf of Aden, which he called the gulf of Eden, thus giving it a biblical hue. His understanding of the location is accurate and comes close to the description of the great port in the thirteenth century account of Ibn al-Mujāwir: Marco Polo, bk. 3, chaps. 35–36 (1903), 2:420, 438–42; Cordier (1920), 124–25; Miles (1993); Smith (1997), esp. article X. The blockade William proposes below would simultaneously dry up the supply of imported commodities from India to Egypt and also severely affect the fortunes of the port of Aden, on which see Bretschneider (1910), 2:305–6; *Book of Knowledge* (1912), 39; Cordier (1920), 124–25; Wright (1925), 299–300; Kammerer (1950), 47–55; Chaudhuri (1985); Steensgaard (1987); Biedermann (2006); Margariti (2007). The importance of the network of Aden with the preeminent ports of Gujarat, Konkan, and Malabar on the western coast of India can hardly be overemphasized. Marco Polo, like Ibn Battuta, noted the arrival of ships at Aden from distant ports and reported how merchants transferred their goods to smaller vessels suitable for sailing in the Red sea, which had many reefs: Pereira (2001); Agius (2002), 184. That Indian merchants (*baniyans* in Arabic texts) regularly frequented this port is evident from the mention of a specific quarter in Aden for Indian merchants.

Omnia enim que in Egipto uenduntur, ut piper, zinziber et alie species, aurum et lapides pretiosi, sericum et panni illi pretiosi, tincti Indie coloribus, et omnia alia pretiosa, propter que emenda mercatores istarum partium eundo in[n] Alexandriam excommunicationis laqueo se exponunt,[o] obedientiam sue matris ecclesie et summi apostolici reuerentiam postponentes, apportantur de India in Egiptum. Nam sicut cibus a capite in gutture et a gutture in stomachum et[p] de stomacho ad ceteras partes corporis se transfundit, ita predicte merces preciose a mari Indico quasi a capite ortum habent, et per predictum gulfum Eden quasi per guttur, dehinc in Egiptum per mare Rubrum quasi in stomachum, et deinde quasi ad partes corporis, ad ceteras mundi prouincias disperguntur. Qui ergo caput prescinderet, totus stomachus ex[q] defectu nutrimenti tabescens per consequens et membra cetera deperirent. Vnde igitur malum prouenit ibi contra morbum remedium apponatur. Quod erit, si uia ista posset aliqualiter impediri, ne scilicet iste merces de maritimis finibus Indiarum possent per gulfum predictum Eden in Egiptum descendere, quia, clauso hoc gulfo, aliud hostium nec locus patet nec[r] aditus unde possint Egiptii hoc habere, propter que per nostros, ut predicitur, in Alexandriam nauigatur.

n in *om.* B   o opponunt C   p et *om.* C   q et *pro* ex C   r uel *pro* nec A

For all of the things that are sold in Egypt, such as pepper, ginger, and other spices; gold and precious stones; silk and those precious materials dyed with the colors of India; and all other precious things are carried from India to Egypt.[103] The merchants of these parts expose themselves to the fetters of excommunication and put aside their obedience to the mother church and reverence for the highest apostle when they go to Alexandria to buy these things. For as food goes from the head through the throat, and from the throat into the stomach, and from the stomach to other parts of the body, so the aforesaid precious goods originate from the Indian sea, as from the head, and are spread through the gulf of Aden, as by the throat, from there by the Red sea to Egypt, as to the stomach, and then, as to the parts of the body, to the other parts of the world. If someone were to cut off the head, therefore, the whole stomach would consequently suffer from lack of food, and the other members would perish.[104] The remedy against the disease is therefore to be applied to the place from which the evil comes. This will occur if that route can be in some way blockaded so that the goods from the shores of the Indies cannot come through the gulf of Aden to Egypt, since if this gulf is closed there would be no other place or approach by which the Egyptians could obtain the goods for which our men sail to Alexandria.

103   The demand for Indian pepper (actually the pepper of Malabar grown in the coastal area of modern Kerala, on the west coast of south India) was constant from the late first century BC until at least the eighteenth century. Thapar (1992) called it the "black gold." Excellent accounts of shipping black pepper from the ports of Malabar/Kerala to the Red sea are available in the accounts of Ibn Battuta, Marco Polo, Ibn al-Mujāwir, and Chau ju-Kua: Appadurai (1936); Nilakantha Sastri (1939); and, on the pepper trade in Alexandria, Atiya (1962). William is mistaken in stating that India supplied gold to the west through Egypt. India has only one major gold-field, Kolar in Karnataka in peninsular India. In fact, gold and silver, as scarce precious metals, were regular and staple imports. On the other hand, a few Indian precious gems and stones, including diamonds (from the Golconda fields) were in sustained demand in western Asia and the Mediterranean area: Chakravarti (1995). Iron was also in steady demand in the western Indian ocean: see Goitein (1973), 185–92; Goitein and Friedman (2008), 594–605. According to Ibn al-Mujāwir camphor (*kafur*, which derives from the Sanskrit *karpura*: Karashima [2002]) was one of the major items of import to Aden: Smith (1995). William is also inaccurate in saying that India exported silk to Egypt. Silk, a product of China, reached the west largely along the overland silk road passing through central and west Asia. Textiles, however, were among the most important export commodities from India: Gopal (1965); Yādava (1973); Ramaswamy (1985). The geniza papers of the eleventh century Jewish merchant Ibn 'Awkal show that indigo from Sindan (Sanjan to the north of Mumbai) in western India reached as far as Old Cairo or Fustat and competed with indigo from Amta near Palestine and from Kirman (southern Iran): Stillman (1973); Chakravarti (1996).

104   The metaphor employed here respectively for India, the gulf of Aden, and Egypt—the head (*quasi a capite*, actually meaning mouth), throat (*quasi per guttur*), and stomach (*quasi in stomachum*)—are unique in the Indian ocean narratives of premodern times. On this and other organic metaphors in the middle ages, of which John of Salisbury presented a famous example, see G. Constable (2007), 7–8. It is from this position that William considered India to be the source of all evils and fountainhead of maritime commerce with Egypt and therefore to be cut off by a naval blockade.

Ad quod autem complendum unicus est modus et facilis, ut scilicet alique galee in mari Indico ponantur, que passum illum predicti gulfi de Eden diligenter custodiant et impediant, ne de cetero aliquis portans predictas merces de[s] India in Egiptum perinde tute ualeant nauigare, et ad hoc explendum tres uel quatuor galee sufficiunt habundanter. Vt autem galee iste haberi ualeant duplex erit modus, unus difficilis et alter facilis. Primus modus est ut tantam pecuniam ecclesia exhiberet[t] quanta pro illis galeis sufficeret, quam sub certa ratione reciperet ille quem ecclesia huic negotio preponere dignaretur. Et quia forte difficile esse uideretur[u] ecclesie hanc pecuniam exhibere, adhibeatur modus secundus, qui sit facilior et melior, ut scilicet dominus papa de thesauro Domini crucifixi largus sit, et pro mille ducentis hominibus a pena et culpa indulgentiam largiatur. Tot enim homines pro quatuor galeis necessarii sunt. Istos autem homines ille habebit eligere, quem dominus papa huic negotio preponere uoluerit, et sibi idem prepositus uoluerit ordinare. Et quia forte huiusmodi homines[v] non possent sufficere ad[w] expensas quas haberent facere in uie longitudine et in predictis galeis, ad hoc necessario componendis predicto preposito concedatur ut centum excommunicatos de Alexandria absoluere ualeat, qui aliquid pro expensis soluant, uel se exponant[x] ad hoc seruitium[y] personaliter exequendum.[z]

Et quia hoc nouum est, et nostris hic temporibus inauditum, per consequens incredibile uidetur aut certe impossibile ex duobus.

Primo quia numquam aliquis[a] attemptauit ecclesie ista suggerere, cum multi fuerint et diuersi qui de diuersis terrarum dispositionibus et marium proprietatibus, admiratione et utilitate digna conscripserint plurima, et quod hoc tam utile et[b] tam facile apud eos incognitum fuerit et sic remanserit indiscussum.

Secundo uidetur impossibile ut tam paruus numerus galearum tanto nauium et lignorum multitudini de India in Egiptum uenientium tam faciliter uiam impediat et precludat, et tot mercatorum milibus Sarracenorum pariter et Indorum[c] tam exilis et paruus numerus hominum se opponat, et insuper quod ibi hoc faciat debilis et infirma quod non potest hic agere ecclesie firma manus.

Quapropter sciendum est[d] quod ex quatuor causis contingere potuit[e] quod nichil de huiusmodi negotio per aliquem ecclesie auribus est suggestum.

Primo quia forte illis qui[f] alia scriptitabant non apparebat ueritas huius facti, quia experientiam non habebant, sicut ego diligenter scrutatus sum, et ego non cognoui scriptura uel narratore uel teste alio mediante, sed de omnibus hiis mihi fidem proprie manus et pedes et oculi prebuerunt. Fui enim in mari Indico fere

---

s   et *pro* de C   t   adhiberet C   u   uideretur esse C   v   huiusmodi homines forte C
w   huiusmodi *add*. C   x   personaliter *add*. C   y   officium *pro* seruitium C
z   exequendum personaliter C   a   et *add*. C   b   et *om*. C   c   Iudeorum C
d   est *om*. C   e   poterit C   f   quia C

The only and easy way to do this is to put some galleys in the Indian sea to guard the passage of the gulf of Aden carefully and furthermore to prevent anyone carrying the aforesaid goods from sailing safely from India to Egypt by that route. Three or four galleys would be more than enough to do this.[105] There are two ways to have these galleys, of which one is difficult and the other easy. The first way is for the church to give enough money for these galleys to someone who is considered worthy to be in charge of this enterprise and would receive it for this purpose. Since it may be difficult for the church to provide this money, a second, and easier and better, way would be for the lord pope to be generous from the treasury of the crucified Lord and to grant an indulgence from punishment and guilt to the twelve hundred men who would be needed for the four galleys and who will have to be chosen by the man whom the lord pope will wish to put in charge of the enterprise, and the captain will wish to arrange this himself. And since there may not be enough men of this type for the expenses which have to be made for the long journey and the galleys necessarily arranged for this purpose, the captain should be allowed to absolve a hundred excommunicated men of Alexandria who will contribute to the expenses or perform this service themselves.

Since this is a new idea and unheard of in our times it may seem incredible or at least impossible for two reasons.

First, since no one ever tried to suggest this to the church, although many and diverse men have written many things worthy of admiration and use about various types of lands and qualities of the seas, and because this advantageous and easy enterprise has been unknown among them, and thus has remained undiscussed.

Second, it may seem impossible for such a small number of galleys to blockade and close the way so easily to such a great number of ships and vessels coming from India to Egypt, and for such a meager and small number of men to oppose so many thousands of Saracen and also Indian merchants and also for a weak and feeble force to do there what the strength of the church cannot do here.

It should for this reason be known that there are four reasons that no one has previously proposed this enterprise to the church.

First, those who have written other things may not have realized the truth of this fact because they lack the experience which I have diligently acquired. I have known not through written works, a narrative, or a text, but my own hands, feet, and eyes are proof to me of all those things. For I was in the Indian sea for about

---

105   William recommends using a small number of war galleys in the gulf of Aden to prevent the movement of ships from India to Egypt. He is fully aware of the novelty of this strategy, saying that "This is a new idea and unheard of in our times." Blockading the gulf of Aden with only four galleys carrying 1,200 men was in his view an attainable target, since he was personally acquainted with the strategic location of the area to be blockaded.

uiginti mensium spatio, et maxime in quadam insula nouem mensibus, que quidem insula est in medio gulfi predicti de Eden, per quem gulfum et per quam insulam est transitus de India in Egiptum. Fui ergo ibi, et que oportuna sunt huic facto inspexi sollicite et diligenter aduerti. Nam oportuit terram mari Indico contiguam et aliquas insulas perlustrare, quia sic uie^g quam causa predicandi in Ethiopiam habebam facere, dispositio requirebat. De qua Ethiopia multa et magna compassio est quod tantus et talis populus^h et tam infinitus sic pereat, et a nostrorum memoria totaliter sit abscisus. Secundo potuit esse quod illi qui me in aliis narrationibus precesserunt nichil de hoc locuti sunt, quia forte non sperabant se posse fauorem debitum et necessarium pro hoc facto ab ecclesia obtinere, et ideo de aliis enarrantes de hoc ex tali diffidentia subticebant. Vel ex alio contingere potuit quod de hoc nichil dixerunt, quia forte habebant se more inuidorum qui bonum quod uident dum pro se obtinere nequeunt, in aliis non promouent uel si uident id posse alium adipisci nituntur totaliter^i impedire, uel etiam ad hoc eorum ingenium et industria non peruenit ut scirent que necessaria erant pro hoc facto et congrua ordinare uel etiam cogitare, quamuis, tempore Argoni imperatoris Tartarorum, Ianuenses, fauente eodem imperatore uno^k potius faciente, inceperint hoc negotium attemptare, facientes tantummodo galeas duas in Baldaco ut per Eufraten, qui est unus de fluuiis Paradisi, in mare Indicum cum dictis galeis descenderent, et sic applicantes ad passum de quo loquor, ipsum clauderent,^{l} ne de cetero merces alique portari possent de India in Egiptum, quod procul dubio perfecissent, nisi eos ille diuisionis et partialitatis spiritus inuasisset qui consueuit Italicos perturbare. Dicentes enim isti se esse Gebellinos et illi Guelfos, mutuo se occidentes, subito ad nichilum sunt redacti.

Qui^m ergo tunc fuit ex indiscreto animo et ex^n zelo fatuo, interceptum totaliter et dimissum, hoc posset nunc reincipi et perfici, si modus hic positus et debitus et cautela et omnia illa^o media haberentur, cum quibus et per que hoc negotium finem debitum et optatum congrue sortiretur. Hoc igitur sufficiat, quantum ad illos quibus prima facie incredibile

---

g   uie *om.* (*cum spatio*) B   h   est *add.* C   i   taliter C   k   *recte* immo
l   et sic … clauderent *om.* C   m   *recte* Quod   n   ex *om.* B   o   alia C

twenty months, and especially for nine months on the island that is in the middle of the gulf of Aden.[106] The route from India to Egypt is by way of this island. I was there and inspected carefully and noted diligently what is suitable for this enterprise. For it was necessary for me to travel over the land next to the Indian sea and some of the islands since the journey which I had to make in order to preach in Ethiopia so required. There is much and great sympathy for Ethiopia and that so great and numerous a people should perish in this way and be totally cut off from the memory of our men. Second, it may be that those who preceded me said nothing of this in other accounts because they had no hope of obtaining from the church the due and necessary support to do this and therefore spoke about other things and were silent about this from diffidence. Or they may have said nothing about this because they were like envious men who do not promote in others a good which they perceive but cannot obtain for themselves or who try to prevent it if they see that it can be obtained by some one else. Or it may even not occur to their ingenuity and industry to know what would be necessary both to arrange suitable things or even to think of doing this, although the Genoese in the time of the emperor Arghun of the Tartars, with indeed his support and cooperation, began to attempt this undertaking and made just two galleys in Baghdad with which they could go down the Euphrates, which is one of the rivers of Paradise, to the Indian sea and thus go to the strait of which I speak and blockade it so that no goods could in the future be carried from India to Egypt.[107] They would doubtless have done this had they not been attacked by that spirit of division and partiality which is accustomed to trouble Italians. For some said that they were Ghibellines and others Guelfs and killing each other they were suddenly reduced to nothing.

What was at that time completely interrupted and dismissed owing to an indiscreet spirit and foolish zeal, therefore, could now be started again and carried out if the proper way described here and the precautions and arrangements are made with which and by which this enterprise can be brought to an appropriate and desired conclusion. This should therefore satisfy those to whom at first sight it seemed incredible

---

106   The island of Socotra (Sokotra, Soqotra) is located just to the east of the horn of Africa, 500 miles southeast of Aden and 300 miles from al Mukalla, the principal port of the Hadhrami coast: see in addition to Doe (1992) and Biedermann (2006), Dauvillier (1948), 271, 277; Kammerer (1950), 501–2; Richard (1968), 48–50 and (1977b), 114; Tibbetts (1971), 445; Von den Brinken (1973), 276; Beckingham and Hamilton (1996), 252; Margariti (2007), 43. Marco Polo, bk. 3, chap. 32 (1903), 2:406–7 called it Scotra; Bembo (2007), 249–51 called it Sacatorà or Cocotorà.

107   In 1290, the Ilkhānid sultan Arghun employed 800 Genoese to build ships in Baghdad for a planned naval attack on Mamluk Egypt: John of Winterthur (1924), 58; Bar Hebraeus (1932), 1:486. See Heyd (1885–86), 2:111; Richard (1968), 49 and (1970), 359–60; Beckingham (1980, 1995), 299; Schmieder (1994), 118–19; Phillips (1998), 98. This was contrary to the current diplomatic policy of Genoa, which had established a treaty with Egypt in 1261. A new treaty between Genoa and the Mamluk sultan derailed the alliance with Baghdad: Jackson (2005), 169–70.

uel^p impossibile uidebatur, ostendendo iterum modum per quem istud perfacile, immo et delectabile et nullius breuiter difficultatis esse uel periculi, apparebit. Igitur, circa hoc quatuor sunt uidenda: primo de modo per quem galee iste haberi ualeant; secundo de portu ubi reduci habeant; tertio de conditione et modo illarum gentium contra quas pugnare conueniat; quarto hiis habitis, uidebitur quedam facilitas^q quomodo^r passus ille custodiri ualeat.

Modus possibilis habendi galeas attendi debet, uel^s quoad locum in quo eas debent facere, uel quoad illos qui eas habent componere, uel quoad homines qui eas habent regere, uel quoad hoc unde habent^t expense procedere. Quoad locum autem ubi fieri ualeant, sciendum est quod multi mercatores et diuites sunt de illa predicta ciuitate Eden, cuius passum claudendum dicimus. Et isti mercatores per se et suos famulos causa mercationum circueunt omnes terras Indie et frequentant, illis exceptis dumtaxat que ditionis^u imperatoris Persidis sunt, et illis que sunt quorumdam Indorum qui in insulis Indie habitant, quia omnes predicti contra homines ciuitatis predicte exercent inimicitias capitales. Aduertendum est igitur quod ibi fiant predicte galee ubi mercatores Eden non appareant, ne per eos factura galearum ualeat impediri. Possent enim saltem in hoc impedimentum inferre, quod domini terrarum illarum, que pacem et confederationem habent cum eis, compositores galearum non reciperent nec tenerent, uel saltem ligna ad componendum galeas nec uenderent nec donarent. Eligendus est ergo locus ad quem mercatores predicti accedere non audeant, et^v in quo lignorum copia decenter ualeat inueniri. Tria sunt ergo loca huiusmodi. Primus locus est Hormutz, insula quedam Indie prime, que dominii^w imperatoris

p et *pro* uel B   q felicitas C   r quam *pro* quomodo B   s et *pro* uel B
t habeant C   u ditionis *om*. C   v et *om*. C   w domini B

or impossible by showing how it will be very easy and indeed both attractive and without difficulty or danger. For this four things should be envisaged: first, how the galleys can be obtained; second, to which port they should be returned; third, the condition and way of the peoples against whom they appropriately will fight; fourth, after these matters have been settled, how easily the strait can be guarded will be apparent.

With regard to how to obtain the galleys, attention should be paid with regard to where they should be made, who should make them, who should direct them, and from where the expenses have to come.[108] With regard to the place where they can be made, it should be known that there are many merchants and rich men in Aden, of which we say the strait should be closed. For the sake of trade those merchants, both by themselves and by their employees, travel around and often visit all the lands of India except those that are subject to the emperor of Persia and those of some Indians who live in the islands of India, since they are all bitterly hostile to the men of Aden. It should therefore be noted that the galleys should be made where the merchants of Aden do not come lest they impede the making of the galleys. For they could make an impediment because the lords of the lands that are at peace and allied with them would not receive or keep the makers of the galleys or at least would not sell or give wood for making the galleys. A place should therefore be chosen where these merchants do not dare to go and where supplies of wood can be properly found. There are three places of this sort. The first is Hormuz, an island of the nearest India, which is in the dominion of the emperor of

108   The following pages contain William's blueprint for the operation of the naval blockade. He recommends the employment of four galleys in the island of Socotra. He also underlines the importance of an adequate supply of raw materials and the availability of appropriate techniques for manufacturing these galleys. In this context he mentions a few places in the western Indian ocean. In addition to Hormuz and Kish, William mentions four places in India as possible sources of wood for manufacturing galleys: Dive Insulide (Diu?), Tana (Thana), Cambay, and Koulam (Kulam). His knowledge of these four important ports on the west coast of India is striking, as is his assessment of the sustained commercial links with the premier Red sea port of Aden.

Persidis est. Secundus locus est insule alie quedam que Diue nominantur, distantes a predicta fere per tria milia miliaria. Tertius locus est terra firma ultime Indie, cuius ciuitates Tana et Cambaeyt[x] et Colom uocantur. Et in

x   Tambaet C

Persia.[109] The second is some islands called Diu,[110] which are fully three thousand miles away from the former place. The third is the mainland of furthest India, of which the towns are called Thana,[111] Cambay,[112] and Kulam.[113] Especially in

109   Hormuz is strategically located at the opening of the Persian gulf and was said by Chaudhuri (1985), 108, to have "held the key to wholesale merchandizing in the Gulf": see also Marco Polo, bk. 1, chap. 19, bk. 3, chap. 39 (1903), 1:107–10, 2:449; Bretschneider (1910), 2:130–38; *Book of Knowledge* (1912), 41, 53; Stübe (1916); Cordier (1920), 24–25; Wilson (1928), 100–109; Steensgaard (1987); Floor (2004). Its rise to prominence probably began in the late twelfth century and marked the revival of the Persian gulf network in the western Indian ocean. The port was in sustained commercial contact with both the Gujarat and Malabar coasts on the western sea-coast of India: Stübe (1916); Jain (1989); Chakravari (2000 and 2007b). William's observation that Hormuz was important for the availability of good quality wood for the construction of the galleys may be incorrect. Hormuz was noted for its ship-building facilities, but the primary raw material, that is, teak, came from India. William sounds more logical when he says that Hormuz and Kish were ideal spots in the Persian gulf for the galleys to retire to during winter or to go for repairs.

110   Dive Insulide was probably the port of Diu in western India, in the Kathiawad area of modern Gujarat. The earliest reference to Diu in the maritime Indian trade is in a twelfth century Jewish geniza business letter showing that a ship from Aden came to al Manjrur (Mangalore, in the coastal belt of the modern state of Karantaka in peninsular India) and from there undertook a coastal voyage to al-Dyyb (Diu), from where it sailed back to Aden: Goitein (1980), also in Chakravarti (2001), 422. Dive Insulide has also been identified with the Maldives or Laccadives in the western Indian ocean: *Recueil*, 552 n. b (Mas Latrie) and cxcii n. 11 (Kohler). The Maldives were possibly conquered in the early eleventh century by Rajaraja, a formidable ruler of the Chola dynasty of south India: Nilakantha Sastri (1955). Ibn Battuta was aware of their commercial importance. For an alternative view see Goitein and Friedman (2008), 316.

111   Tana (Thana) is now a northern suburb of present day Mumbai. It is significant that William follows Marco Polo's spelling of this place, since he very likely knew Polo's account: Marco Polo, bk. 3, chap. 27 (1903), 2:395. It was an important port in the northern part of the Konkan coast and is located on the Thana creek that leads to the port of Thana. A Jewish business letter of 1145 and Marco Polo both refer to the piracy in and around Thana: Chakravarti (1991 and 1998). Northern Konkan (called Kunkan, Kamkam, and Makamkam in Arabic and Persian texts) was famous for the availability of teak, a vital ingredient for ship building in the Indian ocean. The Konkan coast stretched from Daman in the north to Goa in the south—along the western coast of India—and was also noted for coconuts, of which the fiber (coir) was used in the construction of traditional Arabic-Indian ships, being used for stitching the wooden planks of the sea-going vessels.

112   Cambay, on the Gujarat coast, was originally known in Sanskrit as Sristambhatirtha/Stambhapura and was the greatest port in western India: Marco Polo, bk. 3, chap. 28 (1903), 2:397–98; Beckingham (1980), 299; Chaudhuri (1985), 108–9; Steensgaard (1987), 130–31; Biedermann (2006). The name Cambay has a close phonetic correspondence with the Arabic name Khambayat. It figures prominently in the accounts of Marco Polo and Ibn Battuta. Cambay was endowed with an agriculturally rich hinterland in Gujarat, maintained overland linkages with Ujjayini in Madhyapradesh (a major nodal point in central-western India), and reached out to far-flung forelands, like Aden and Hormuz. In the early sixteenth century the Portuguese writer Pires commented that Cambay's two arms spread respectively to Aden and Malacca and that it overshadowed all other ports in the Indian ocean: Jain (1987); Arasaratnam (1994).

113   Koulam is the port of Kollam (Quilon) on the Malabar coast, in the modern state of Kerala. Marco Polo called it Coilum: Marco Polo, bk. 3, chap. 22 (1903), 2:375–76. In Persian and Arabic texts and also in the Jewish geniza business letters it appears as Kulam or Kulam Mali, which distinguished it from another Collam on the same Malabar coast, known as Pantalayani Kollam (the

hiis locis ultimis maxime est tanta lignorum copia, ut numquam in aliqua mundi parte uiderim tam altas arbores et tam solidas et[y] minus nodosas, magis rectas. Domini uero terrarum istarum[z] libenter[a] darent contra Sarracenos predicte ciuitatis Eden consilium, auxilium et fauorem, non solum de suis rebus, sed libentius de personis,[b] aliqui propter odium, aliqui propter lucrum. Quoad magistros qui galeas habent componere, et quoad illos qui eas habent regere, quoad expensas etiam et sumptus necessarios, satis est ostensum. Tamen etiam[c] hoc addo, quod meo iudicio numquam per aliquos alios quam per Ianuenses posset hoc negotium adimpleri. Et hoc uel[d] quia in mari ceteris gentibus probiores et magis exercitati existunt, uel quia ad circueundum et uidendum ceteras mundi partes, facilius se exponunt nec retrahit eos amor proprie patrie, nec retardat, uel etiam quia magis auidi sunt ad lucrum. Iam enim Ianuenses soli naues faciunt in mari predicto Indie, non tamen causa hic posita sed spe lucri. Et si dominus papa uellet hoc facere, quod omnes marinarii Ianuenses, qui sunt pro facto Alexandrie excommunicati, uel saltem tot sicut sunt necessarii pro hoc facto, ut supra dixi, possent absolui ab excommunicatione, ita quod tenerentur[e] de persona certo tempore huic negotio deseruire, expeditio facilior redderetur.

Portum[f] uero habere poterunt in locis diuersis maris Indie ad hoc plurimum oportunus. Est enim mare Indicum, ut supradixi, refertum insulis[g] innumerabilibus, que, ut uulgariter asseritur, sunt plusquam ·xx·m·, licet sint plurime in hiis omni habitatore carentes. Quarum due sunt tantum de dominio sepe nominati imperatoris Persidis, que quidem sunt plurimum accomode, ut galee iste ad eas diuertant quando reparatione aliqua indigebunt, uel ad hiemandum, illo scilicet tempore quo non in mari Indico nauigatur,[h] uel etiam ad deponendum merces a Babiloniorum[i] mercatoribus per modum istum piraticum acquisitas. Vna uero istarum insularum[k] uocatur Chyx, altera Hormutz, de qua feci superius mentionem. Quod autem galee ad has duas insulas causis predictis tute ualeant declinare, ut imperator Persidis assensum prebeat oportebit, quia eo inuito non possent ad[l] terras suas moram facere sine discrimine, nec etiam declinare.

y et *om.* C   z istarum terrarum C   a liberenter C   b particulis *pro* personis C
c etiam *om.* C   d uel *om.* C   e tenebitur AB   f autem *add.* C   g et *add.* C
h nauigetur B   i babilonicorum C   k que *add.* C   l in *pro* ad B

these furthest places are such great supplies of wood that in no other part of the world have I ever seen such tall and solid trees, with fewer knots and straighter. The lords of these lands would willingly give advice, assistance, and support, both of their own possessions and more willingly of persons, against the Saracens of the town of Aden, some owing to hate and some for the sake of profit. Enough has been said concerning the masters who should build the galleys, those who should direct them, and the expenses and necessary supplies. I should add, however, that in my opinion this undertaking can be carried out only by the Genoese, both because they are more skillful and experienced on the sea than other peoples, and because they show themselves more prepared to visit and see other parts of the world and are not deterred or held back by love of their fatherland, or even because they are more eager for money. For the Genoese alone already build ships in the sea of India, though not for the reasons given here but in hope of gain. And if the lord pope wishes to absolve from excommunication all the Genoese sailors who are excommunicated on account of Alexandria, or at least as many as are needed for this project, on condition that each will serve on this enterprise for a certain amount of time, the expedition will be made more easily.

They can have a very suitable port in several places in the sea of India, which, as I said above, is full of innumerable islands, of which it is commonly said that there are more than twenty thousand, though many of them are uninhabited.[114] Only two of these are in the dominion of the emperor of Persia and are indeed very well suited for the galleys to go when they need repairs, or to winter when there is no navigation in the Indian sea, or even to deposit goods seized from the merchants of the Babylonians in this piratical way. One of these islands is called Kish[115] and the other Hormuz, which I mentioned above. In order for the galleys to put in safely at those two islands, for the aforesaid reasons, however, the emperor of Persia must give his consent, without which they cannot without danger stay or even put in on his lands.

---

same as Fandariyana in the Persian and Arabic texts and the geniza documents). Kollam derived major benefits from its overseas connections both with Aden and with Kish and Hormuz in the Persian gulf. That Kollam yielded excellent wood for boat-building purposes is confirmed by Arabic and Persian authors before AD 1500: *Receuil*, 552 n. e; Nainar (1942), 47–49 and, on Kollam teak, 206; Goitein (1974); Nilakantha Sastri (1955); Chakravarti (2001).

114   See the note to Marco Polo, bk. 3, chap. 34 (1903), 2:425 n. 6, on the proverbial number of islands in the Indian ocean, and Richard (1968), 50.

115   The island of Kish (Qays) in the Persian gulf became a major seat of maritime trade, especially with India and the Oman peninsula, after the gradual waning of the port of Siraf: *Receuil*, 553 n. b; Bretschneider (1910), 2:129–30; Chaudhuri (1985), 47, 129; Biedermann (2006), 78–88. Like Aden and Hormuz, it was, according to Marco Polo, a major supplier of war horses by ships to India: Chakravarti (1991) and, for a description of Kish by Benjamin of Tudela, who visited in 1170, Wilson (1928), 98–99. In about 1135 the sultan of Kish made an unsuccessful maritime attack on Aden, after which business at the port of Aden was adversely affected for a brief period: Goitein (1954); Margariti (2008); Goitein and Friedman (2008), 337–51; and (on the types of ships used in this raid) Chakravarti (2002), 46–47.

Imperator enim predictus gauderet plurimum si ad claudendum passum predictum[m] posset uiam aliquam inuenire. Et ideo, non solum dico tuitionem prestaret, sed insuper magna ex parte uel forte complete[n] expensas necessarias procuraret[o] sed, esto quod tuitionem huiusmodi denegaret, adhuc aliis predictis insulis Diue, que omnino remote sunt ab omni dominio Tartarorum et etiam nomine, reduci·poterunt et reparari et moram contrahere, et etiam si uoluerint continue permanere.

Conditionem illorum contra quos pugnandum moneo talem esse experientia noui. Gens est pauida, consilio et scientia caret, ita ut non eos rationabiles extimem, sed homines bestiales. Gens est[p] omnino ignara belli, sic ut inuadere uel euadere nesciat. Iaculis nisi forte lanceis non utitur, non pugnat cum arcubus uel balistis. Quas si haberent non uidentur idonei, non dico ad loricas uel alia arma ferri sed nec ad paleas penetrandas, et, ut dicam breuius, non habent arma inuasiua, nec etiam defensiua, sed, cum solum a morte uel captiuitate defensionis necessitas imminet, tunc non probitatis audacia uel aliqua bellandi industria mori,[q] sed quasi bestie, quedam sensualitatis[r] instinctu, non rationis, pusillanimitatem cordis excutiunt, et se[s] utrumque[t] defendunt[u] cum lapidibus et quibusdam aliis[v] ferramentis, et contra iacula in eos missa quedam scuta obiciunt, facta de feno et de palmarum foliis consuta, que omnia hostes ad eos capiendum magis incitant et inuitant quam deterreant, sic[w] non ut mortem uel seruitutem euadere, sed uitam et libertatem aliquantulum uelle protendere uideantur. Magis ergo uidentur preda quam hostes, et ad bellum magis se ligatos exhibent quam armatos. Certe patet quod nostri de istis tot caperent quot uiderent. Et quamuis tales sint, tamen per eorum manus transit quicquid[x] portatur ad alias mundi partes de speciebus et serico et aliis mercibus pretiosis.

Facilitas autem per quam[y] passus predictus ualeat custodiri patebit ex duobus, primo ex dispositione passus ipsius, secundo ex adiutorio illorum et fauore qui illis inimicantur, contra quos passus ipse custodiendus est. Dispositio passus illius[z] talis est quod, preter illa que de eius conditione supraposita[a] sunt, habet in suo introitu tres Christianorum insulas, quibus non[b] clausus esse uidetur, sed potius obturatus, ita ut de dicta ciuitate Eden ad quam, ut predictum est, merces pretiose portantur de India in Egiptum denuo transportande, nullus potest exire in Indiam profecturus, nec inde iterum in dictam ciuitatem, cum lignis uel nauibus transmeare, quin de necessitate ad dictas tres insulas, uel ad earum alteram appropinquet, et est talis conditio populi in hiis insulis habitantis ut omnem hominem recipiant undecumque siue pirata siue mercator existat, qui ad eos uelit declinare, uel cum eis pacifice habitare. Quapropter, cum sint aliqui qui contra mercatores

m illum *pro* predictum B   n complete *om.* C   o procuraret necessarias B
p enim *pro* est C   q *recte* moti   r insensualitatis C   s se *om.* C
t *recte* utcumque?   u defendunt *om.* C   v aliis *om.* B   w sed *pro* sic C
x quicquam C   y quem AB   z illius *om.* C   a habet *add.* C   b non *om.* C

For the emperor would greatly rejoice if the aforesaid strait could in some way be closed. And he will therefore not only give protection, I say, but will also furnish a large part or perhaps all of the necessary expenses. Should protection of this sort be denied, however, they could be brought back and repaired and be withdrawn temporarily, or even if they wished remain permanently, in the other of the aforesaid islands of Diu, which are far from any even nominal control of the Tartars.

I know from experience the character of the people against whom I advise fighting. They are fearful people, lacking purpose and knowledge, so that I consider them not as rational but as animal-like men. They are entirely ignorant of war and do not know how to attack or escape.[116] They do not use javelins except perhaps as spears and do not fight with bows or crossbows. Those they have are apparently not suited to pierce chain mail or other arms of iron or even of straw. To put it briefly they do not have arms for attack or even for defense, and only when they are forced to defend themselves from death or capture do they shake off their cowardice of heart, moved not on account of the bravery of prowess or some diligence in fighting, but like certain beasts of instinct not of reason but of feeling. They defend themselves as best they can with stones and some iron implements, and against the javelins thrown at them they interpose some shields made of hay and sewn together from the leaves of palms, all of which incites and encourages rather than deters their enemies to capture them, so that they seem to want to prolong life and liberty for a time rather than to avoid death or servitude. They therefore appear to be booty rather than enemies and in battle show themselves bound fast rather than armed. It is certainly clear that our men would capture as many of these men as they could see. Such as they are, however, whatever spices, silk, and other precious goods are carried to other parts of the world pass through their hands.

The ease with which the strait can be guarded will be clear from two things: first, the disposition of the strait itself and second, the help and support of those who oppose the men against whom the strait is to be guarded. The layout of the passage is such that in addition to what has been said above about its condition it has at its entrance three islands of Christians, by which it seems not closed but rather blocked, so that from the town of Aden, to which the precious goods are carried from India for transport to Egypt, no one can leave to travel to India nor from there to the same town, to pass through in wooden ships or vessels, without approaching one or other of the three islands, and the condition of the inhabitants of these islands is such that they receive anyone from anywhere, whether he is a pirate or a merchant, who wants to put in or live peacefully with them. Since therefore there are some men who want to make piratical raids against the merchants

---

116   This comment relates to the martial, particularly naval, incapability of the ruler of Aden.

dicte ciuitatis Eden, uel quoscumque alios uelint insidias piraticas exercere, ad dictas accedunt insulas, ibidem quem capiant prestolantes. Et ideo, homines istarum insularum omnibus Sarracenis in illo mari mercantibus sunt redditi odiosi, tum quia Christiani sunt tum quia, per illas insulas uel occasione earum, insidias perpetes patiuntur. Et ex hoc est edicto communi prohibitum et per modum cuiusdam sententie excommunicationis et pene anathematis confirmatum, ut nullus det eis consilium, auxilium uel fauorem. Attemptauerunt insuper aliquando, manu potenti et quasi quodam magno passagio, eos inuadere et delere, quod procul dubio perpetrassent, nisi homines predictarum[c] insularum trium ad solita presidia confugissent. Habent enim non castra fortia nec ciuitates munitas et fortes, ad quas possint cum necessitas imminet confugere et defendi, sed quedam antra subterranea et petrosa foramina in prcruptis montibus et inaccessibilibus, ad que habent pro singulari defensione intuitum, in quibus latitant et imponunt omnia sua mobilia et abscondunt, cum a suis hostibus inuaduntur. Hostes uero ibi moram non adessent contrahere, propter multa que causa[d] breuitatis obmitto. Igitur in hiis insulis galee predicte constituent nidum suum, et quia recipientur gratanter et hilariter ab eorum incolis in Sarracenorum odium, et quia melius et utilius poterunt per eos Sarracenis Egipti dampna inferre, et contra eosdem cum maiori quiete insidias exercere. Dispositionem autem hanc scio, non narratore alio[e] mediante, nempe quia fui in dictis insulis nouem mensibus commoratus, quando uolebam causa predicande fidei, cum quibusdam aliis ordinis mei meis sociis in Ethiopiam proficisci.

De qua Ethiopia, et de quibusdam insulis possem stupenda narrare nisi quod materia[f] libelli huiusmodi[g] id rennuit et quam intendo in hoc opusculo breuitas non requirit. Adiutorium uero quod habere poterunt dicte galee ad hoc tantum et tam[h] affectandum negotium exequendum erunt homines de quibus supra dixi, in aliis insulis habitantes. Que quidem insule supra nominate dicuntur esse certissime plus quam sex milia habitate, et habent piratarum tam numerum copiosum, ut quadraginta uel quinquaginta naues, quarum quelibet sexcentos uel octingentos habent homines simul congregatos, de facili uideritis modum bellandi risu dignum et extraneum obseruantes. Hii igitur omnes non uidentur ad aliud anhelare, nisi quomodo possent ciuitatem predictam Eden et alias etiam ciuitates maritimas destruere et delere. Quod certe complerent si essent consueti remorum adiutorio uti. Omnes ergo isti, cum uiderent nostrorum modum et artem bellandi, non dico uenire in nostrorum adiutorium, sed pre multitudine pluere uiderentur, et tunc sequeretur aliud bonum inextimabile quod scilicet esset[i] possibile predictam ciuitatem Eden eorum adiutorio capi. Iam enim per se solos hactenus fuit

c   dictarum C   d   tam *pro* causa B   e   aliquo B   f   huius *add.* C

g   huiusmodi *om.* C   h   causa *pro* tam B   i   esset *om.* C

of Aden and others, they come to these islands and wait there for whom they capture. All the Saracens trading in that sea therefore hate the men of those islands both because they are Christians and because of the constant attacks suffered by them from these islands or owing to them. It is consequently prohibited by a common edict confirmed by a sentence as of excommunication and almost of anathema for anyone to give them advice, assistance, or support. They have furthermore tried to invade and destroy them by force and almost by a great crusade, and they would certainly have done so if the men of the three islands had not fled to their usual places of safety. For they have no strongholds or fortified and strong towns to flee to and to be defended when necessity requires but certain underground caves and rocky chasms in precipitous and inaccessible mountains on which they rely for their only defense and in which they lie hidden and put and hide all their moveable possessions when they are invaded by their enemies, who do not stay there, however, for many reasons which I omit for the sake of brevity. The galleys will therefore establish a base in these islands both because they will be received gratefully and joyfully by their inhabitants who hate the Saracens and because from there they will be able to damage the Saracens of Egypt better and more effectively and attack them with less trouble. I know this arrangement not from another narrator but because I stayed for nine months in these islands when I wanted to go to Ethiopia with some associates of my order in order to preach the faith.

I could tell marvelous things about Ethiopia and certain islands except that the material does not belong in a booklet of this sort and is not required by the brevity which I intend in this little work. The men living in the other islands, of whom I spoke above, will give the help needed by the galleys to carry out such a great and desirable enterprise. For those islands are said to have certainly more than six thousand inhabitants, and they have so many pirates that you would readily see forty or fifty ships, each with at least six or eight hundred men gathered together who observe a laughable and strange way of fighting. All these men seem to want only to destroy and defeat the town of Aden and other coastal towns, and they would certainly do this if they were accustomed to the use of oars. When all these men see the method and art of fighting of our men, therefore, I do not say they will just come to help our men but will be as plentiful as rain. Another inestimable advantage is that with their help it will be possible to take the town of Aden, which they previously took by themselves, but

capta, quam quia tenere non poterant, occisis de ea quos ceperant et secum portare non poterant,[k] acceptis spoliis pretiosis et totam ciuitatem incendio superponentes ad propria redierunt.

Tales sunt ergo[l] isti qui uolunt et possunt, si scirent ut nostri omnes Sarracenos de mari Indico eiusque ciuitatibus maritimis extirpare. Iuuentur ergo per nostros et in hoc negotio dirigantur ut inimici Christi,[m] ueritatis et fidei, ad nichilum redigantur, et potentia babilonici principis deprimatur uel etiam conuertatur. Amen.

Indulgeat mihi indigno uestro seruulo, pater et domine reuerende, uestra benignitas copiosa, quia incomposita et incompacta[n] uerba piis uestris auribus deprimere ausus fui. Zelus autem fidei non attendit quid stilus sed quid deuotio dicat, nec caritas respicit quid locutio uerbis depingere sed quid uideatur et debeat[o] ueritas continere. Ardorem ergo deprecor uestri zeli, et uestram superhabundantem flagito caritatem, ut me in hoc excusatum habeat et pro labore huius libelli qualiscumque sua copiosa gratia superfundat et benedictionis sue munere benedicat, protegat et defendat, et ad promouendum hec que predixi manum porrigat adiutricem.[p]

---

k occisis . . . poterant *om*. B   l ergo sunt C   m Christi *om*. C   n incompactata C
o debeat *om*. C   p Amen. Et sic est finis huius opusculi *add*. C

since they could not hold it they killed whomever they captured and could not take with them, took precious spoils, put the entire town to fire, and returned to their own lands.

Such are the men who are willing and able—if they knew how, like our men—to extirpate all the Saracens from the Indian sea and its coastal cities. Our men should help and direct them in this enterprise in order that the enemies of Christ, truth, and the faith may be annihilated, the power of the prince of Babylon may be suppressed, and he may even be converted. Amen.

May your great kindness, father and reverend lord, forgive your unworthy little servant for daring to oppress your pious ears with ill-arranged and loosely joined words. The zeal of faith pays attention to what devotion rather than the pen says, however, and love considers not what speech says in words but the truth they seem to and should contain. I therefore pray the flame of your zeal and solicit your overflowing love to excuse me for this and to cover me with your abundant grace for the work of this little book and to bless, protect, and defend me by the reward of your blessing and stretch out your helping hand to accomplish what I have said.

ABBREVIATIONS

DHGE   *Dictionnaire d'histoire et de géographie ecclésiastiques* (Paris, 1912–)

History   *A History of the Crusades*, vol. 3, *The Fourteenth and Fifteenth Centuries*, edited by Harry W. Hazard, 2nd ed. (Madison, 1975)

JESHO   *Journal of the Economic and Social History of the Orient*

ODB   *Oxford Dictionary of Byzantium*, edited by Alexander Kazhdan et al., 3 vols. (New York and Oxford, 1991)

Recueil   *Recueil des historiens des croisades: Documents arméniens*, vol. 2 (Paris, 1906)

Repertorium   *Repertorium fontium historiae Medii Aevi* (Rome, 1962–)

ROL   *Revue de l'Orient Latin*, 12 vols. (Paris, 1893–1911; repr. 1964)

S   Series

BIBLIOGRAPHY

* *denotes primary sources*

Abel, Felix-Marie
    1923   Ecrits des dominicains sur la Terre Sainte. In *Miscellanea dominicana in memoriam VII anni saecularis ab obitu sancti patris Dominici (1221–1921)*. Rome.

Agius, Dionisius Albert
    2002   Classifying Vessel-Types in Ibn Baṭṭūṭa's Riḥla. In Parkin and Barnes (2002), 174–208.

Ahrweiler, Hélène
    1965   L'histoire et la géographie de la région de Smyrne entre les deux occupations turques (1081–1317), particulièrement au XIIIᵉ siècle. *Travaux et mémoires* 1:1–204.

Allen, Rosamund
    2004   *Eastward Bound: Travel and Travellers, 1050–1550*. Manchester.

Allsen, Thomas T.
    1987   *Mongol Imperialism: The Policies of the Grand Qan Möngke in China, Russia, and the Islamic Lands, 1251–1259*. Berkeley, Calif.

Alphandéry, Paul
    1954–59   *La Chrétienté et l'idée de croisade*, edited by Alphonse Dupront. 2 vols. L'évolution de l'humanité 38–38A. Paris.

Altaner, Berthold
    1924   *Die Dominikanermissionen des 13. Jahrhunderts*. Breslauer Studien zur historischen Theologie 3. Habelschwerdt.

Amitai, Reuven
    1995   *Mongols and Mamluks: The Mamluk-Īlkhānid War, 1260–1281*. Cambridge Studies in Islamic Civilization. Cambridge.
    2005   The Resolution of the Mongol-Mamluk War. In *Mongols, Turks, and Others: Eurasian Nomads and the Sedentary World*, edited by Reuven Amitai and Michal Biran. Brill's Inner Asian Library 11. Leiden and Boston.

Appadurai, Angadipuram
    1936   *Economic Conditions in Southern India 1000–1500*. 2 vols. Madras.

Arasaratnam, Sinnappah, and Aniruddha Ray
    1994   *Masulipatnam and Cambay: A History of Two Port-towns 1500–1800*. New Delhi.

Argenti, Philip P.
    1958   *The Occupation of Chios by the Genoese and their Administration of the Island, 1346–1566*. Cambridge.

Ashtor, Eliyahu

    1969   *Histoire des prix et des salaires dans l'Orient médiéval*. Monnai, prix, conjoncture 8.
            Paris.

    1983   *Levant Trade in the Later Middle Ages*. Princeton.

Atiya, Aziz

    1938   *The Crusade in the Later Middle Ages*. London.

    1962   *Crusade, Commerce and Culture*. Bloomington and London.

Ayalon, David

    1951   L'esclavage du Mamelouk. *Oriental Notes and Studies* 1:1–66. [Reprinted in idem,
            The Mamlūk Military Society. Variorum CS 104. London, 1979, art. I.]

    1994   *Islam and the Abode of War*. Variorum CS 456. Aldershot and Brookfield, Vt.

Balard, Michel

    1978   *La Romanie génoise (XIIᵉ–début du XVᵉ siècle)*. 2 vols. Bibliothèque des Ecoles fran-
            çaises d'Athènes et de Rome 235. Genoa and Rome.

    1989   The Genoese in the Aegean (1204–1566), translated by Sharon Neeman. In *Latins
            and Greeks in the Eastern Mediterranean after 1204*, edited by Benjamin Arbel, Ber-
            nard Hamilton, and David Jacoby. *Mediterranean Historical Review* 4, no. 1:158–74.
            London.

Bar Hebraeus

* 1932   *The Chronography of Gregory abû'l Faraj, . . . Commonly Known as Bar Hebraeus*,
            translated by Ernest A. Wallis Budge. 2 vols. Oxford.

Baumgärtner, Ingrid, and Hartmut Kugler (editors)

    2008   *Europa im Weltbild des Mittelalters. Kartographische Konzepte*. Orbis mediaevalis.
            Verstellungswelten des Mittelalters 10. Berlin.

Beazley, C. Raymond

    1906   *The Dawn of Modern Geography*, vol. 3, *A History of Exploration and Geographical
            Science from the Middle of the Thirteenth to the Early Years of the Fifteenth Century
            (c. A.D. 1260–1420)*. Oxford.

Beckingham, Charles F.

    1980   The Quest for Prester John. *Bulletin of the John Rylands Library* 62:291–310.
            [Reprinted in idem, *Between Islam and Christendom*. Variorum CS 175. London,
            1983, art. II, and in Beckingham and Hamilton (1996), 271–90.]

Beckingham, Charles F., and Bernard Hamilton (editors)

    1996   *Prester John, the Mongols and the Ten Lost Tribes*. Aldershot and Brookfield, Vt.

Bembo, Ambrosio

* 2007   *The Travels and Journal of Ambrosio Bembo*, edited by Anthony Welch. Berkeley.

Biedermann, Zoltán

    2006   *Soqotra. Geschichte einer christlichen Insel im indischen Ozean vom Altertum bis zur
            frühen Neuzeit*. Maritime Asia 17. Wiesbaden.

Book of Knowledge

* 1912   *Book of the Knowledge of All the Kingdoms, Lands, and Lordships that are in the
            World*, translated and edited by Clements Markham. Hakluyt Society 2S 29. London.

Boswell, John

    1980   *Christianity, Social Tolerance, and Homosexuality*. Chicago and London.

Bosworth, Clifford E.

    1996   *The New Islamic Dynasties*. New York.

Boussac, Marie-Françoise, Jean-François Salles, and Federico De Romanis (editors)

    2005   *A Gateway from the Eastern Mediterranean to India: The Red Sea in Antiquity*. New
            Delhi and Lyons.

Brand, Charles M.

    1962   The Byzantines and Saladin, 1185–1192: Opponents of the Third Crusade. *Speculum*
            37:167–81.

Brătianu, George Ioan

    1929   *Recherches sur le commerce génois dans la mer noire au XIIIᵉ siècle*. Paris.

Bréhier, Louis

    1928   *L'église et l'Orient au moyen âge. Les Croisades*. 5th ed. Bibliothèque de l'enseignement de l'histoire ecclésiastique. Paris.

Bretschneider, Emil

    1910   *Mediaeval Researches from Eastern Asiatic Sources*. 2 vols. Trübner's Oriental Series. London.

Brinken: *see* Von den Brinken.

Cahen, Claude

    1970   Le Recueil des historiens des croisades. A propos d'une réimpression anastatique. *Journal des Savants* Apr.–June, 94–104.

Carozzi, Claude, and Huguette Taviani-Carozzi (editors)

    2007   *Faire l'événement au Moyen Age*. Aix-en-Provence.

Chabot, Jean-Baptiste

    1905–8 Review of *Recueil*. In *ROL* 11:486–95.

Chakravarti, Ranabir

    1991   Horse Trade and Piracy at Tana (Thana, Maharashtra, India): Gleanings from Marco Polo. *JESHO* 34:59–82.

    1995   Rulers and Ports: Visakhapattinam and Motuppalli in Early Medieval Andhradesa. In *Merchants, Mariners and Oceans*, edited by K. S. Mathew, 57–82. New Delhi.

    1996   The Export of Sindani Indigo from India to the "West" in the Eleventh Century. *Indian Historical Review* 18:18–30.

    1998   Coastal Trade and Voyages in Konkan: The Early Medieval Scenario. *Indian Economic and Social History Review* 35:197–224.

    2000   Nakhudas and Nauvittakas: Ship-Owning Merchants in the West Coast of India (c. AD 1000–1500). *JESHO* 43:34–64.

    2002   Seafarings, Ships and Ship-Owners: India and the Indian Ocean (AD 700–1500). In Parkin and Barnes (2002), 28–61.

    2007a *Trade and Traders in Early Indian Society*. 2nd ed. New Delhi.

    2007b Reaching Out to the Distant Shores: Indo-Judaic Trade prior to AD 1500. In *Indo-Judaic Studies in the Twenty-First Century: A View from the Margin*, edited by Nathan Katz, Ranabir Chakravarti, B. M. Sinha, and Shalva Weil, 19–40. New York.

Chakravarti, Ranabir (editor)

    2001   *Trade in Early India*. New Delhi.

Chandra, Satish (editor)

    1987   *The Indian Ocean: Explorations in History, Commerce and Politics*. New Delhi, Newbury Park, and London.

Chaudhuri, K. N.

    1985   *Trade and Civilization in the Indian Ocean: An Economic History from the Rise of Islam to 1750*. Cambridge.

    1990   *Asia before Europe: Economy and Civilization in the Indian Ocean from the Rise of Islam to 1750*. Cambridge.

Chau ju-Kua (Zhao ru Gua)

*   1911   *His Work on the Chinese and Arab Trade in the Twelfth and Thirteenth Centuries Entitled Chu-fan-chï*, translated by Friedrich Hirth and W. W. Rockhill. St. Petersburg.

Chevalier, Ulysse

    1894–1903 *Répertoire des sources historiques du Moyen Age. Topo-bibliographie*. 2 vols. Montbéliard.

Chronique d'Amadi
* 1891–93   *Les chroniques d'Amadi et de Strambaldi*, edited by René de Mas Latrie. 2 vols. Collection de documents inédits sur l'histoire de France. Paris.

Constable, Giles
    2007   Medieval Latin Metaphors. *Viator* 36:1–20.
    2008   The Fourth Crusade. In *Crusaders and Crusading in the Twelfth Century*, 321–47. Farnham and Burlington, Vt.

Constable, Olivia Remie
    2003   *Housing the Stranger in the Mediterranean World: Lodging, Trade, and Travel in Late Antiquity and the Middle Ages*. Cambridge.

Constantinidi-Bibikou, H.
    1950   Yolande de Montferrat, impératrice de Byzance. *Hellénisme contemporain* 4:425–42.

Cordier, Henri
    1920   *Ser Marco Polo: Notes and Addenda to Sir Henry Yule's Edition*. London.

Curtius, Ernst Robert
    1990   *European Literature and the Latin Middle Ages*, translated by Willard Trask. Bollingen Series 36. Princeton.

Cutler, Anthony
    1996   Les échanges de dons entre Byzance et l'Islam (IXe–XIe siècles). *Journal des Savants* Jan.–June, 51–66.

Dagron, Gilbert
    2007   Une rhétorique de l'événement: l'astrologie. In Carozzi (2007), 193–200.

Dalché, Patrick Gautier
    2008   Représentations géographiques de l'Europe—septentrionale, centrale et orientale— au Moyen Age. In Baumgärtner and Kugler (2008), 63–79.

Daniel, Norman
    1975   *The Arabs and Mediaeval Europe*. London and Beirut.

Darrouzès, Jean, and Vitalien Laurent
    1976   *Dossier grec de l'Union de Lyon (1273–1277)*. Archives de l'Orient chrétien 15. Paris.

Dauvillier, Jean
    1948   Les provinces chaldéennes "de l'Extérieur" au Moyen Age. In *Mélanges offerts au R. P. Ferdinand Cavallera*, 261–316. Toulouse.

Dehérain, Henri
    1919   Les origines du Recueil des "Historiens des Croisades." *Journal des Savants* NS 17:260–66.

Delaville Le Roulx, Joseph
    1886   *La France en Orient au XIVe siècle*. 2 vols. Bibliothèque des Ecoles françaises d'Athènes et de Rome 44–45. Paris.

Directorium
* 1906   Brocardus, *Directorium ad passagium faciendum*. In *Recueil*, 368–517.
* 1906–8 *Directorium ad faciendum passagium transmarinum*, edited by C. Raymond Beazley. *American Historical Review* 12:810–57, 13:66–115.

Doe, Brian
    1992   *Socotra: Island of Tranquility*. London.

Doehaerd, Renée
    1941   *Les relations commerciales entre Gênes, la Belgique et l'Outremont*, vol. 1, *Introduction*. Institut historique belge de Rome. Études d'histoire économique et sociale 2. Brussels and Rome.

Dols, Michael
    1977   *The Black Death in the Middle East*. Princeton.

Douais, Célestin
* 1894   *Acta capitulorum provincialium ordinis fratrum Praedicatorum. Première province de Provence. Province romaine. Province d'Espagne (1239–1302)*. Toulouse.

Dubois, Pierre
* 1956   *The Recovery of the Holy Land*, translated by Walther I. Brandt. Records of Civilization 51. New York.

Dürrholder, Gottfried
    1913   *Die Kreuzzugspolitik unter Papst Johann XXII. (1316–1334)*. Diss. Freiburg im Breisgau. Strassburg.

Edbury, Peter
    1991   *The Kingdom of Cyprus and the Crusades, 1191–1374*. Cambridge.

Ehrle, Franz
    1890   *Historia bibliothecae Romanorum pontificum tum Bonifatianae tum Avenionensis*, vol. 1. Rome.

Epstein, Steven A.
    1996   *Genoa and the Genoese, 958–1528*. Chapel Hill.
    2007   *Purity Lost: Transgressing Boundaries in the Eastern Mediterranean, 1000–1400*. Baltimore.

Eubel, Conrad
    1897   Die während des 14. Jahrhunderts im Missiongebiet der Dominikaner und Franziskaner errichteten Bisthümer. In *Festschrift zum elfhundertjährigen Jubiläum des deutschen Campo Santo in Rom*, edited by Stephen Ehses, 170–95. Freiburg im Breisgau.

Evert-Kappesowa, Halina
    1949   La société byzantine et l'Union de Lyon. *Byzantinoslavica* 10:28–41.
    1952   Une page de l'histoire des relations byzantino-latines. Le clergé byzantin et l'Union de Lyon (1274–1282). *Byzantinoslavica* 13:68–92.

Faral, Edmond
    1947   Recueil des historiens des croisades. In *Les travaux de l'Académie des Inscriptions et Belles-lettres. Histoire et inventaire des publications*. Paris.

Fasolt, Constantin
    1991   *Council and Hierarchy: The Political Thought of William Durant the Younger*. Cambridge Studies in Medieval Life and Thought 4S 16. Cambridge.

Ferrand, Gabriel
    1922   Une navigation européenne dans l'océan indien au XIVe siècle. *Journal asiatique* 11S 20:307–9.

Fidentius of Padua: *see* Paviot (2008), 53–169.

Floor, Willem
    2004   Hormuz. In *Encyclopaedia Iranica* 12:471–76.

Foss, Clive
    1991   Smyrna. In *ODB* 3:1919–20.

Frescobaldi, Leonardo, and Giorgio Gucci
* 1948   *Visit to the Holy Places of Egypt, Sinai, Palestine, and Syria in 1384*, translated by Theophilus B. Bellorini and Eugene Hoade. Publications of the Studium Biblicum Franciscanum 6. Jerusalem.

Gatto, Ludovico
    1956   Per la storia di Martino Zaccaria signore di Chio. *Bullettino dell' "Archivio paleografico italiano"* NS 2:325–45.

Geanakoplos, Deno J.
    1959   *Emperor Michael Palaeologus and the West, 1258–1282: A Study in Byzantine-Latin Relations*. Cambridge, Mass. [Reprinted Hamden, Conn., 1973.]

Geanakoplos, Deno J. (*continued*)

1966   *Byzantine East and Latin West.* Harper Torchbooks 1265. New York and Evanston.

1975   Byzantium and the Crusades, 1261–1354. In *History*, 69–103.

1976   *Interaction of the "Sibling" Byzantine and Western Cultures in the Middle Ages and Italian Renaissance (330–1600).* New Haven and London.

Germon, Louis de, and Marie-Louis Polain

1899   *Catalogue de la bibliothèque de feu M. le Comte Riant. Deuxième partie.* 2 vols. Paris.

Gesta Francorum et aliorum Hierosolymitanorum

*   1962   edited and translated by Rosalind M. T. Hill. [Nelson's] Medieval Texts. London and Edinburgh.

Ghosh, Amitav

1992   *In an Antique Land.* New Delhi and London.

Giese, Wolfgang

1978   Asienkunde für den kreuzfahrenden Westen. In *Secundum regulam vivere. Festschrift für P. Norbert Backmund O. Praem.,* edited by Gert Melville, 245–64. Windberg.

Gill, Joseph

1974   The Church Union of the Council of Lyons (1274) Portrayed in Greek Documents. *Orientalia Christiana Periodica* 40:5–45. [Reprinted in Gill (1979b), art. V.]

1979a   *Byzantium and the Papacy 1198–1400.* New Brunswick, N.J.

1979b   *Church Union: Rome and Byzantium (1204–1453).* Variorum CS 91. London.

Goitein, Shlomo Dov

1954   Two Eyewitness Reports on an Expedition of the King of Kīsh (Qais) against Aden. *Bulletin of the School of Oriental and African Studies* 16:247–57.

1966–87 *A Mediterranean Society.* 6 vols. Berkeley.

*   1974   *Letters of Medieval Jewish Traders: The Jewish Communities of the World as Portrayed in the Documents of the Cairo Geniza.* Princeton.

1980   From Aden to India: Specimens of the Correspondence of Indian Traders of the Twelfth Century. *JESHO* 23:43–66.

Goitein, Shlomo Dov, and Mordechai Friedman

*   2008   *India Traders of the Middle Ages: Documents from the Cairo Geniza.* Leiden and Boston.

Golubovich, Girolamo

1919   *Biblioteca bio-bibliografica della Terra Santa e dell' Oriente francescano,* vol. 3 (*dal 1300 al 1332).* Quaracchi.

Gopal, Lallanji

1965   *The Economic Life of Northern India c. A.D. 700–1200.* Delhi.

Gottron, Adam

1912   *Ramon Lulls Kreuzzugsideen.* Berlin and Leipzig.

Grabar, Oleg

1997   The Shared Culture of Objects. In *Byzantine Court Culture from 829 to 1204,* edited by Henry Maguire, 115–29. Washington, D.C.

Gregory, Timothy E.

1991   Chios. In *ODB* 1:423–24.

Guenée, Bernard

2005   *Ego,* je. L'affirmation de soi par les historiens français (XIVe–XVe siècles). *Académie des Inscriptions et Belles-Lettres: Comptes rendus* 597–611.

Habicht, Christian

2012   Eudoxius of Cyzicus and the Ptolemaic Exploration of the Sea Route to India. Forthcoming in the proceedings of the 2009 conference "Ptolemaic Waterways and Power." Athens.

Haenel, Gustaf

1830   *Catalogi librorum manuscriptorum.* Leipzig.

Hagenmeyer, Heinrich
    1908   Review of *Recueil*. In *Byzantinische Zeitschrift* 17:521–25.
Harris, Jonathan
    2003   *Byzantium and the Crusades*. New York.
Hartog, François
    2005   *Évidence de l'histoire. Ce que voient les historiens*. Cas de figure 5. Paris.
Hennig, Richard
    1953   *Terrae incognitae*, vol. 3, *1200–1415*. 2nd ed. Leiden.
Heyd, Wilhelm
    1885–86 *Histoire du commerce du Levant au moyen âge*, translated by Furcy Raynaud. 2 vols.
            Leipzig.
Holt, Peter M.
    1986   *The Age of the Crusades*. London.
Hölzle, Peter
    1980   *Die Kreuzzüge in der okzitanischen und deutschen Lyrik des 12. Jahrhunderts*.
            Göppinger Arbeiten zur Germanistik 278. Göppingen.
Honigmann, Ernst
    1935   *Die Ostgrenze des byzantinischen Reiches von 363 bis 1071*. Brussels.
Hourani, George Fadlo
    1999   *Arab Seafaring in the Indian Ocean in Ancient and Early Medieval Times*, rev. ed. by
            John Carswell. Princeton.
Housley, Norman
    1992   *The Later Crusades, 1274–1580: From Lyons to Alcazar*. Oxford.
*   1996   *Documents on the Later Crusades, 1274–1580*. Houndmills and London.
    2003   Costing the Crusade: Budgeting for Crusading Activity in the Fourteenth Century.
            In *The Experience of Crusading*, vol. 1, *Western Approaches*, edited by Marcus Bull
            and Norman Housley, 45–59. Cambridge.
Hussey, Joan M.
    1990   *The Orthodox Church in the Byzantine Empire*. Oxford.
Ibn Batuta (Baṭṭūṭa)
*   1929   *Travels in Asia and Africa, 1325–1354*, translated by Hamilton A. R. Gibb.
            London.
Ibn Majid: *see* Tibbetts (1971).
Ibn al-Mujāwir, Yūsuf ibn Yaʾqūb
*   2008   *A Traveller in Thirteenth-Century Arabia: Ibn al-Mujāwir's Tārīkh al-mustabsir*,
            translated by Gerald Rex Smith. Hakluyt Society 3S 19. Aldershot and London. [*See
            also* Miles (1993).]
Itinerarium
*   1997   *Chronicle of the Third Crusade: A Translation of the Itinerarium peregrinorum et gesta
            regis Ricardi*, translated by Helen J. Nicholson. Aldershot.
Jackson, Peter
    2005   *The Mongols and the West, 1221–1410*. The Medieval World. London.
Jacoby, David
    2001   The Supply of War Materials to Egypt in the Crusader Period. *Jerusalem Studies in
            Arabic and Islam* 25:102–32.
Jain, Vardhman Kumar
    1989   *Trade and Traders in Western India AD 1000–1300*. New Delhi.
Jaspert, Nikolas
    2003   *Die Kreuzzüge*. Darmstadt.
    2008   Interreligiöse Diplomatie im Mittelmeerraum. Die Krone Aragón und die islamische
            Welt im 13. und 14. Jahrhundert. In *Aus der Frühzeit europäischer Diplomatie*, edited
            by Claudia Zey and Claudia Märtl, 151–89. Zürich.

Jireček, Constantin J.

1877   *Die Heerstrasse von Belgrad nach Constantinopel und die Balkanpässe.* Prague.

John of Winterthur

*   1924   *Die Chronik Johanns von Winterthur,* edited by Friedrich Baethgen and Carl Brun.
Monumenta Germaniae historica: Scriptores rerum germanicarum NS 3. Berlin.

Kaeppeli, Thomas

1970–93   *Scriptores Ordinis Praedicatorum Medii Aevi.* 4 vols. Rome.

Kammerer, Albert

1950   Le périple de l'Afrique à travers les âges. *Comité des travaux historiques et scientifi-
ques. Bulletin de la section de géographie* 59:21–58.

Karashima, Noboru (editor)

2002   *Ancient and Medieval Commercial Activities in the Indian Ocean: Testimony of
Inscriptions and Ceramic Sherds.* Tokyo.

Kazhdan, Alexander

1991a   Phokaia. In *ODB* 2:1665.

1991b   Nymphaion, Treaty of. In *ODB* 3:1506.

Kedar, Benjamin Z.

1976   *Merchants in Crisis: Genoese and Venetian Men of Affairs and the Fourteenth-Century
Depression.* New Haven.

1977   Segurano-Sakrân Salvaygo. Un mercante genovese al servizio dei sultani mamaluc-
chi, c. 1303–1322. In *Fatti e idee di storia economica nei secoli XII–XX. Studi dedicati a
Franco Borlandi,* 75–91. Bologna.

1985   L'*Officium Robarie* di Genova. Un tentativo di coesistere con la violenza. *Archivio sto-
rico italiano* 143:331–72.

Kedar, Benjamin Z., and Sylvia Schein

1979   Un projet de "passage particulier" proposé par l'ordre de l'Hôpital, 1306–1307.
Bibliothèque de l'Ecole des Chartes 137:211–26.

Kohler, Charles

1903–4   Documents relatifs à Guillaume Adam archevêque de Sultanieh, puis d'Antivari, et
son entourage (1318–1346). *ROL* 10:16–56. [Reprinted in idem, *Mélanges pour servir à
l'histoire de l'Orient latin et des croisades,* 2:475–515. Paris, 1906.]

1909–11 Quel est l'auteur du *Directorium ad passagium faciendum*? *ROL* 12:104–11.

Laiou, Angeliki E.

1972   *Constantinople and the Latins: The Foreign Policy of Andronicus II, 1282–1328.* Cambridge, Mass.

2002a   The Agrarian Economy, Thirteenth–Fourteenth Centuries. In *The Economic History of Byzantium from the Seventh through the Fifteenth Century,* edited by Angeliki
Laiou, 1:311–75. 3 vols. Washington, D.C.

2002b   Economic and Noneconomic Exchange. In *The Economic History of Byzantium from
the Seventh through the Fifteenth Century,* edited by Angeliki Laiou, 3:681–96. 3 vols.
Washington, D.C.

Lapina, Elizabeth

2007   "Nec signis nec testis creditur . . .": The Problem of Eyewitnesses in the Chronicles of
the First Crusade. *Viator* 38:117–39.

Lefort, Jacques

2002   The Rural Economy, Seventh–Twelfth Centuries. In *The Economic History of Byzantium from the Seventh through the Fifteenth Century,* edited by Angeliki Laiou, 1:231–
310. 3 vols. Washington, D.C.

Leopold, Anthony

2000   *How to Recover the Holy Land: The Crusade Proposals of the Late Thirteenth and
Early Fourteenth Centuries.* Aldershot and Burlington, Vt.

Lewis, Archibald
    1973   Maritime Skills in the Indian Ocean 1368–1500. *JESHO* 16:238–64.

Lilie, Ralph-Johannes
    1993   *Byzantium and the Crusader States 1096–1204*, translated by J. C. Morris and Jean E. Ridings. Oxford.

Lloyd, Simon
    1995   The Crusading Movement, 1096–1274. In *The Oxford Illustrated History of the Crusades*, edited by Jonathan Riley-Smith, 34–65. Oxford and New York.

Loenertz, Raymond Joseph
    1937   *La société des frères pérégrinants. Etude sur l'orient dominicain*, vol. 1. Institutum historicum FF. Praedicatorum Romae ad S. Sabinae. Dissertationes historicae 7. Rome.

Lombard, Maurice
    1958   Arsenaux et bois de marine dans la Méditerranée musulmane (VIIᵉ–XIᵉ siècle). In *Le navire et l'économie maritime du moyen âge au XVIIIᵉ siècle principalement en Méditerranée*, edited by Michel Mollat, 53–106. Paris.

Lopez, Roberto
    1933   *Genova marinara nel duecento. Benedetto Zaccaria, ammiraglio e mercante.* Messina and Milan.

Magnocavallo, Arturo
    1901   *Marin Sanudo il Vecchio e il suo progetto di crociata.* Bergamo.

Ma Huan: *see* Mills (1970).

Mansi, Giovanni Domenico
*   1901–27 *Sacrorum conciliorum nova et amplissima collectio.* 53 vols. Paris.

Margariti, Roxani Eleni
    2007   *Aden and the Indian Ocean Trade: 150 Years in the Life of a Medieval Arabian Port.* Islamic Civilization and Muslim Networks. Chapel Hill.
    2008   Mercantile Networks, Port Cities and "Pirate" States: Conflict and Competition in the Indian Ocean World of Trade before the Sixteenth Century. *JESHO* 51:543–77.

Mas Latrie, Louis de
    1891   Note sur le voyage du dominicain Brochard l'Allemand dans l'hémisphère austral, au XIVᵉ siècle. *Académie des Inscriptions et Belles-Lettres. Comptes rendus 1890* 4S 18:21–22.
    1892   L'Officium Robarie ou l'office de la piraterie à Gênes au Moyen Age. *Bibliothèque de l'Ecole des Chartes* 53:264–72.

Miles, Samuel Barrett
    1993   Extract from an Arabic Work Relating to Aden [Ibn al-Muǧāwir: Tārīḫ al-Mustabṣir). In *Texts and Studies on Historical Geography and Topography of Central and South Arabia*, collected and reprinted by Fuat Sezgin, 2:147–60. Islamic Geography 92, Frankfurt. [Reprint of Frederick Mercer, *An Account of the British Settlement of Aden in Arabia.* London, 1877. 183–96.]

Miller, William
    1911   The Zaccaria of Phocaea and Chios (1275–1329). *Journal of Hellenic Studies* 31:42–55.

Mills, John V. G.
*   1970   *The Overall Survey of the Ocean's Shore, Translation of Ma huan's Ying-Yai She-lan.* Hakluyt Society, Extra Series 42. Oxford.

Molinier, Auguste
    1903   *Les sources de l'histoire de France des origines aux guerres d'Italie (1494)*, vol. 3, *Les Capétiens, 1180–1328.* Paris.

Monneret de Villard, Ugo
    1948   *Il libro della peregrinazione nelle parti d'Oriente di Frate Ricoldo da Montecroce.* Institutum historicum FF. Praedicatorum Romae ad S. Sabinae. Dissertationes historicae 13. Rome.

Monumenta
*   1857   *Monumenta conciliorum generalium seculi decimi quinti. Concilium Basileense. Scriptorum tomus primus,* edited by František Palacký and Ernst von Birk. Vienna.

Moule, Arthur C.
    1930   *Christians in China before the Year 1550.* London.

Müller, Anne
    2002   *Bettelmönche in islamischer Fremde.* Vita regularis 15. Münster.

Nainar, S. Muhammad Husayn
    1942   *Arab Geographers' Knowledge of Southern India.* Madras. [New ed.: *Southern India as Known to Arab Geographers.* New Delhi, 2004.]

Niccolo of Poggibonsi
*   1945   *Libro d'Oltramare, 1346–1350,* edited by Alberto Bacchi Della Lega and Bellarmino Camillo Bagatti. Studium Biblicum Franciscanum, Collectio maior 2. Jerusalem.

Nicol, Donald M.
    1989   Popular Religious Roots of the Byzantine Reaction to the Second Council of Lyons. In *The Religious Roles of the Papacy: Ideals and Realities, 1150–1300,* edited by Christopher Ryan, 321–39. Papers in Mediaeval Studies 8. Toronto.

Nilakantha Sastri, K. A.
    1939   *Foreign Notices of South India from Megasthenes to Ma Huan.* Madras University Historical Series 14. Madras.
    1955   *The Cōlas,* rev. ed. Madras University Historical Series 9. Madras.

Norden, Walter
    1903   *Das Papsttum und Byzanz.* Berlin.

Odo of Deuil
*   1948   *De profectione Ludovici VII in orientem: The Journey of Louis VII to the East,* edited and translated by Virginia Gingerick Berry. Records of Civilization 42. New York. [Rev. ed. 2001.]

Oikonomides, Nikolas
    1991a   Diplomacy. In *ODB* 1:634–35.
    1991b   Prisoners, Exchanges of. In *ODB* 3:1722.

Omont, Henri
    1898   *Bibliothèque nationale. Nouvelles acquisitions du département des manuscrits pendant les années 1896–1897.* Paris.
    1921   Guillaume Adam, Missionnaire. In *Histoire littéraire de la France* 35:277–84.

Pachymeres, Giorgios
*   1984–2000 *Georges Pachymérès. Relations historiques,* edited by Albert Failler, translated by Vitalien Laurent. 5 vols. Corpus fontium historiae byzantinae 24. Paris.

Pall, Francisc
    1942   Les croisades en Orient au Bas Moyen Age. Observations critiques sur l'ouvrage de M. Atiya. *Revue historique du Sud-Est européen* 19.1:527–83.

Parkin, David, and Ruth Barnes (editors)
    2002   *Ships and the Development of Maritime Technology in the Indian Ocean.* London.

Paviot, Jacques (editor)
*   2008   *Projets de croisade (v. 1290–v. 1330).* Documents relatifs à l'histoire des croisades 26. Paris.

Pearson, Michael N.
    2004   *The Indian Ocean.* New York.

Pelliot, Paul

    1951   Deux passages de *La Prophétie de Hannan, fils d'Isaac*. In *Mélanges sur l'époque des croisades*, 73–97. Paris. [Reprinted in Beckingham and Hamilton (1996), 113–37.]

Pelzer, Auguste

    1947   *Addenda et emendanda ad Francisci Ehrle historiae bibliothecae Romanorum pontificum tum Bonifatianae tum Avenionensis tomum 1*. Vatican City.

Pereira, José Manuel Malhão

    2001   *The Mighty Red Sea. Comunicação apresentada no "International Seminar on Maritime Activities in India with Reference to the Portuguese 1500–1800," Universidade de Goa*. Lisbon.

Phillips, Jonathan R. S.

    1998   *The Medieval Expansion of Europe*. Oxford.

Polo, Marco

*   1903   *The Book of Ser Marco Polo the Venetian Concerning the Kingdoms and Marvels of the East*, edited and translated by Henry Yule, 3rd ed. by Henri Cordier. 2 vols. London.

Prescott, Hilda F. M.

    1954   *Jerusalem Journey*. London.

Prutz, Hans

    1883   *Kulturgeschichte der Kreuzzüge*. Berlin.

Purcell, Maureen

    1975   *Papal Crusading Policy: The Chief Instruments of Papal Crusading Policy and Crusade to the Holy Land from the Final Loss of Jerusalem to the Fall of Acre (1244–1291)*. Studies in the History of Christian Thought 11. Leiden.

al-Qaddumi, Ghadah al-Hijjawi

*   1996   *Book of Gifts and Rarities: Kitab al-hadaya wa al-tuhaf*. Harvard Middle Eastern Monographs. Cambridge, Mass.

Ramaswamy, Vijaya

    1985   *Textiles and Weavers in Medieval South India*. New Delhi.

Raymond of Aguilers

*   1968   *Historia Francorum qui ceperunt Iherusalem*, translated by John Hugh Hill and Laurita Hill. Memoirs of the American Philosophical Society 71. Philadelphia.

Ricaldus (Riculdus, Riccoldo) of Monte Croce

*   1997   *Liber peregrinationis. Pérégrination en Terre Sainte et au Proche Orient*, edited and translated by René Kappler. Textes et traductions des classiques français du moyen âge 4. Paris.

Richard, Jean

    1960   Les premiers missionnaires latins en Ethiopie (XIIe–XIVe siècles). In *Atti del Convegno internazionale di studi etiopici*, 323–29. Accademia nazionale dei Lincei quad. 48. Rome.

    1968   European Voyages in the Indian Ocean and the Caspian Sea (12th–15th Centuries). *Iran: Journal of the British Institute of Persian Studies* 6:45–52.

    1970   Les navigations des occidentaux sur l'océan indien et la mer caspienne (XIIe–XVe siècle). In *Sociétés et companies de commerce en Orient et dans l'océan indien,* edited by Michel Mollat, 353–63. Bibliothèque générale de l'École pratique des hautes études, VIe section. Paris.

    1977a   The Eastern Mediterranean and its Relations with its Hinterland (11th–15th Centuries). In *Les relations entre l'Orient et l'Occident au Moyen Age*. Variorum CS 69. London, art. I.

    1977b   *La papauté et les missions d'Orient au Moyen Age (XIIIe–XVe siècles)*. Collection de l'Ecole française de Rome 33. Rome.

Richard, Jean (*continued*)

1984   Le royaume de Chypre et l'embargo sur le commerce avec l'Egypte (fin XIIIᵉ–début XIVᵉ siècle). *Académie des Inscriptions et Belles-Lettres. Comptes rendus* 120–34. [Reprinted in idem, *Croisades et Etats latins d'Orient*. Variorum CS 383. Aldershot and Brookfield, Vt., 1992, art. XVI.]

Roberg, Burkhard

1964   *Die Union zwischen der griechischen und der lateinischen Kirche auf dem II. Konzil von Lyon (1274)*. Bonner historische Forschungen 24. Bonn.

Robert the Monk

*   2005   *Historia Iherosolimitana: Robert the Monk's History of the First Crusade*, translated by Carol Sweetenham. Crusade Texts in Translation 11. Aldershot and Burlington, Vt.

Röhricht, Reinhold

1890   *Bibliotheca geographica Palaestinae. Chronologisches Verzeichniss der auf die Geographie des Heiligen Landes bezüglichen Literatur von 333 bis 1878*. Berlin.

Rouse, Mary, and Richard Rouse

2006   Context and Reception: A Crusading Collection for Charles IV of France. In *Courtly Arts and the Art of Courtliness: Selected Papers from the Eleventh Triennial Congress of the International Courtly Literature Society, University of Wisconsin-Madison, 29 July–4 August 2004*, edited by Keith Busby and Christopher Kleinhenz, 105–78. Woodbridge and Rochester, N.Y.

Runciman, Steven

1954   *A History of the Crusades*, vol. 3, *The Kingdom of Acre and the Later Crusades*. Cambridge.

1955   *The Eastern Schism: A Study of the Papacy and the Eastern Churches during the XIth and XIIth Centuries*. Oxford.

Salomon, Richard

1936   *Opicinus de Canistris. Weltbild und Bekenntnisse eines avignonesischen Klerikers des 14. Jahrhunderts*. Studies of the Warburg Institute 1. London.

Salonen, Kirsi, and Ludwig Schmugge

*   2009   *A Sip from the "Well of Grace": Medieval Texts from the Apostolic Penitentiary*. Studies in Medieval and Early Modern Canon Law 7. Washington, D.C.

Sanudo, Marino (the Elder)

*   1972   *Liber secretorum fidelium crucis* (Hanover, 1611), reproduced with introduction by Joshua Prawer. Toronto.

Sarton, George

1947   *Introduction to the History of Science*, vol. 3, *Science and Learning in the Fourteenth Century*. Baltimore.

Schein, Sylvia

1991   *Fideles Crucis: The Papacy, the West and the Recovery of the Holy Land, 1274–1314*. Oxford.

Schmieder, Felicitas

1994   *Europa und die Fremden. Die Mongolen im Urteil des Abendlandes vom 13. bis in das 15. Jahrhundert*. Beiträge zur Geschichte und Quellenkunde des Mittelalters 16. Sigmaringen.

Schon, Peter M.

1960   *Studien zum Stil der frühen französischen Prosa*. Analecta Romanica 8. Frankfurt.

Setton, Kenneth M.

1975   *Catalan Domination of Athens*, rev. ed. London.

1976   *The Papacy and the Levant (1204–1571)*, vol. 1, *The Thirteenth and Fourteenth Centuries*. Memoirs of the American Philosophical Society 114. Philadelphia.

Shahîd, Irfan A., Alexander Kazhdan, and Anthony Cutler

1991   Arabs. In *ODB* 1:149–51.

Siberry, Elizabeth
    1983   Missionaries and Crusaders, 1095–1274: Opponents or Allies. In *The Church and War*, edited by W. J. Sheils, 103–18. Studies in Church History 20. Oxford.

Sidebotham, Steven E.
    2011   *Berenike and the Ancient Maritime Spice Route*. California World History Library 18. Berkeley.

Silvestre de Sacy, Antoine-Isaac
    1822   Mémoire sur une correspondance inédite de Tamerlan avec Charles VI. *Histoire et mémoires de l'Institut royal de France. Académie des Inscriptions et Belles-Lettres* 6:470–522.

Sinor, Denis
    1975   The Mongols and Western Europe. In *History*, 513–44.
    1999   The Mongols in the West. *Journal of Asian History* 33:1–44.

Smith, Gerald Rex
    1995   Have You Anything to Declare? Maritime Trade and Commerce in Ayyubid Aden: Practices and Taxes. *Proceedings of the Seminar for Arabian Studies* 25:127–40. [Reprinted in idem (1997), art. X.]
    1997   *Studies in the Medieval History of Yemen and South Arabia*. Variorum CS 574. Aldershot.

Soranzo, Giovanni
    1930   *Il papato, l'Europa cristiana e i Tartari. Un secolo di penetrazione occidentale in Asia.* Pubblicazioni della Università cattolica del Sacro Cuore 5S: Scienze storiche 12. Milan.

Spuler, Bertold
    1968   *Die Mongolen in Iran. Politik, Verwaltung und Kultur der Ilchanzeit 1220–1350*, 3rd ed. Berlin.

Steensgaard, Niels
    1987   The Indian Ocean Network and the Emerging World Economy, circa 1500–1750. In Chandra (1987), 125–50.

Stevenson, Henry, and J. B. de Rossi
    1886   *Codices palatini latini bibliothecae Vaticanae*, vol. 1. Rome.

Stillman, Norman A.
    1973   The Eleventh Century Merchant House of Ibn ʿAwkal (a Geniza Study). *JESHO* 16:15–88.

Stübe, Rudolf
    1916   Hormuz. In *Encyclopedia of Islam* 2:315–16.

Suny, Ronald G.
    1994   *The Making of the Georgian Nation*. Bloomington.

Symon Semeonis
 * 1960   *Itinerarium Symonii Semeonis ab Hybernia ad Terram Sanctam*, edited and translated by Mario Esposito. Scriptores latini hiberniae 4. Dublin.

Talbot, Alice-Mary
    1991a   Catalan Grand Company. In *ODB* 1:389.
    1991b   Irene-Yolanda of Montferrat. In *ODB* 2:1010.
    1991c   Roger de Flor. In *ODB* 3:1802.
    1991d   Zaccaria. In *ODB* 3:2217–18.

Taŭtu, Aloysius L.
 * 1953   *Acta Urbani IV, Clementis IV, Gregorii X (1261–1276)*. Vatican City.
 * 1958   *Acta Benedicti XII (1334–1342)*. Vatican City.

Thapar, Romila
    1992   The Black Gold: South Asia and the Roman Maritime Trade. *South Asia* 15:1–28.

Tibbetts, Gerald R.

* 1971   *Arab Navigation in the Indian Ocean before the Coming of the Portuguese, Being a translation of Kitāb al-fawāi 'dfī usūl al-bahr wa'l-quwā'id of Ahmad b. Mājid al-Najdī.* Oriental Translation Fund 42. London.

Trapp, Erich (editor)

1996   *Prosopographisches Lexikon der Palaiologenzeit.* Vienna.

Trexler, Richard

1995   *Sex and Conquest: Gendered Violence, Political Order, and the European Conquest of the Americas.* Cambridge.

Tyerman, Christopher J.

1982   Marino Sanudo Torsello and the Lost Crusade: Lobbying in the Fourteenth Century. *Transactions of the Royal Historical Society* 5S 32:57–73.

1985   The Holy Land and the Crusades in the Thirteenth and Fourteenth Centuries. In *Crusade and Settlement: Papers Read at the First Conference of the Society for the Study of the Crusades and the Latin East Presented to R. C. Smail*, edited by Peter Edbury, 105–12. Cardiff.

van der Veen, Marijke

2011   *Consumption, Trade and Innovation: Exploring the Botanical Remains from the Roman and Islamic Ports at Quseir al-Qadim, Egypt.* Journal of African Archaeology, Monograph Series 6. Frankfurt.

Vasiliev, Alexander A.

1935–68 *Byzance et les Arabes.* 4 vols. Corpus bruxellense historiae byzantinae 1–3. Brussels.

Viollet, Paul

1921   Guillaume Durant le Jeune, évêque de Mende. In *Histoire littéraire de la France* 35:1–139.

Von den Brinken, Anna-Dorothée

1973   *Die "Nationes christianorum orientalium" im Verständnis des lateinischen Historiographie von der Mitte des 12. bis in die zweite Hälfte des 14. Jahrhunderts.* Kölner historische Abhandlungen 22. Cologne and Vienna.

2008   Europa um 1320 auf zwei Weltkarten süditalienischer Provenienz. Die Karte zur "Chronologia magna" des Paulinus Minorita (BnF Lat. 4939) und die Douce-Karte (Bodleian Douce 319). In Baumgärtner and Kugler (2008), 157–70.

William of Tripoli

* 1883   Tractatus de statu Saracenorum. In Prutz (1883), 575–98.

Williamson, Joan

1994   Philippe de Mézières and the Idea of Crusade. In *The Military Orders: Fighting for the Faith and Caring for the Sick*, edited by Malcolm Barber, 358–64. Aldershot and Brookfield, Vt.

Wilson, Arnold T.

1928   *The Persian Gulf.* Oxford.

Wright, John Kirtland

1925   *The Geographical Lore at the Time of the Crusades.* American Geographical Society: Research Series 15. New York.

Yādava, B. N. S.

1973   *Society and Culture in Northern India in the Twelfth Century.* Allahabad.

Zachariadou, Elizabeth A.

1983   *Trade and Crusade: Venetian Crete and the Emirates of Menteshe and Aydin (1300–1415).* Venice.

1991a   Aydin. In *ODB* 1:239–40.

1991b   Menteshe. In *ODB* 2:1342–43.

1991c   Saruhan. In *ODB* 3:1844–45.

Zhao ru Gua: *see* Chau ju-Kua.

GENERAL INDEX

Page numbers refer as a rule to the English text and notes on the odd-numbered pages. The following abbreviations are used:

abp	archbishop
abt	abbot
bp	bishop
Byz	Byzantine
emp	emperor
k	king
n	note
pat	patriarch

Acre, 5, 41
Adelheid (Irene) of Brunswick-Grubenhagen, wife of Andronicus III, 93n
Aden (Eden), 99, 107, 109n, 111, 113, 115
  attacked by sultan of Kish ca. 1135, 111n
  attacked by islanders, 115–17
  gulf of, 99n, 101, 103–5
  merchants of, 113–15
  unwarlike character, 113
Aegean sea, 51n
Africa, 8
Alans, 29
Alexander III, pope, 27n
Alexandria, 7n, 9, 27, 35, 37, 43, 49, 51, 53, 55, 63, 101, 103, 111
Alexandrini (Christian merchants trading with Alexandria), 9, 36, 38, 42, 48, 52
Alfonso X, k of Castile, 93n

Amadi, chronicle of, 43n
Amta, 101n
Anatolia, *see* Asia Minor
Andronicus I, Byz emp, 10
Andronicus II, Byz emp, 6, 43n, 45n, 51n, 79, 87–91, 93n, 95–97
  conditions imposed by monks, 91–93
  imprisoned Catholics, 95
Andronicus III, Byz emp, 7, 93n
Anselm of Havelberg, bp, 45n
Antioch, 75, 77
Antivari (Bar), 2–3
Arabia, 99
Aragon, k, 49n
Arghun, Ilkhānid sultan, 105
Armenia, 2, 15
  prince, *see* Haython
Asia Minor (Anatolia, Turkey), 3, 10, 25n, 51, 53, 55, 65, 67, 73, 79
Augustine, St., 85n
Avignon, 2, 43n
  papal library, 12
Aydin, emirate, 51n, 53n, 65n

Babylon, *see* Cairo, Egypt
Baghdad, 59, 61
  ships built by Genoese, 105
Balkans, 3, 69
Bar, *see* Antivari
Barcelona, 27n
Barlaam the Calabrian, 43n
Basel, council (1431–49), 11, 12
  Dominican house, 12
Baybars II, sultan, 55n

Bekkos, John, pat of Constantinople, 87n, 95
bells in Christian churches, 49
Benedict XII, pope, 43n
Black sea, 47n
Bohemond of Taranto (Antioch), 75n
Bosphorus, 3, 71, 73
  "arm of St. George," 75, 77
bread, supply in Byz empire, 69
  poisoned, sold to crusaders, 77
Brocardus (Brochard, Burchard), 7–8
Bulgaria, Bulgars, 29, 71
  k, *see* Ivan III
Byzantium, emp, 7, 27, 41–43, 69, 75–77
  see also Andronicus I, II, III, Isaac II, John III, Michael VIII

Cairo (Babylon), 27, 101n
Cambay, 107n, 109
camphor, 101n
Carcassonne, 2
Castile, *see* Alfonso X
castrum, 19
Catalan Company, 49n, 95n
Catalonia, 27
Cathay (eastern Mongols), 45–47
Chaghatay, son of Chinggis kahn, 47n
Chaldea, 61, 85
Charles of Anjou, k of Naples, 93n
Charles IV, k of France, 5n, 11
Chau ju-Kua, 101n
Chinggis (Ghengis) khan, 47n

Chios, 3, 7n, 49, 51, 53n, 65, 67
Clement IV, pope, 43n
Clement V, pope, 2, 35, 55, 59n
coconut fiber, 109n
Condom, 1
Conrad III, emp, 77n
Constantinople, 2, 3, 7, 9, 10, 11,
    43n, 45, 49, 53, 63–67, 71–75,
    79, 95
  Blachernai; palace, 89n
  patriarch, *see* Bekkos,
    Germanos III, Joseph I
  Pera (Galata), 67
  Sta. Sophia, 89
  synod (1273), 87n
  see also Bosphorus, Byzantium
Corinth, abp, 2n
Crusades, crusading,
  first, 67, 75, 77
  indulgence, 53
  nomenclature, 19
  planning, 5, 55–61
  role of kings, 61
  role of pope, 61
  route, 69–71, 75, 85
  second, 10, 77n
  supplying, 65, 67–69, 77
  third, 10
  see also Louis IX, William of
    Adam
Cumans, 29, 73
Cyprus, 37n, 39–41
  k, *see* Guy of Lusignan,
    Henry II

Daman, 109n
David, k of Georgia, 59
Directorium, 3, 5–11, 12
Dive Insulide (Diu), islands, 107n,
    109, 113
Dominicans, 12, 93
  expelled from Constantinople,
    95
dominium, 19
Dubois, Pierre, 5
Duwa (Du'a) ("middle" empire of
    Mongols), 47

Eden, *see* Aden
Egypt, Egyptians (Babylonians,
    Saracens), 3, 4, 8, 9, 25n,
    27–29, 47n, 51, 73, 75, 79,
    99–101, 111
  crusade to, 37n

famine, 41–43
  qualities as fighters, 73–75
  sultan, 9, 41–43, 45, 47–49, 51,
    55, 57, 61, *see also* Baybars II,
    Muhammad I, Qalāwūn
  trade with India, 97–113
  see also Alexandria, Cairo,
    Mamluks, Nile
England, English, 71
Ephesus, 53, 65
  abp, *see* Raymond Stephen
Ethiopia, 3, 99, 105
Euphrates, river, 105

Fidentius (Fidenzio) of Padua, 5,
    9, 39n
France, French, 71
  k, *see* Louis IX, Philip VI
Franciscans, expelled from
    Constantinople, 95
Frederick II, emp, 95n
Frescobaldi, Leonardo, pilgrim, 39n
funduq (trading house), 27n
  see also hospice

Garcias de Ayerbe, bp of León, 5n
Genoa, Genoese, 9, 27, 33–35, 47n,
    49, 65, 67, 93, 105, 111
  Officium Robariae, 13, 37–39
  ships built in Baghdad, 105
  treaty with sultan, 105n
Georgia, Georgians, 59, 73
  k, *see* David
Germanos III, pat of
    Constantinople, 89n, 95
Germany, Germans, 71, 93
  emp, *see* Conrad III,
    Frederick II
Ghengis, *see* Chinggis
Ghibelline, among Genoese in
    Baghdad, 105
Goa, 109n
gold, 101
Golden Horde, *see* Khazaria
grain produced in Byz empire, 69
  shortage in Egypt, 43
Greece (Romania), Greeks, 3, 29,
    67–69, 77, 85, 93
  qualities as fighters, 71–73, 75,
    87
  sold as slaves, 79–85
  treachery, 69n, 75–79, 97
Gregory X, pope, 89n
Gucci, Giorgio, pilgrim, 39n

Guelf, among Genoese in
    Baghdad, 105
Gujarat, 99n, 109n
Guy of Lusignan, k of Cyprus, 93

Haython (Hethoun, Hayton,
    Het'um), Armenian prince
    and historian, 5, 14n, 59n
Henry II, duke of Brunswick-
    Grubenhagen, 93n
Henry II, k of Cyprus, 27n
Holobolos, Manuel, anti-unionist
    official, 91n
Holy Land (Palestine), 3, 23, 27, 51,
    57, 71, 73, 77, 79
homosexuality in Egypt, 31–33, 35,
    41, 47, 49, 51
Hormuz, 107–9, 111
horses, shipped to India, 111n
hospices, pilgrim, 41
  see also funduq
Hospitallers, 37n, 55n, 65n, 67
Hülegü, Mongol khan, 41n, 59n,
    61n
Hungary, Hungarians, 29, 71, 77

Ibn 'Awkal, Jewish merchant, 101n
Ibn Battuta, traveller, 99n, 101n,
    109n
Ibn al-Mujāwir, traveller, 101n
Iconium (Konya), 10
Idumea, 99
Ilkhānids (southern Mongols),
    25n, 47n, 59n
India, 3, 9, 55
  trade with Egypt, 97–113
  see also William of Adam
Indian ocean (sea), 9, 27, 97–99,
    103, 109n, 111, 117
  islands, 107, 111, *see also* Dive
    Insulide, Laccadives,
    Maldives
indigo, 101n
Innocent III, pope, 27n
iron, 29, 101n
Isaac II, Byz emp, 10
Ivan III, k of Bulgaria, 95n

Jerusalem, 9, 10, 23, 39
  pat, 41
Jews, owning slaves, 79
Jochī, son of Chinggis kahn, 47n
John XXII, pope, 2, 3, 59n
John III Vatatzes, Byz emp, 65n

John of Cora, abp of Sultanieh, 3n, 8
John of Ragusa, Dominican theologian, 12n
John of Salisbury, 101n
Joseph I, pat of Constantinople, 89n

Karantaka, 109n
Khazaria (Khwarazim) (northern Mongols, Golden Horde), 47
emp, 47–49, 51, 53, 57–59
Kirman, 101n
Kish, 107n, 109n, 111
Kolar (gold-field), 101n
Konkan, 99n, 109n
Koulam (Kulam, Kollam, Quilan), 107n, 109, 111n

Laccadive islands, 109n
León, 5n
bp, *see* Garcias
Lombards, 67
Louis IX, k of France, 59, 61n, 75
Lyons, second council (1274), 45n, 87n, 89, 91n

Malabar, 99n, 101n, 109n
Malacca, 109n
Maldive islands, 109n
Mamluks, 25n, 27n, 29n, 31n, 49n, 59n
Mangalore, 109n
Marco Polo, 99n, 101n, 109n, 111n
Maria, daughter of Ivan III, wife of Roger de Flor, 95n
Marino Sanudo (the Elder), 5, 9, 37n
Marseille, 27n
mastic, 49n, 51n
meat, supply in Byz empire, 69
Mediterranean sea, 99
Meliteiniotes, Theodore, patriarchal official, 87n
Menteshe, emirate, 51n
Metochites, George, pro-union patriarchal official, 87n
Michael VIII, Byz emp, 43n, 49n, 65n, 79n, 87, 89–91
lack of burial, 91–93, 95–97
miracle at tomb, 93, 95–97
Möngke, Mongol khan, 47n
monks, Byz (fakirs), 43–45, 47–49, 51, 87–91, 95

imposed conditions on emp, 91–93
punished by Michael VIII, 91
Mongols (Tartars), 9, 25n, 27, 29, 45, 73, 79, 95, 113
see also Cathay, Duwa, Ilkhānids, Khazaria
Monte Cassino, abt, 89
Montpellier, synod (1162), 27n
Morisco, Andrea, Byz admiral, 93
Muhammad Khadābanda Ölyeytü, Ilkhānid khan, 59n
Muhammad I b. Qalāwūn, sultan, 25n, 31n, 33–35, 55n
Mumbai, 101n, 109n
Muslims, trade with, prohibitions, 9, 27, 29n, 35–37, 51n
Mustansir, al-, Abbasid caliph, 59n

Narbonne, 2
Niccolo of Poggibonsi, 39n
Nicholas of Chalcedon, bp, 89n
Nile, river, 29, 43n
Nymphaeum, treaty (1261), 65n

Oman, 111n
Ottoman Turks, 25n, 51n

Palestine, *see* Holy Land
Parastron, John, Byz envoy to council of Lyons, 89n
pepper, 101
Persia (southern Mongols), 3, 4, 7n, 47, 55, 75, 85, 108
emp, 57, 59, 75, 107, 111–13
gulf, 109n
Philip VI, k of France, 2n, 11
Philip of Commines, 5
Philip of Mézières, 5
Phocaea, 49n, 67
pilgrims to Holy Land, 9, 27, 39–41
Pisa, 27
pope (supreme pontiff), 23, 39, 43–45, 53n, 103
role in crusade, 61
see also Alexander III, Benedict XII, Clement IV, Clement V, Innocent III, John XXII
Prester John, 99n
prophecies (Muslim), 55

Qalāwūn, sultan, 31n, 37n
Qaydu (Qaidu), great-grandson of Chinggis kahn, 47n

Raetia, 71
Ramón Lull, 5
Raymond of Farges, cardinal-deacon of Sta. Maria Nova, 23, 25, 27, 31, 117
Raymond Stephen, abp of Ephesus, 2, 8
Recueil des historiens des croisades, 14–16
Red sea, 3, 9, 99, 101
reunion of Roman and Greek churches, 45
Rhodes, 37n, 43
Roger de Flor, *megas dux*, 95
Romania, *see* Byzantium, Greece
Rome, Roman
bp, *see* pope
curia, 59
fourth Lateran Council (1215), 27n
third Lateran Council (1179), 27n
Russia, 47n
Ruthenia, Ruthenians, 29, 77

Saladin, 10
Saruhan, emirate, 51n
schism, Greek and Roman churches, 85–87
seasickness, 69–71
Seguranus Salvago, 33
Seljuk Turks, 10, 25n
Siberia, 47n
Sicily, 43n
silk trade, 101
Sindan (Sanjan), 101n
Siraf, 111n
slaves, slavery, 19, 79–85
in Asia Minor and Persia, 53
in Egypt, 29–31, 35, 41
numbers of Greek slaves, 83
Smyrna, 2, 49n, 65
Socotra, 3n, 105, 107n, 113–15
attacks by Saracens, 115
Spain, 59
see also Aragon, Castile
Sultanieh, 2, 3n, 8
abp, *see* John of Cora, William of Adam
Symon Semeonis, Irish pilgrim, 27n
Syria, 3, 25n, 27n

Tana (Thana), 107n, 109
Tartars, *see* Mongols

Taurus, 81
teak, 109n, 111n
Templars, 55n, 93
Thessalonica, 93n
Thessaly, 69n
Thrace, 69n
Timur (Tamerlane), 65n
Transoxania, 47n
Turkestan, 47n
Turkey, *see* Asia Minor
Turks, 29, 51, 53, 55, 63, 67, 73, 75, 79
    cruelty, 79–81
    see also Ottoman, Seljuk

Venice, Venetians, 27, 67
Vienne, council (1311–12), 27n, 55n
villa, 19
virtus, 19

William of Adam, 1–11, 23
    attitude to Greeks, 10
    crusading plans, 9–10, 25–27
    life, 1–3
    missionary, 81–83
        in Ethiopia, 115
        in India, 83–85, 103–5
        in Socotra, 105, 115
    name, 1
    plan to blockade Red sea,
        103–15
    style, 4
    travels, 3, 55
    Treatise, 9–11
    writings, 2, 3–4
William of Mende, crusade
    publicist, 5n
William VII of Montferrat, 93

William of Nogaret, 5
wine, supply in Byz empire, 69
wood, for building ships, 111
    supplies in Egypt, 29
    see also teak

Yolanda (Irene) of Montferrat,
    wife of Andronicus II, 93

Zaccaria, Bartolomeo, 49n, 55
Zaccaria, Benedetto (I), 49
Zaccaria, Benedetto (II), 49n,
    55, 81
Zaccaria, Manuele, 49n
Zaccaria, Martino, 49n, 55, 81
Zaccaria, Paleologus, 49
Zaccaria family, 51n, 53, 65, 67